Educated in
Romance

Educated in Romance

Women, Achievement, and College Culture

Dorothy C. Holland
& Margaret A. Eisenhart

The University of Chicago Press   *Chicago & London*

DOROTHY HOLLAND is professor of anthropology at the University of North Carolina at Chapel Hill. MARGARET A. EISENHART is associate professor of anthropology and education at the University of Colorado at Boulder.

The University of Chicago Press, Chicago 60637
The University of Chicago Press, Ltd., London

© 1990 by The University of Chicago
All rights reserved. Published 1990
Printed in the United States of America
99 98 97 96 95 94 93 92 91 90   5 4 3 2 1

The University of Chicago gratefully acknowledges the contribution of the Exxon Education Foundation toward the publication of this book.

Library of Congress Cataloging in Publication Data

Holland, Dorothy C.
    Educated in romance : women, achievement, and college
culture / Dorothy C. Holland & Margaret A. Eisenhart.
        p.   cm.
    Includes bibliographical references.
    ISBN 0-226-34943-8
    1. Women college students—United States—Social life and
customs.   2. Women—Education (Higher)—United States—Case
studies.   3. Sex differences in education—United States.
4. College students—United States—Case studies.   5. Educational
anthropology—United States.   6. Educational sociology—United
States.   I. Eisenhart, Margaret A.   II. Title.
LC1756.H65   1990
376'.65'0973—dc20   90-34489
                                                               CIP

∞ The paper used in this publication meets the
minimum requirements of the American National Standard
for Information Sciences—Permanence of Paper for Printed
Library Materials, ANSI Z39.48-1984.

Contents

Foreword

A revolution is developing in the social sciences that promises to transform not only existing fields of knowledge, such as anthropology, sociology, and education, but the very way we understand 'knowledge' and mark out fields of study. Its strongest stimulus is the growth of modern feminism. Feminist scholars have provided devastating proof of the blindness of Western intellectual traditions to the crucial importance of gender to social life and human culture in almost all of its aspects. Alongside the (re)discovery of gender are reconsiderations of method. There are critiques of the ideal of an impersonal, disembodied knower; a search for ways of combining personal experience with awareness of large-scale structures; new ways of interrogating data and defining and addressing audiences. We are, I think, involved in a change away from a professionalized, hierarchical, masculine model of social science toward a democratic, participatory, and inclusive model. It is no accident that women are leaders in this move.

Dorothy Holland and Margaret Eisenhart have made a notable contribution to this process of change. Their method is concrete, indeed they make use of one of the most concrete methods known in social science, close-focus ethnography. But their intellectual concerns are very broad, as they discuss the shift in the conceptual foundations of debate about education and society. This is a fast-moving area which in twenty years has passed through several distinct paradigms. Starting from a descriptive and largely social-psychological view of social inequality and education, theory in the area moved to the macro level and emphasised the determining power of a whole social system, but got stuck with a one-sided emphasis on structure. More recent work has tried to find ways to hold onto structural issues while acknowledging that social structures themselves are built and changed through history by the practices of people and groups. Holland and Eisenhart present the dialectic of theory with notable clarity and constructiveness.

Next, they are concerned not just to register the importance of gender but also to learn how gender can be understood and theorised. There is intellectual movement here, as active and complex as in the debates about education. Holland and Eisenhart make some intriguing suggestions about how current theory can be developed. They explore the ambiguities of the concept of resistance; show how important it is to analyse the specific supports women have to contest hegemonic definitions of femininity; and throughout the book show how the coercive cultural forms of patriarchy are grounded in the flow of everyday life.

Finally, they are not only concerned with theory as abstraction, but also with theory as strategy, as reflection within a process of social change. After reading this book we have a much clearer idea of both the possibilities and the difficulties of moving toward more equal gender relations in settings like universities.

Ethnography and life-history work is slow work. It does not lead quickly to publication, and it is difficult to get fully funded by granting agencies which seem to prefer quick-and-shallow surveys. But close-focus research of this kind can illuminate issues, reveal the depths and complexities of social problems, far beyond the capacities of conventional quantitative research. When ethnographic work is well done it can be astonishingly fruitful. *Educated in Romance* shows how careful observation and patient reflection, opens up perspective after perspective beyond the original issues. Here, a vivid description of student life is merely the starting-point for a train of argument that ranges from the language of romance to the interplay of gender and race, and the social relevance of universities.

As a contribution to the ethnography of education, *Educated in Romance* will have a secure place. It is well crafted, carefully observed, even more carefully reasoned. A non-American reader notes with pleasure the authors' familiarity with research and theory from Europe and Australasia; this is social science firmly grounded in a global consciousness. Yet the work does not simply follow existing models. European theories of cultural reproduction have all too often led to research where a heavy theoretical framework overwhelms the fieldwork. *Educated in Romance* strikes the delicate balance between sophisticated theory and a willingness to learn from observation and let the evidence speak.

The book also has urgency and relevance to its time. On this score, two points impress me particularly. The first is the evidence the authors marshal for the importance of the heterosexual peer group in the transmission of patriarchal gender relations through time. They suggest that in this regard patriarchy is structurally different from class and racial oppression. In the last ten years there has been a good deal of argument about the connections between these three structures of power. But this has been caught in a dilemma between an over-formal conception of interacting systems, and a poststructuralist abandonment of any conception of weighty and organised power structures. Holland and Eisenhart's line of argument just might provide the way out of this dilemma. And it also has important implications for strategies of change in gender relations. Holland and Eisenhart map an implicit politics of difference between *peer networks*, not just between sexes, and this opens up very interesting possibilities for practice, among them the opportunity for progressive movements in sexual politics based on heterosexual groupings. Such a politics would be very different from the movements we find familiar from the experience of the 1970s and 1980s.

The second point is Holland and Eisenhart's demonstration that the academic culture of the university is largely irrelevant to the daily lives of most of the students studied. This evidence should worry everyone working in universities who thinks of them as having an intellectual, let alone a critical, mission. A terrifying failure of the teaching enterprise is suggested here—which may be partly explained by the strength of the peer culture, but which I suspect is also in part a cause of that culture. As Holland and Eisenhart show, the official grading of academic attainment goes on in eerie counterpoint to the unofficial grading of sexual attractiveness in peer-group life.

It is hard to imagine a better demonstration of the need to investigate the realities beneath the comfortable myths of education. We are much in the authors' debt for showing, with clarity and verve, how this can be done.

R. W. Connell
Macquarie University, Sydney

Preface

This book follows the lives of a group of black and white women while they were attending two universities in the American South and entering the world of work. It describes the cultural systems and social practices they encountered and participated in; it traces their interpretations of the academic experience, their ups and downs with campus life and the culture of romance, and the ebb and flow of their views of themselves as learners and as workers; it recounts their efforts to direct their own lives and to make sense of their experiences; and it explores their dissent and moments of protest against male privilege.

The anthropological and sociological analyses we do here illuminate small-scale events, primarily the day-to-day happenings and the everyday, often minute "choices" that paved the entry into adulthood of a small number of college women in the early 1980s. In the scope of the historical struggle over women's rights and women's place in Western society, we present but a brief moment. Yet that moment has much to tell us. When we compare the experiences of the women in this study with those of girls and women in other schools in the United States, in Britain, and in Australia, we begin to see the forms that young women's confrontations with gender inequality can take. We begin to see the ubiquity of the culture of romance and attractiveness. We begin to see similar logics behind what girls and young women do with the educational "opportunities" offered them by sexist societies. We begin to see why young women's forms of protest differ from working-class and racial minority forms of dissent.

The struggle over women's rights is both amazingly fast-paced and inexorably slow. Since the time of the study, for example, women's studies programs have grown on university campuses, including the two studied here, and the women's movement has become more visible in the media and in politics. Because of its expansion, the movement presumably provides intellectual resources for a much larger proportion of students than it did at the time of our study. On the other hand, we continue to hear statistical reports of working women's entrenchment in second-sector jobs and domestic chores. And, some of the institutional barriers to gender equality have grown even stronger. The Supreme Court has just now—July 1989—ruled that the state of Missouri can prevent abortions in public clinics and hospitals. Clearly the lives of women now entering the two universities cannot be the same as the lives of the women described here. And yet they cannot be altogether different. There is no stasis to the picture we describe, but, many of its important features remain the same.

The paradox of change in stability and stability in change must also be true for the individual women we studied. Though the experiences we describe are now several years in the past, they undoubtedly are still powerful in the presents of the women who lived them. In treating their lives as revelatory of the lives of young women in a system of patriarchy, we take up only one aspect, albeit an important one, of who they are and superimpose upon it anthropological and sociological analyses that some of them possibly would reject. In other words, we have risked violating the study participants' own sense of themselves and memories of their experience. We have tried to minimize that risk by letting their ideas and feelings come through, in their own words and in the actual complexities of their lives. Yet by revealing so many details we have run another risk, of violating the anonymity we promised the women. Where pseudonyms did not seem protection enough, we have altered or omitted background details in their stories. We hope that only the women themselves will recognize the real individuals behind the pseudonyms we use. We have been especially mindful and long-thinking about these dilemmas because the women's participation in our study was, in a profound sense, a gift. In the end we hope that they will feel that we have treated their gift with respect and put it to good use.

There are many others to thank as well. Next in importance to the women in the study were the women who helped us do the interviews and carry out the observations: Rae Bennett, Mari Clark, Kathy Luchok, Pat Roberts, Debra Skinner, Isabel Terry, and Wende Watson. Amanda Sandell and Barbara Reid helped with the later interviews. Carole Cain, Alison Greene, Bradley Levinson, Karen Mickelsen, and Amanda Sandell helped us process and analyze the interviews and observations and carried out related library and documentary research.

A large number of people made valuable comments on the manuscript and earlier related articles: Jeff Boyer, Carole Cain, Alex Cuthbert, Valerie Fennell, Jean Harris, Carole Hill, William Lachicotte, Bradley Levinson, Wendy Luttrell, Holly Mathews, Judith Meece, Sandi Morgen, Don Nonini, Laura Oaks (who also did a lot of first-rate editing), Laurie Price, Naomi Quinn, Karen Sacks, Judith Shrum, Sheila Slaughter, Claudia Strauss, Lois Weis, and several anonymous reviewers.

The main period of research was supported by the National Institute of Education. The University Research Council of the University of North Carolina at Chapel Hill provided funds for two small related studies. Virginia Polytechnic Institute and State University and the University of Colorado provided leaves of absence and support for Eisenhart; the University of North Carolina at Chapel Hill, for Holland.

Two people stand out among the members of our intellectual and emotional communities. For Joe Harding and William Lachicotte we have a special feeling of appreciation. Frequently offering humor and help, they endured the highs and lows of this ten-year project at especially close range.

The book is dedicated by Holland to her mother, Catherine Fancher Balch, who has been offered lots of rubbish—including male-privilege rubbish—in her day and has generally refused, with her own style of wisdom, grace, and humor, to take it.

The book is dedicated by Eisenhart to the Brown sisters—Helen, Henrietta, Irene, and Maryanna—four strong women whose hard-won achievements in a male-dominated society were an inspiration to her.

Part 1 *Introduction*

1 *Why Study Women's Responses to Schooling?*

In 1979 the United States National Institute of Education (NIE) wanted to know why so few women were becoming scientists or mathematicians. We received some of their funds to investigate this question in two southern universities: a predominantly black university that we have called "Bradford," and a predominantly white university that we have called "Southern University" (SU). About halfway through the first part of the study—the ethnographic portion—we designed and administered the second part—a survey—to randomly selected samples of women at each school. The ethnographic sample had been skewed toward women with strong academic records and career aspirations; from the survey sample we learned that the ethnographic findings could be generalized.

As it turned out, the study went beyond the question of why so few American college women were going into the high-paying traditionally male-dominated fields of math and science. It revealed young women's paths into traditional female positions in society in general. When the women in our ethnographic sample began their college careers, they had reputations as good students, and approximately half said they would major in a math- or science-related field. All stated that they expected to pursue a career after graduating from college. Yet from following these women's unfolding lives—during the study (1979–81), when the women were due to graduate from college (1983), and again when they had begun their adult lives (1987)—we know that less than a third of these bright and privileged women met their own expectations for the future. By the time they left college, they had arrived at practices—to put the outcome in terms of the critical educational and feminist literature—that are key in sustaining women's subordinate positions in the society. Most had ended up with intense involvements in heterosexual romantic relationships, marginalized career identities, and inferior preparation for their likely roles as future breadwinners. The cases of Linda and Paula illustrate the pattern.

WHY DID LINDA AND PAULA DROP THEIR CAREER PLANS?

When Linda began college in 1979, she told us, she was determined to do well academically, to get a degree she could "use," and afterwards "to have a professional career." She said: "I'm going toward a professional career that I will use the rest of my life. I'm going to college to establish a career that I can use to help people . . . and to make a decent living." She intended to become a physical therapist.

Once in college, Linda had difficulty maintaining the high grade-point average she had come to expect of herself in high school. She spent long hours laboring over schoolwork. "I'm working all the time," she told us. "I even feel guilty if I'm not studying." After barely a semester at college, she decided that despite her hard work she could not make the grade-point average required to get into the specialized therapy program she was interested in. She was very much disappointed. After discussions with her parents, friends, and other adults, she chose to aim for a specialized nursing field instead. Because a somewhat lower average was required for admittance into the program, Linda was hopeful she would make the cut. She continued to work hard during her freshman and sophomore years, and by the middle of her sophomore year she had been admitted to the nursing program she wanted. She was excited and relieved, and she began to anticipate the next hurdles and her future as a nurse. "If you don't have your B.S. in nursing, you're not going to get a decent job. You're going to be stuck on late night shift, emptying bed pans, and that's not what I want to do. . . . I'm hoping for private practice or a special hospital . . . so it would end up satisfying as a career."

Linda also seemed to realize that she and her boyfriend, whom she planned to marry someday, would soon be on their own financially. Speaking about the two of them, she said: "We're getting older and closer to careers and being completely independent of our parents. In three or four years we're going to be looking for jobs to support ourselves and then a family of our own. It's kind of scary to be completely independent."

To us, Linda seemed seriously committed to pursuing a career and, at least compared to others in our study, well-informed about the steps she needed to take and the course she needed to be on in order to achieve the kind of career she desired. She had difficulty with her schoolwork, but she kept at it, and she kept her career goal in mind. For these reasons, we were surprised when one day near the end of our study, Linda said: "If I had to make a decision between my family [my husband and children] and my career, then there's no question— my family. If I have to give up my career, that's fine. . . . If I had to choose, it would be family over career, with no qualms at all."

Subsequently Linda married her college boyfriend and took a full-time hospital job. When we interviewed her in 1987, she explained that her marriage had ended in divorce, but that she was engaged to be married again within the year. Asked about her career goals, Linda said, "I'd like to work half-time for a while, then quit and have at least two children."

When we first met Paula, she had come to college with a straight-A average from high school and planned to major in biology and become a doctor. During her freshman year she did not find her courses, including calculus and chemistry, particularly difficult, but she did find them "boring." Often she could not make herself go to class or study. By the end of her freshman year, she decided to switch her concentration to nursing, "because my grades aren't high enough for med school." During the first semester of her sophomore year, she missed the deadline for application to the nursing program and decided instead to try for an education degree. In the middle of her sophomore year, Paula had this to say about her career-related decisions during college: "Since I've been here, I've changed my mind about a thousand times. . . . And, like right now, I feel like . . . just not working would be the greatest thing in the world—just take care of children and not studying."

Paula eventually settled on a social-science field as her major and graduated in 1983. After graduation she enrolled in a management-trainee program, worked in a department store, and got married. In 1987 she had this to say about careers: "[My husband and I] want to have successful careers . . . his is a career, where I feel like mine is a job. So, my career goals are for his career more so than mine. . . . I'm trying to be there to help [him] when I can."

Linda's and Paula's actions, as well as those of many other women in this study, would seem to reproduce the traditional gender roles and system of male privilege in the United States. They seem to have willingly scaled down their aspirations for careers and entered into marriage in economic positions inferior to those of their husbands.

If we want to account fully for the continuation of male privilege, we must ask why Linda and Paula "chose" such paths for themselves. This question is an essential question of social reproduction theory. Why do working-class people, women, and members of racial minorities willingly accept positions that are inferior, accept jobs that yield a low standard of living, and continue in jobs that endanger life and limb? Paul Willis, a contributor to this literature, refers to this question in the title of his book *Learning to Labor: How Working Class Kids Get Working Class Jobs* (1977, rev. ed. 1981b). In a more recent study about clerical jobs, which are mostly held by women, Valli (1983:3) poses the question directly: "Why, then [given the negative aspects of such jobs], would students consciously prepare themselves to become office workers?"

Feminist scholars would go beyond these issues of jobs and ask: Why do women enter into positions of economic and emotional dependency on men? Why do women, even college women who supposedly have the means to escape, enter without a fight into the domestic labor market in a one-down position? Why, Adrienne Rich (1980) might ask in an even more radical vein, do they accede to "compulsory heterosexual relations"?

STRUCTURE, CULTURE, AND SOCIAL REPRODUCTION

The issue of young women's "choices" and willing entry into low-paying occupations and traditional domestic roles is closely interlocked in the critical education and feminist literature with the question of the role of schools in society. As presented in detail in chapter 3, social reproduction theorists (e.g., Althusser 1971; Bourdieu and Passeron 1977; Bowles and Gintis 1976) have argued that in countries such as France and the United States, schools reproduce structures of class privilege. The same has been argued for the reproduction of male privilege (e.g., Barrett 1980; Deem 1978; Wolpe 1978).

According to the usual rhetoric, schools are the gateway to social and economic opportunity for those who are willing to study and learn. In the critical literature, the reverse is argued: schools maintain class, race, and gender structures. They do so, the argument goes, by differentially training students and by supplying ideologies that mystify the systems of privilege in this society.

This picture of the school's role in social reproduction has been significantly modified and refined over the years. As originally presented, it was far too simplistic. The early versions implied by omission that students are simply ciphers, that they passively absorb school ideologies and docilely acquiesce in school practices. The theories left out a crucial element that ethnographic studies of schools have revealed all along, namely that students come to school from homes and communities where they have developed values and orientations not encompassed by the schools.[1] As revisors of the early formulations of reproduction theory (e.g., Apple 1982; Apple and Weis 1983; Giroux 1981; MacDonald 1980; Willis 1977, 1981a, 1981b) pointed out, working-class students, including girls and young women, *react to and sometimes oppose* the ideologies and practices they meet in school.[2] School ideologies and practices do not fully determine their reactions. Rather, students bring values and understandings from other realms of their lives and, together with fellow students, generate a system of meaning and practice in response to the social barriers they face.

This latter-day reproduction theory—which itself is currently undergoing revision—does not at all deny the schools a crucial role in social reproduction. In the case of gender, for example, it is certainly important that school materials reflect a gender bias, that patterns of staffing and treatment of the mostly female teaching staff reflect nationwide patterns of a gender-based occupational structure, that teachers treat girls differently from the ways they treat boys, that schools valorize skills, talents, and ways of knowing that are associated with males and not females. Rather, the revised position is that the values and orientations of the working class, women, and racial minorities are not fully determined by the schools. Students have some autonomy in their reactions, and their reactions affect how and even whether class, gender, and race hierarchies are maintained. The students' reactions may, in the end, despite the students' opposition to and "penetration" of school ideologies, lead them willingly to embrace stereotyped roles (e.g., working-class jobs, as in the case described by Willis 1977, 1981b). Yet in other instances, their reactions may seriously challenge the existing system of class, race, or gender privilege. Even when they ultimately pose no threat, students' responses to schooling are clearly a part of the dynamic struggle over societal structures that must be taken into account.

Women's Resistance to the Gender Hierarchy

Comparatively speaking, we know little about the roles of schools in reproducing gender hierarchies. Social reproduction theory, in its early stages and as modified since the early 1970s, has first and foremost considered the reproduction of class structures. But patterns of class reproduction are not easily transferred to gender. Feminist scholars have conclusively argued that gender hierarchies cannot be collapsed into class hierarchies (See chapters 3 and 4).

Gender structures are differently constituted. Not surprisingly, women's patterns of resistance to the gender hierarchy have not turned out to be simple analogues of working-class patterns of resistance to the class hierarchy. There are several directly relevant studies of schoolgirls and young women, including those of McRobbie (1978a, 1978b), Lees (1986), and Griffin (1985) in Britain, Thomas (1980), Connell, Ashenden, Kessler, and Dowsett (1982), and Kessler, Ashenden, Connell, and Dowsett (1985) in Australia, and Weis (1988) and Valli (1986) in the United States. Piecing these studies together with ours, we find some important points of difference between the mediation of class hierarchies in schools and the mediation of gender hierarchies in schools. The primary difference has to do with the role of the peer group. For class, the ideologies and practices promulgated by the school and reflected in texts and classroom materials are the targets of working-class opposition. For gender, agemates are more virulent purveyors of gender privilege than school authorities and school materials.

As we followed the women's experiences during the period of our study, we found that the peer system promoted and propelled the women into a world of romance in which their attractiveness to men counted most. The women were subjected to a "sexual auction block." In the shadow of the peer society, academics commanded only limited attention. The women were more or less left on their own by the university, by their peers, and to a lesser extent by their parents, to develop—or not—careers, to prepare themselves—or not—as future breadwinners.

Our study revealed a pattern of women's opposition that may be fairly common. None of the women in the study participated in any rebellious counterculture groups that opposed gender structures. Yet despite their superficial acquiescence, it would be a mistake to assume that they neither criticized male privilege or were lackadaisical about gender issues. To the contrary, they very actively tried both to avoid the parts of the peer system of romance that they disliked (one woman even temporarily dropped out of it), and to maneuver their status within romantic relationships. They had various critiques—some quite radical—of the consequences of the gender hierarchy. And they were actively engaged with those internal divisions and factions within the peer community that struggled over competing constructions of feminine and masculine attractiveness.

This book traces the paths of Linda and Paula and the other women in our study, through college into adulthood. We describe their college experiences, their academic strategies, their responses to the system of male privilege that they encountered, and the effect of their responses on their life courses. We also relate their cases, and our general findings, to issues within the critical education and feminist literature on gender and schooling, including the question of how the culturally constructed world of romance relates to women's school careers.

2   *The Odyssey behind the Case*

It is customary to cast a scholarly book as though it is solely a turn in an ongoing rational dialogue. The corollary is that more personal debates—internal and external—are omitted. Yet these are the ones that give life and drama to the questions that researchers have traditionally reported so matter-of-factly. Further, in the social sciences especially, these more personal debates are too integral a part of the research to be omitted.

For a variety of good reasons, more recent practice in our own discipline of anthropology—as well as in feminist research (see McRobbie 1982; Weiler 1988)—dictates that the personal be made public and that the traditional scholar's guise of total objectivity, emotional uninvolvement, and implied superiority to "subjects," "respondents," and "informants" be dropped. In matters of meaning—and in anthropologists' view human behavior always involves meaning—the subject of study must be recognized and treated as a partner in a sort of dialogue, not as an object under a microscope. All researchers are fettered by the taken-for-granted meanings that they bring to their projects and impose on those they would understand. A researcher can only begin to break the fetters if she allows her informants' words and deeds to break through her preconceptions. The guise of the all-knowing, "objective" researcher simply does not serve for such a task. Good ethnographers have recognized all along that their "native informants" were partners; the difference is that the research reports no longer need to be written as though the research had been conducted otherwise. In fact, for the report to be complete and accurate it must reveal the researcher's foundation for understanding. Otherwise, how is the reader to know the researcher's contribution to the research dialogue? How is the reader to assess the researcher's likely blind spots?[1]

For us the immediate impetus to describe the course of our unfolding understanding came from the reactions that we received when presenting the findings of our research. Many, including students in our classes, found the parts of women's lives that we described enlightening and engrossing but did not much enjoy the description of the difficult theoretical debate in which the study is embedded. Except to readers or listeners who were well-versed in the subject, the theoretical material often seemed opaque and even annoying. Many of the women who participated in the study would no doubt react in the same way. We hope we have fairly presented some of the dilemmas they faced and have adequately shown the cleverness of their solutions. It would be both tragic and ironic, given our aims, to lose the richness of their lives in a sea of theory. Nevertheless, their experiences and solutions, if they are to be best appreciated and most useful for assessing the nature of gender oppression, must in our opinion be highlighted by, and in return reflect back upon, current theories of cultural production and practice.[2] In this chapter we tell the more personal odyssey of our involvement in the study, not only because the story contains some of our "breakthrough" realizations and provides a basis for assessing our still-unrecognized blindnesses, but also because it brings to light and enlivens some of the issues and distinctions in the literature (more formally discussed in Part 2). The remainder of the chapter should, in fact, provide enough of an orientation that the reader can upon its completion make a temporary detour around Part 2 and move directly to the case itself, beginning with chapter 5.

THE STORY OF THE STUDY

Although the study was not even conceptualized until 1979, its formation began in 1975 with a project we did in an elementary school in "Bradford," the home city of the black university described in this book. In that study we literally sat and watched a set of "focal students" go through the fifth grade and then the sixth grade. The school had recently been desegregated, and our task was to describe the student groups that formed and the patterns of interaction that occurred between teachers and students. We interviewed the students, we watched with whom they interacted, we listened to the ways they talked to and about each other and their teachers, and we watched what they did in class, in the lunchroom, out on the playground, and in the morning before school.

Because we followed specific individuals and knew a great deal about who their friends were, what seemed to make them happy, what seemed to make them sad, how they talked about themselves, and so forth, it would have been virtually impossible to miss their myriad efforts to shape and affect their own social environment. They were hardly passive recipients of the messages of the school, as either re- production or socialization theory would have led us to expect. The creativity of their responses was forever amazing us. One of the white focal students had fallen in with a group of friends who liked to upset her by saying they didn't like her anymore. This girl was trying, like many of the other students, to form friendships across race lines. The girls with whom she wanted to be friends were black. We knew from watching that attempted friendships across race lines were difficult to maintain and usually failed. This girl succeeded longer than most. After several weeks of being "in" and then "out" with this group, the girl, who was "slow" according to tests and her teachers' opinions, came up with the idea of forming a club. She drew up an insignia and talked the other girls into becoming members. She created an orga- nization of a type—a girls' or young women's club in a coed school— that is, judging from the literature, relatively rare. When one of us asked her about the club, she explained that she had thought it up in order to keep the girls from dropping her. She figured that the club bonds would make the friendships stronger.

Creative opposition to school adults was particularly evident in the rooms of white teachers whom black students thought to be preju- diced. The librarian, for example, had to contend with "disappearing" students who silently dropped out of their chairs and crawled away under the library tables while she was lecturing.

There was one focal student, a white boy from a working-class family, who appeared to be extremely passive. In all the many months that we observed him, he did not initiate even one interaction, and he quickly did whatever the teachers told him to do. But as it turned out, he was not a passive recipient of social forms, either. We learned, by finding out about his life outside school, that his passivity was a stra- tegic reaction to minimize contact with his black peers and teachers. His parents eventually withdrew him from the school and put him in a private, segregated school.

In addition to noticing individual creativity in response to school and to social situations posed by friends and enemies, we were struck by the power of the peer group compared to that of the teachers and other school adults. We eventually came to the conclusion that the peer group was an extremely important site of elaboration and de- velopment of the basic structural divisions in the society—namely, race, class, and gender (see also Schwartz 1972). Gender was especially elaborated and developed in the peer groups at the school. In fact, we concluded that the peer group, not school adults or school materials, was the major mediator of gender. Gender, especially as constructed in romantic relationships, was emphasized in the peer group but downplayed by the teachers and principal. And to the students, peers tended to be much more exciting and riveting than school adults. Like Willis (1981b), we concluded that traditional gender relations were being promoted in the school, but not so much through direct socialization from teachers and school materials. Instead, the route to reproduction of gender relations was a circuitous one. The gender structure of the larger society affected the culture of the peer group, which in turn canalized the boys' and girls' present and future relationships with one another. The peer group, which we speculated was reacting in part to societal restrictions placed on the students because of their age, was grasping at markers of adult status, including romantic involvements. Especially among the white students, romantic themes were emphasized to the point that gender encounters were almost always interpreted by peers as romantic in nature. The effect was to severely limit and channel social exchanges between boys and girls (Clement et al., 1978[3]; Eisenhart and Holland 1983; Schofield 1982).

When it came time to write the proposal for the NIE study of university women, we carried two strong hunches into the task. First, as justified by other literature and by our own observations (albeit from the position of faculty) of student life on college campuses, we guessed that the peer group remained important at the university level. Second, we guessed that university students were no more passive recipients of "cultural transmissions" from the school than were elementary school students. Thus we focused on the women's peers and on following a number of individuals through part of their college careers. We wanted to know how individuals interpreted their college experiences, what influenced their choice of majors, and how their peers figured in their lives.

Our two general hunches were borne out. But our initial hypotheses as to *how* peers affected women's careers in math and science and other fields were wrong. We guessed that women's choices of a major would be affected by their peers' ideas of appropriate majors for males versus females. We anticipated that women would be steered by their peers toward majors and careers traditionally associated with women, such as teaching and nursing, and away from majors and careers traditionally associated with men, such as law and business. As it turned out, we were wrong. The women we focused on—twenty-three in total—arrived at the university with at least some idea of their possible majors and careers. The formation of their ideas about themselves in future careers had occurred *before* they came to college.

A further assault on our hypotheses came when we realized, much to our chagrin as faculty, that the student cultures were devoted to other activities, not to schoolwork and learning. The student peer cultures were not organized around classes and majors. There was not much talk about majors. It was clear from our interviews and observations that friends might not even know each others' majors.[4] Academic progress and related decisions were considered more or less personal business, of concern primarily to the individual student. Peers were not directly influential in choices of a major.

We learned that peers did affect the student careers of the women we studied, but not in the ways we had thought. We came up with the metaphor of a train on a track. The women had come to school on track toward certain majors or careers. Once at college they could remain on track, change tracks, or be derailed. For some, lower-than-expected grades signaled a need to reconsider the track. For others, low grades were associated with boredom and taken as a sign to leave school, to derail. Just how low grades and other negative experiences were interpreted depended in part upon advice from peers. Peers affected students' careers in other ways as well. Competing demands on time from boyfriends and girlfriends were a potential encouragement to derailment. In other words, peers did not determine the track, as we had originally guessed, but did influence whether the women stayed on track, changed tracks, or were derailed (Holland and Eisenhart 1981).

A more embarrassing discovery, embarrassing because it now seems obvious, concerned our implicit background assumptions about the women's views of the university. We were mistaken in our taken-for-granted notions of their views in several ways, especially in the case of Bradford, the historically black school.[5] These bogus assumptions came to light when we looked at the results of the survey. Halfway through the ethnographic study, we sketched out a model of the myriad ways in which friends seemed to affect women's commitments to their majors, drew up a survey, and administered it to random samples of women from the two universities. Table 1 shows the factors that were significantly correlated with commitment to completing a degree in the chosen major. As can be seen, the significant correlations are different for Bradford and for SU. The model was drawn up from the ethnographic work at both schools, but the overall results from the survey showed that the model had better explanatory capa-

TABLE 1. Survey: Correlations between women's assessments and "commitment to their major," by university

	Bradford	SU
Validity of the costs of an education	.175	−.012
	(p = .06)	(NS)
Legitimacy of the institution's standards	.166	−.064
	(p = .06)	(NS)
Attachment to rewards/identities associated with the major	.159	.075
	(NS)	(NS)
Perceived costs to get desired ends from major	.042	.019
	(NS)	(NS)
Assessment of ability to succeed in chosen major/career	−.002	−.034
	(NS)	(NS)
Comparative evaluation of present major	.278	.527
	(p = .01)	(p = .0001)
Financial difficulties	−.158	−.030
	(p = .07)	(NS)
Competing peer identities/rewards	−.187	.006
	(p =.08)	(NS)
Importance of hometown activities and family	−.091	.057
	(NS)	(NS)
Energy available for study	.173	.151
	(p = .05)	(p = .03)
Direct help with coursework	.041	.009
	(NS)	(NS)
Indirect help (happiness) from others	.155	.124
	(NS)	(NS)

SOURCE: Adapted from Holland and Eisenhart 1981:89.
NOTE: Figures are observed path coefficients. Computations were carried out by the SYSREG procedure (SAS) for a block recursive model. See Holland and Eisenhart (1981) for full details of questions, formation of composite variables, and analyses.

The top figure of each pair is the standardized b value or path coefficient. The figure in parentheses is the probability of the parameter estimate of the b value. Probabilities greater than .10 are *not* listed.

bility for SU than for Bradford. The amount of variance in commitment to major explained for SU was 46 percent, whereas for Bradford it was 35 percent (both multiple correlation coefficients were significant at the .0001 level) (Holland and Eisenhart 1981:88). Compared to many social science studies, the amount of variance explained for Bradford was impressive and, of course, it was even more so for SU. But it was clear that something was different between the two schools and that we had not grasped the situation at Bradford as well as we had that at SU. Both of us are more familiar with predominantly white universities and are white ourselves. We had missed something.

Going back through the ethnographic interviews and observations—which were complete by the time we were analyzing the results of the survey—we began to realize that the Bradford women had an overall view of the university that differed from the view that the white SU students had. In terms of its relevance to careers, the Bradford women tended to see the university as providing a necessary credential, but not necessarily a relevant education. Getting through was a trial, and not necessarily an edifying one, that had to be gotten over. The Bradford women's orientation was consistent with the black community's view of schools as described by Ogbu (1974, 1985, 1987). They had a suspicion that school—the institution in general—was likely to be unfair to black students and somewhat irrelevant to their interests and concerns (see also Fordham and Ogbu 1986). The SU women were much more likely to accept the university as a legitimate gatekeeper to future careers and to believe that their schoolwork was meaningful beyond enabling them to get a degree (see Holland and Eisenhart 1981, 1988b).

In short, we were forced to recognize that we could not take the women's or their peer groups' orientation to the university for granted. We had implicitly assumed that their orientations were close to our own. Not surprisingly, as both of us were and are college teachers and both were putting a lot of effort into our classes, we had been implicitly assuming that the women shared our view of the importance of college work and appreciated what to us was its relevance, intrinsic worth, and authority. The ethnographic work clearly told us that these values (and thus we ourselves?) were relatively unimportant in students' lives, black and white. But the fact was and still is hard for us to grasp emotionally.[6] It took the added weight of the otherwise inexplicable survey differences to sensitize us, in our role as researchers, to the need to tease out the women's interpretation of schooling and its purpose. Chapter 12, "Schoolwork for What?" describes the three major orientations we found. "Work for doing well" was found primarily at SU; "work for getting over" was found predominantly at Bradford; "work for learning from experts" was found at both.

By the time we submitted the final report to NIE (Holland and Eisenhart 1981), we knew that we were just beginning to understand the ways in which the peer group affected women's careers and that we were just beginning to understand that there were differences among the women as to how they interpreted the purpose and authority of the university. The report to NIE encompassed the survey results and preliminary analyses of the ethnographic materials. NIE was not interested in waiting for the amount of processing that the ethnographic materials would take. They denied our request for an extension of time, and we had to submit the final report before being able to piece together a full picture of the student culture, before we had worked out the different interpretations of the university, and before we were able to trace the paths of particular individuals and their particular problems, triumphs, and resolutions. As we look back on that report now, it seems fairly accurate, but difficult to interpret— somewhat like a precisely described but nonetheless limited portion of a much larger picture.

The final piece of our approach fell into place as we reflected on changes taking place in the theory of cultural-production studies. We had not initially analyzed the research from the structural perspective represented in the social-reproduction or subsequent cultural-production literature. The anthropology of education, in common with most other approaches to American education, had generally not, up to the early 1980s, explicitly dealt with social theory. Anthropologists had provided good analyses of the variety of meaning systems that students brought to schools and the socialization problems that arose when culturally different students came to schools, but they had not related those meaning systems and problems of cultural difference to structural aspects of society. With some exceptions (e.g., Gearing et al. 1979), anthropology had remained dependent upon socialization theory and thus was unable to account for students' reactions to their situations, except insofar as they could be explained by cultural differences.

By the time we submitted the NIE report, the 1981 edition of Willis's *Learning to Labor* had been published, and John Ogbu was beginning to summarize his many years of work on minority educational outcomes, particularly black outcomes in the United States. Although arising from different theoretical traditions, Willis's account of working-class education in England and Ogbu's account of minority education in America had some important convergent findings. Both argued that students do at some level grasp the nature of their society and recognize the positions that people like them are conventionally afforded. Both argued that students respond to schooling in light of their apprehension of their society and that they draw upon their cultural resources and heritage to forge their responses to schooling. And, finally, both argued that educational outcomes are a joint product of the schools' stance toward student groups and the students' responses to schooling.

The convergence of Willis's and Ogbu's conclusions made it possible for us to see how studies of structure and locally important meaning systems—the "lived culture"—could be joined. We now had more explicit terminology and theory for talking and thinking about structural barriers and their relationship to the meaning systems created by racial minorities, the working class, and women. But there was a problem. Holland remembers puzzling over Ogbu's arguments and asking him, in so many words: "You say black students see—at some level—that they face an arbitrarily imposed job ceiling and adjust their efforts in school accordingly. By the same reasoning, since American women face similar job ceilings, they should respond as do blacks. Why do so many girls and young women take school so seriously? Why don't they rebel in school? If black American students form oppositional identities in school in the face of white denigration, they why haven't American women students similarly responded to their characterization as inferior to men? How are women reacting to gender oppression?"

Those questions—questions, it turned out, that were similarly motivating other researchers—led us back to our interviews, observations, and survey. Aided by some additional research (described in chapter 5), we worked out a major component of student culture—its organization around romance and attractiveness—and, even more important, its differential constitution for women versus men. In addition, we traced out individual women's lives and the clash of their goals for their schoolwork with the sexually charged, peer-dominated world of gender relations. We began to see that the women in the study were constantly exposed to societal evaluation—to judgments of their worth—on the basis of their sexual attractiveness to men and that much of what they did was addressed to improving or avoiding that evaluation.

Again, as with the women's orientation to their coursework and studies, our "discovery" of the importance of romance and attractiveness and its implications for the women's response to schooling came relatively slowly and with some discomfort. We found it difficult to realize the students' views of academics because we ourselves were college professors, immersed in our teaching and studies. The source of the blinders was different in the matter of romanticized/sexualized gender relations, and the effects, in some ways, were more complex.

The women's experience and understanding of gender relations were familiar to us. We had had experiences like theirs in high school and college. We too had discovered, from even more years of personal experience and more years of hearing about the experiences of our friends, colleagues, and acquaintances, that as women we are open both to insulting treatment (such as uninvited evaluations of

sexual attractiveness, sexual harassment, even rape) and to opportunities for romantic involvements that shape the direction and texture
of our lives. The problem was not so much to notice the women's
views, but rather to make a critical assessment of the system of romance and attractiveness that we were beginning to trace out from the
interviews and observations. What was the *significance* of such a system
in their lives?

The desire for romance is popularly talked about in American culture as though it were a universal human desire. Students at SU and
Bradford talked to each other as though everyone were naturally and
obviously in or wanting to be in a romantic/sexual relationship (Holland n.d.). While it is easy to make assessments from inside the cultural meaning system of romance (to see and evaluate, for example,
apparent miscreants who exploit romantic partners for selfish ends),
it is much more difficult for someone raised in the system to see and
evaluate the whole idea of romance. For us, thinking and writing
about romance as culturally constructed—deconstructing its seeming
naturalness—posed difficulties and discomforts. This was true even
though our training and previous experience as sociocultural anthropologists had equipped us for such a task (Peacock 1988). After all, we
too have grown up in the culturally constructed world and have
learned to experience the pleasures and satisfactions, as well as the
pains, that go along with it. Not only have we learned to see the system
as natural, we also have learned to interpret and feel our emotions in
relation to the system. What would we lose if we became fully con-
scious of romance as culturally constructed? Certainly many feminist
writings, such as Simone de Beauvoir's *The Second Sex*, to cite a classic,
and Rich's (1980) serious questioning of the naturalness of heterosexual relationships, have invited us to such critical awareness, but
reflection continues to necessitate both a cognitive and emotional
process that is not altogether comfortable.

Looking back at our original research proposal, we realized that we
had scarcely attended to the significance of gender relations, and
upon reflection it seemed that we were likely to underestimate it
again in the analysis. What was the source of our lack of emphasis?
Beyond having learned to see romance as natural, we had also
learned to navigate gender relations interpreted in the idiom of romance. As girls and as young women growing up in this culture, we
had had no choice but to be exposed to the system, to participate in it,
and to come to terms with it in some way. We had had a modicum of
choice about whether to become more or less experienced in the
conduct of romantic relationships, and more or less self-invested in

sexual attractiveness and in romanticized/sexualized gender relations. But we had had no choice other than to devise some way to think about, feel about, and be in (or out of) such relationships.

What many of the women in our study seemed to us to be spending inordinate amounts of time doing, we came to realize, was working out their own particular ways of dealing with the system of gender relations that they were encountering on campus. How had we forgotten going through such a process ourselves? Why had we not anticipated that romantic involvements would be consuming a lot of the women's time and energy and would become confounded with their steps toward future careers? We had been taking not only the ideas of romance and attractiveness for granted, but also the very existence of the system and the part it plays in women's lives. We had devised our own ways to stay in or out of the system and to minimize our discomforts with it. The system had become a part of us and thus difficult to imagine as not a part of us. Having more or less mastered it, we had lost sight of its having mastered us. We had learned to deal with the system without having to think about it much and without reflecting upon whether and how it constrained our lives.

As with academics, the data forced us to recognize and examine our assumptions. The women's interviews and the observations of their peer activities were full of references to gender relations. Eventually we began to notice that many of the women did not feel truly involved or confident in the world of romance. We began to notice that some of them seemed to be camouflaging their real feelings about the men they were involved with; others, only feigning interest in meeting men. It also became clear that, in the process of adjusting to the gender relations promoted on campus, many of the women were making choices that ultimately would affect their future careers and future financial independence.

Thus we began to see that gender relations, as constructed through the peer culture's emphasis on romance and attractiveness, had a great deal of significance in the women's lives. And we began to see that the women's patterns of opposition to patriarchy had to be interpreted in light of the importance of peers in conveying gender relations. We came to see that for women of the age we studied, it was peers, not school or community authorities, who were the primary mediators of gender oppression and patriarchy. From the literature we knew that for race and class, *groups* of students oppose and resist; from our study we began to see that for gender, *individual* women oppose and resist. For race and class, the primary mediators are clearly separate and distinct from self and similar others: a school adult, a community official.[7] For gender, at least when one is young and still in school, the mediator is more like self. The mediator is an agemate who may well sleep in the same room.

The next two chapters complete the theoretical prelude to the case. Chapter 3 discusses theories of patriarchy and cultural production that take account of gender. Chapter 4 summarizes the existing ethnographic contributions on women in the cultural-production and practice literature. Though few in number, these studies, most of which were carried out in England, combined with the present research, suggest a consistent pattern. In the British school described by Lees (1986), girls were dominated by fear of being labeled a "slag," a promiscuous girl (see also Griffin 1985). At Bradford and SU, women were not so vulnerable to the threat of a ruined reputation; a different component of the cultural idiom of romance and attractiveness was important. But the results were very similar: the women faced constant evaluations of their worth on the basis of their sexual appeal to men, and they made life "decisions" in the shadow of that reality.

Part 2   *The Theoretical Framework and Existing Studies*

3   *Reproduction Theory and the Gender Status Quo*

What can the lives of women at Bradford and SU tell us about schools and the reproduction of patriarchy in the United States? In this chapter we place our study in the framework of the questions posed in the literature.

We began asking questions about schooling and the reproduction of patriarchy in the mid-1970s.[1] During that period the social theory underlying liberal views of education was exposed and severely challenged. At the same time, feminist social theory broke the silence about gender and its importance as a structuring feature of society. Both areas of theory—critical educational theory (articulated by sociologists of education, anthropologists, and Marxist theoreticians) and feminist theory—have since undergone successive waves of reformulation, some interrelated and some independent. Current views of women and schooling, including our own, draw upon both sources of theory.

Here we will discuss the two streams of theory as they have informed the development of social-reproduction theories of education and of feminist theories, particularly those related to schooling and gender. Reproduction theory originally asked how exploitative class hierarchies were perpetuated from generation to generation.[2] Feminist theorists borrowed from this stream of thought to explain the reproduction of male privilege as a functional component of capitalism. Only later did they begin to see that gender systems might be independent from, but intertwined with, class systems. Gender structures are complex; even today, insofar as it applies to gender and schooling, feminist theory has not resolved the debate about what constitutes the significant, intrinsic nature of gender relations and hierarchies.

In this chapter we recount the historical path of critical education and feminist theory through three conceptual distinctions: (1) prejudice versus social reproduction, (2) reproduction versus production, and (3) production versus practice. We follow the changing conceptions of gender structures as they have intersected with these three ideas of how social structures, including gender hierarchies, are reproduced.

PREJUDICE, BIAS, AND STEREOTYPES VERSUS SOCIAL REPRODUCTION

In the 1970s European social theoreticians began to argue that schools reproduced the social relations of production in capitalism (Althusser 1971; Bourdieu and Passeron 1977).[3] Schools were viewed as instrumental in the reproduction of the class structure because they selectively transmit skills and attitudes according to class, sort people through credentialing into class-related social positions, and profoundly shape identities to fit class destinies. Similar analysis of the political economy of schooling in America soon appeared; perhaps the best known, Bowles and Gintis's *Schooling in Capitalist America,* was published in 1976. According to Bowles and Gintis, the schools promote the interests of the upper classes by unobtrusively reproducing a nonrebellious working class, one that is trained and willing to take a subordinate place in the capitalist system.

Aside from Bowles and Gintis and a few other scholars who were also writing about schools and cultural and social reproduction (e.g., Anyon 1981; Apple 1979, 1982; Giroux 1981; Leacock 1969), most American social scientists continued a tradition of educational research founded upon an unexamined, mostly implicit, social theory.[4] The immediate causes of differential educational outcomes—those correlated with class and race (or minority status)—were debated but not in explicit connection with social theory. Instead, researchers in the empirical tradition studied student characteristics, such as "cultural differences," and school mechanisms, such as tracking, that lead to differential outcomes. Anthropology also had its version of this trend, which resulted in numerous ethnographic studies of schools and analyses of the communicative and attitudinal barriers faced by lower-income and minority children in the classroom (e.g., Gallimore, Boggs, and Jordan 1974; Heath 1983; Philips 1983; Rist 1973).

In this *"traditional* educational theory," in contrast to *"critical* educational theory," American society is implicitly conceived to be

> given, not changeable in any serious way, and desirable. . . .
> When schools are criticized (and they are increasingly
> blamed for everything from drug use to the success of

Japanese industry), it is because they fail to achieve their unstated but assumed function of reproducing and maintaining an idealized vision of U.S. society, one in which everyone finds his or her proper place: the inadequate fail and the deserving and talented rise on their merit. (Weiler 1988:4)

(See also Hawthorn 1987:chapter 9, for a discussion of the underdevelopment of social theory in American social science in general.)

Many, including the anthropologists cited above, would strenuously object to Weiler's characterization of their assumptions, arguing that their research has revealed the prejudice and bias, as well as cross-cultural miscommunication, that seriously impede the educational careers of minority students. Anthropological studies, for example, have made it quite clear that disruptions of socialization will occur when children with different communicative codes and languages encounter school materials and texts not developed with them in mind and face school officials who retain negative stereotypes about their abilities. Nonetheless, the implication of traditional studies is that the schools *would* function to distribute individuals fairly in society if only discriminatory practices and negative stereotypes were dropped and ways of teaching the "culturally different" were mastered.[5]

Traditional educational theory rests on an implicit social theory, which is rather similar to what undergirds the "sex-role theory" of patriarchy (Connell 1987:47–54): society is arranged according to a set of customary or traditional social principles and social roles. These roles are constituted by an aggregate of customs learned through socialization. In sex-role theory, change comes about when outmoded traditional sex roles are cast aside and invalid stereotypical views about the differences between women and men are exposed (see also Arnot 1982:67–69).

Social-reproduction theory challenges these liberal views of social injustice as too shallow. Prejudicial treatment is a reality, mishandling of cultural differences is a fact, but the basis of social injustice is more fundamental.[6] In one sense social-reproduction theory seems quite similar to the traditional functionalist conceptualizations of society just discussed. In Bourdieu and Passeron's analysis of the French schools, for example, students are socialized to certain jobs and certain roles and to a "mindset" and view of society that justifies the class hierarchy. As in socialization theory, they learn what they are taught—the skills proffered them, the positions to which they are destined, and the understandings and values shared by other members of the society. Where Bourdieu and Passeron differed was that they linked socialization to power. They analyzed how what is learned undergirds the structure of power and privilege in the society.

By a sleight of hand, as Bourdieu and Passeron describe it, the schools in France justify the exploitation of the working classes by the beneficiaries of capitalism. The schools convey the message that intellectual virtuosos are entitled entry to the upper echelons of French society, whereas lesser lights are suited for lower-level jobs. They pass off the "cultural arbitrary" (the style of thinking and acting) of the upper class as characteristic of native, inborn intellectual brilliance. All students are trained to this cultural arbitrary and compete in examinations that measure mastery of it. Not surprisingly, the children of the upper classes turn out to be "better" students and more "intellectually brilliant" and are therefore entitled to better-paying, higher-status jobs with more workers and citizens at their direction. By means of this "symbolic violence" that it never recognizes, the working class is led into a docile and passive acceptance of a system that places it from the outset at a disadvantage.

Social-reproduction theory differs from traditional educational theory and from sex-role theory by insisting that the social system itself must be critically considered. In traditional theories of education, which presume a meritocracy, there are no natural interest groups—working classes or upper classes, in one case, women or men, in the other—and no reason for misleading any members of the society as to its true nature and their positions in it. The system is the way it is because of custom, and there are no interest groups that strive to maintain the status quo. In neither of these theories is it the issue to challenge misleading and purposely mystifying mechanisms in the society; rather, the goal is to enlighten misinformed and out-of-date teachers, administrators, parents, and other child socializers about more modern and more valid conceptualizations of society and its members. The recalcitrants, the conventional or traditional types, the male chauvinist pigs, the racist teachers, the well-intentioned but misinformed administrators all simply need to brought to see the world in a different way or suffered until they are outlived by a new, enlightened generation.[7] In social-reproduction theory, by contrast, the system of power and privilege itself needs to be changed, and change is likely to involve more than overcoming prejudice. The groups benefited by a system are unlikely to give up without a contest. Scientific facts on sex differences and scholarly rejections of racist theories are unlikely to convince the privileged groups to give up their prerogatives.

Social-Reproduction Theories of Gender

Although the earliest "reproduction theorists," including Althusser and Bourdieu, emphasized class, their theories and research had implications for gender. Bourdieu and Saint Martin's (1970) statistical tables, for example, clearly show an inverse correlation between coming from the working class and succeeding in the top ranks of the French educational system *and* show the same for being female, though the authors do not specifically discuss gender differences. Similarly, the schools' standards for academic excellence, exposed by Bourdieu and Passeron as a "cultural arbitrary" associated with the elite classes, could no doubt be further unmasked to show their favoring of males of the elite classes. Bourdieu and Passeron certainly did not totally neglect gender bias. They recognize it through the idea of "feminization" of occupations (1977:76–97, 182–83). But their primary focus was on the class system.

Feminist researchers followed up the implications of reproduction theory for gender inequalities. They blamed the schools for sealing women's fate in the paid labor force, where women clearly received wages below those of men of their social class. A stream of feminist research on gender and schooling developed to counter biological and psychological explanations of women's lower economic achievements. Barrett (1980) adapted an Althusserian perspective to argue that schools shape gender relations within class structures. Wolpe's (1978) analysis of British school policy argued that some major educational policies rested on ideological biases that served to limit women's futures to unpaid domestic labor and lower-paying salaried jobs. Deem (1978) documented the curriculum that working-class women were taking and analyzed the limitations it placed on their opportunities for advanced schooling and better jobs. Like the social reproductionists, both Wolpe and Deem linked the ideological position of the school to the subordination of women, in terms not only of actually channeling them into lower-paying jobs but also of outfitting them with an ideology to explain their lower levels of achievement.

"REPRODUCTION" VERSUS "PRODUCTION"

Althusser, Bourdieu and Passeron, Wolpe, Barrett, and Deem may have differed in whether they focused on class or gender, but they shared a similar limitation. Although they illuminated the ideological messages promulgated by schools, the differential tracking of students, and the symbolic violence perpetuated by the schools, they took for granted what was actually going on in the classroom.

They did not look closely at actual encounters between students and teachers, nor did they engage in detailed theorizing about students' internalization of school ideology. In Connell's (1983:152) appraisal, even Bourdieu, despite his influential concept of "habitus," relegated the schoolday-to-schoolday processes of reproduction to "black box" status. Exactly how, on a day-to-day basis, the school differentially trained people, instilled a valorization of some students' backgrounds and not of others', or shaped class members' identities was not their major concern (see also Valli 1986:17). Perhaps as a result of this omission, they missed a crucial fact—student resistance. Giroux (1983a:271) comments on Bourdieu's failure to note student opposition: "The power of reflexive thought and historical agency are relegated to a minor theoretical detail in Bourdieu's theory of change."[8]

This lacuna in social reproduction theories began to be filled in the late 1970s. For the neo-Marxists, the processes of social reproduction were considerably illuminated by the work of researchers associated with the University of Birmingham's Centre for Contemporary Cultural Studies (CCCS). The CCCS group joined the questions posed by social-reproduction theory to the ethnographic study of youth cultures, adolescents, and schooling. The result was insight into the dynamics of cultural reproduction and the role of oppressed groups in societal reproduction. The classic study from this group is Willis's *Learning to Labor* (1977, 1981b).

At this point the British studies and anthropological studies of education in the United States began to converge.[9] Comparing the work of Willis (1981a, 1981b) with that of the anthropologist John Ogbu (1974, 1978, 1985, 1987), we find similar methods (namely, reliance upon ethnographic case studies) and a convergence of focus on the responses of oppressed groups (working-class males for Willis, ethnic and racial minorities for Ogbu) to schooling.[10] In essence, both concluded that students are likely to act in school from a collective sense of the "opportunities," or lack of them, afforded by society to people of their group. Students are critical of the school and society's misrepresentations of them, sometimes to the point that they disrupt the smooth functioning of the school. But often, for various reasons and despite their oppositional character, student actions result in reproducing cultural values and patterns that in turn contribute to the reproduction of structured inequalities and of traditional class and race relationships. In the earlier reproduction theories of Althusser, Bowles and Gintis, and Bourdieu and Passeron, which focus on the policies, texts, exams, and practices of school officials, the lower classes are, by implication, silent and presumably passive and submissive to the programming of the state. Willis's dramatic study of the "lads" of Hammertown Boys, a "non-selective" modern secondary school in Britain, and Ogbu's decade-and-a-half of work on minorities in the United States, especially blacks, suggest otherwise.

Willis, his fellow researchers at CCCS, Ogbu, feminist researchers, and others as well (see Apple 1982:91–134; Giroux 1983b:71–111) emphasized the active role of working-class students, minority students, and female students in responding to schooling. In contrast to the arguments of earlier social-reproduction theorists, schools do not smoothly, unilaterally function to "cool out" those who do not fit the profile of the privileged student (Clark 1960; Lakomski 1984). These students do not blindly follow the path prescribed by the schools, nor do they swallow whole the schools' justification of their probable futures in the lower strata of the social hierarchy.

From his research for *The Next Generation* (1974) Ogbu began to argue that black students oriented themselves to school on the basis of their perceptions of the labor market and their likely future in it. Although his social theory was neither explicit nor informed by neo-Marxism, Ogbu could have applied the concepts that Willis used to interpret the lads' apprehension of their society. Black students, Ogbu found, were cognizant of the job ceiling faced by blacks. They "penetrated" the official ideological premises of the school to ascertain that no matter how hard they worked in school they would still face a society predicated on white privilege. Over the years, Obgu has refined his analysis to include as major components: (1) the identity-relevant legacy of the opposition between blacks and whites in the United States; (2) "folk theories of making it" that differ from school and mainstream social ideology; and (3) blacks' apprehension of unfair constraints on their participation in the labor market. His analyses emphasize the oppositional identities that have developed in the black community over the long history of struggle since slavery, as well as the styles of speaking, fashions of dress, ways of succeeding, and ways of acting in institutional contexts, that signal these identities.

Willis's look at the Hammertown students showed a similarly complicated picture. Students reacted to the structural barriers facing the working class and, in their reaction, produced social practices and a meaning system, a culture, that celebrated working-class masculinity and the sorts of jobs held by their fathers. They rejected school ideology but produced a culture that ironically led them to the same positions in society as were occupied by their fathers. The lads constantly walked on the edge of dismissal, flaunting their disdain for the rules and symbolically challenging the school's ideology. Willis, like others associated with CCCS (e.g., Hall and Jefferson 1976; Hebdige 1979), analyzed working-class youth cultures as an appropriation of various cultural codes and paraphernalia from the media and from the youths' home communities. The resulting counterculture was put together in reaction to society's idea of the young people as future members of the working class. The lads were far from passive; they certainly did not internalize the school's view of themselves. And yet, although rejecting the school's ideology, they ended up in working-class jobs. In fact, they embraced working-class jobs with gusto.

In contrast to prior social-reproduction theory, Willis's interpretation contained the possibility of radical social change. There was no reason that the next generation would produce a meaning system like that of the lads, or indeed one that would lead its members to the same willing acceptance of working-class jobs. The outcome was in doubt each generation. There was a dynamic, open-ended interaction of the classes, so that the existing exploitative relations might or might not be reproduced. By animating the working class in the scenario of reproduction, Willis escaped the determinism of Althusser and others.

Willis's portrait of the lads emphasized a creative or productive element. In their day-to-day responses to events, informed by an apprehension of the structural position of the working class, the lads made sense of their lives and forged an identity for themselves. To generate this acted-out and sometimes articulated sense of their lives, they drew upon ideas and practices from their working-class background, but also from other sources. "Structural determinations act," Willis remarks, "not by direct mechanical effect, but by mediation through the cultural level where their own relationships become subject to forms of exposure and explanation" (1981b:174). This collective generation of an outlook and way of being and acting in the world he terms "cultural production" (1981a:49). As we shall see, a number of writers use this concept of cultural production, as well as its implication that people forge their own meaning systems in response to the societal position they face and its material implications.

Weiler (1988) refers to the theories of Althusser, Bourdieu and Passeron, and Bowles and Gintis as "reproduction" theories and the later ones heralded by Willis as "production" theories. "Production" theory builds upon "reproduction" theory. It admits that power and privilege are granted to some groups and not to others by capitalism and patriarchy (and, we might add, by race and age hierarchies). It attends to the ideology and practice of school officials, but it adds a crucial look at the reactions of the students to school practices and school officials. The distinction highlights the tendency of "production" theorists to look first to the "lived culture" of the students and their cultural productions, rather than to the policies and practices of the school that, if effective, reproduce the status quo. "Production" further suggests a potential for change in the structure, whereas "reproduction," because of its early association with Althusserian Marxists, connotes invariant structures. "Production" is a felicitous term also because it is compatible with the current emphasis on "practice."[11]

With these caveats, we have for now adopted Weiler's labels and put our own work here into the "productionist" camp. Later, in the chapter on peer-related gender politics, we will review and revise these labels.

Cultural-Production Theories and Gender

Feminist scholars of gender and schooling arrived at the position that conflict and resistance had to be incorporated into their analyses, as had Willis and others writing on class heirarchies. Weiler (1988:36–37) credits the British sociologist of education Arnot (1982) and Kelly and Nihlen (1982) in the United States, with being among the first to articulate the need for production theories of gender and schooling. Kelly and Nihlen focused on schools' roles in reproducing the sexual division of labor. They summarized available studies on school patterns of staffing showing that women occupied lower rungs of school administration, studies showing sex-stereotyping in texts and classroom materials, and studies of differences in the attention that teachers give students depending on their race and gender. They did not, however, assume that girls and women simply internalize the apparent messages about women's roles that are embedded in discriminatory school policies and practices. They suspected that women may resist these messages and called for an investigation of what students do with the information presented to them.

More explicitly than Kelly and Nihlen, Arnot (1982) emphasized the importance of incorporating resistance into views of schooling and gender. In order to avoid the implication of inevitable reproduction, she proposed to substitute the Gramscian (1971) concept of "hegemony" for reproduction and modified Bernstein's (1971, 1980) concept of "codes" to suggest that young women might contest and contradict gender codes learned from their families, peers, and schools. Feminist theory on gender and schooling thus began to incorporate an explicit production component.

Meanwhile a number of feminist researchers in Britain, including a group associated with CCCS, were working to remedy the virtual absence of ethnographic information on girls' involvement in youth culture (e.g., Cowie and Lees 1981; Griffin 1985; Lees 1986; McRobbie 1978b, 1980; McRobbie and Garber 1976). They were influenced by and contributed to production theories and were especially motivated to complement, expand on, and critique Willis's study of working-class lads in *Learning to Labor* (McRobbie 1980; see also Acker 1981).

As it turned out, women's patterns of response and resistance were different from those of working-class males found by Hebdige (1979) and Willis (1981b). We will return to details of these ethnographic studies in chapter 4. For the moment we must take up these feminist critiques of *Learning to Labor*, because they presaged further theoretical distinctions and raised some issues particularly germane to our study.

In Willis's book the reader sees the world, the school, the other students, and the teachers primarily from the perspective of the lads. Willis gives a plausible account of the lads' response to schooling and the ultimate outcome of this response in their working lives. Unfortunately, his relatively exclusive focus on the lads produced some myopic theoretical conceptualizations. At least by implication, Willis presents the lads as though they were *the* working class. We do learn about internal divisions among the working class—the lads versus the "ear'oles" (conformist students), the lads versus the girls, the lads versus the Pakis and the West Indians—but not much about the dynamic interactions of the groups or about the significance of internal class divisions for the theory of production (see also Connell 1983; Giroux 1983a:287; Jenkins 1983). In other words, Willis virtually neglected the process of the construction and emergence of groups (e.g., lads, girls, Pakis) within the working class. Many conceivable interests crosscut student groups in institutions, and how they coalesce is a matter of cultural politics and struggle. If the process is not studied, one group, like the lads, is apt to be seen as representing the whole.

In a related vein, Willis's (1981b:199) vivid account of the lads leaves no doubt about their sexism. The final line of the first edition of the book quotes Joey's response to Willis's query about going back to college: "I don't know, the only thing I'm interested in is fucking as many women as I can if you really wanna know." Willis analyzes the dynamics by which sexist attitudes from the lads' working-class background are culturally reproduced and highlights the grave consequences of these attitudes for the lads' understanding ("penetration") of and response to the British class system. By opposing themselves to females and femininity and associating mental work with femininity, the lads had closed themselves off to more powerful means of representing and understanding the social system in which they were enmeshed. They could act out their opposition through clothing and symbolic acts of defiance, but they could go no further. These symbols did not lend themselves to fine-grained analysis of the society and so circumscribed the lads' recognition of ways to remedy their social problems, and change the society.

Although Willis does link these dire limitations of the lads' ability to effect social change to sexism (e.g., 1981b:147) and although he does speak of the lads' role in recreating patriarchal gender relations, he never specifically addresses the question of patriarchy and its relationship to capitalism. His explanation of the lads' embracing and recreating the sexism of their fathers implies that their sexist behavior was epiphenomenal to their response to schooling and capitalism. In forming their response to the capitalist system they drew upon the sexist patterns of the working class to forge a celebration of their masculinity, in opposition to the school's proffered student identity. But were their actions in relation to women, and hence their role in perpetrating patriarchy, really epiphenomenal, as Willis describes? Or could it be that gender struggles are just as central as class struggles?

This point ties in with another concern raised by McRobbie and her colleagues: the possibility that male researchers were ethnocentrically ("gendrocentrically") blind to the significance of "female" culture for working-class culture in general. As their feminist anthropologist counterparts (e.g., Reiter 1975) have recognized and continue to point out, male ethnographers tend either to miss "female domains" or to assume that they are unimportant to the "male domains" they are describing. The difficulty seems to lie in persuading male scholars that gender has to be incorporated into theory that guides all social analysis—not just covered in a chapter on women and women's activities.

The limited appreciation of gender structures can be attributed, in part, to the origins of social-reproduction theory. Because the reproductionist and later productionist theories of gender and schooling began in the context of Marxist analysis of class, they tended to focus on the reproduction of the sexual division of labor. The wider entailments of gender hierarchies eluded the theorists' gaze. The early ethnographic studies of women's youth cultures and responses to schooling were particularly influenced by this restricted view of gender relations (see McRobbie 1982, for example). Nonetheless, because ethnographic research is not especially tethered by theory, these early ethnographic studies stimulated a reconceptualization of gender hierarchies. While conceptualizations of schools as sites in the reproduction of class, gender, and race relations were becoming sophisticated, ideas of the nature of gender hierarchies were developing as well.

GENDERED SOCIAL THEORY

Putting gender into social theory began in earnest in the 1970s. Still not in accord with one another, these feminist theories center on different aspects of the social relations of gender and on different determinants of these relations. In some feminist theories, which Connell (1987:41) calls "extrinsic," gender hierarchies are seen as subordinate features of a society organized around class relations. In other theories, categorized as "intrinsic" by Connell, gender relations are a social phenomenon unto themselves.[12]

Extrinsic theories of gender hierarchies are important to consider here because the reproduction theories discussed above originally drew their visions of society from Marxist theories of capitalism and did not ordinarily feature gender, except as an aspect of the sexual division of labor. That is, Marxist feminist theorists began by assuming that gender relations lie in the shadow of class relations. They suspected that the subordination of women plays a functional role in the maintenance of capitalism. Women figure into the capitalist equation as a reserve, cheap labor force and, more importantly, as the primary cogs in reproducing the male labor force. They give birth to children, take care of children, and meet male workers' domestic needs.[13] Thus the gender hierarchy is handy for capitalism, but is not necessary, and gender relations do not enter into the key component of the capitalistic system—the relations of production. On this basis, gender was presumed a weaker natural interest group than class.

To account for its origin and maintenance, theorists relegated the gender hierarchy to the important but peripheral area of ideology. They explained it as a truncated social structure arising from universal, though perhaps surmountable, psychodynamic tendencies (such as those theorized by Lacan) or cognitive structures (such as those adduced by the anthropologist Levi-Strauss). Because ideologies are permeable and, unless sustained by necessity, expendable, the gender hierarchy was seen as deriving from a sort of universal understanding or idea of male-female differences that conceivably could be cast aside. For example, in the twentieth century, because of technological advances in birth control and life-prolonging advances in medicine and public health, it is no longer necessary for women to spend their adult lives bearing children. Thus, supposedly, the strong symbolic association between women and childbearing will tend to weaken, and with it, support for the ideological differentiation between males and females. When considered in this fashion, gender relations are less fundamental and "less comprehensive" than class relations (Connell 1987:45). They are important in the biological reproduction and nurturance of the labor force but not in the central economic arena of production, and thus are presumably not a direct basis of competing interests between women and men.

Mono Systems versus Dual Systems

By the end of the 1970s, serious doubts arose about the validity of theoretically subordinating gender to class. Given that gender hierarchies predate capitalist modes of production, could they really be relegated to a peripheral position in social theory? Given their obvious effects on women's lives today, could they really be considered of peripheral importance?

The idea that the gender hierarchy constitutes a structure or system of equal importance to, and related to, the class hierarchy emerged in the late 1970s, articulated by Hartmann (1979) and by a collection of papers edited by Eisenstein (1979). It crystalized into a "dual-systems theory," in which gender subordination is viewed as a separate system with its own logic and basis. Class relations and gender relations crucially intertwine in different ways in different moments of history, but neither determines the other.[14]

The dual-systems approach opened up two major issues, neither of which has been resolved much to anyone's satisfaction. The first was the challenge of interrelating the two systems or structures. Recently Weiler (1988:29) has summed up the challenge as follows: "The immediate task for socialist feminists is to create a synthesis of these two lines of analysis, to create a theory that can relate to what Rubin has called 'the sex/gender system' and the economic system through an analysis of the sexual division of labor and an understanding of the intersection of these two forms of power." That Weiler's comment echoes a statement made by Hartmann almost a decade before, in 1979, reveals that the task is still in progress.

The second issue is related to the first. Not only does the intertwining of class and gender—and we would add race and age—hierarchies have to be worked out, but the nature of gender hierarchies, intrinsically defined, has to be theorized as well. If the economic interests that define and determine class relations in capitalism do not define and determine gender relations, then what does?

A number of theories have been proposed that purport to answer this question, or at least establish the preliminary terms and arena for analysis. Connell (1987:54–65) has divided the competing theories into two very abstract types, "categorical" and "practice." The distinction depends upon whether the investigation or explanation *presupposes* the categories to be investigated. If so, the theory qualifies as "categorical." If, instead, the investigation presumes that interest groups emerge around culturally constructed "sexual" activities, the theory qualifies as a "practice" theory.

Categorical theories posit a priori gender types, usually two—women and men—related to one another by power and conflict of interest. Mary Daly's account of global patriarchy in *Gyn/Ecology* (1978), for example, takes it for granted that men and women are the relevant categories and that the explanation or core of their relationship is the violence of males toward females. Another categorical theory, more commonly encountered in academic literature, is that of "sexual stratification." It too posits two categories—men and women—and proceeds to map inequalities between the two. On the whole, categorical theories concentrate on *describing* the relationship between the genders, which varies from theory to theory, but not on how the categories are formed. The categories may be biologically given, as in Mary Daly's writings, or socially predicated, as are the gendered persons in a "family." Connell (1987:56) gives an example from Delphy's (1977) analysis along Marxist feminist lines, in which the institution of marriage defines gendered categories and the "core of the relations between them is the husbands' appropriation of a surplus from the wives' unpaid labour." Another form of categorical theory comes from the positing of Weberian ideal types: typical males or females with typically male or female attitudes who do typically male or female things, and so forth, the world over. This type of categorical model turns out to be quite prevalent in common-sense or cultural models, as well as in scientific theories (Quinn and Holland 1987).

In practice theory, by contrast, the whole area of sexual activities, sexual politics, and the interest groups that emerge are considered a question for research. It is assumed that sexual activities such as intercourse are culturally constructed in different ways across cultures and historical periods, and that they may influence, but not determine, the groups that form socially in relation to the conflicts of interest that arise. These cultural definitions may or may not strike us, in our twentieth-century Western world, as familiar. They may or may not seem related to our "biologically given" categories of male and female. Yanagisako (1988), for example, cites Halperin's account of classical Greece in which sexual intercourse was important in the creation of political identities and was defined in terms of the active person and the passive person, both of whom could be male.[15]

By their nature, practice theories are apt to be more complex than categorical theories. They are subject to the vagaries of varied, culturally fired imaginations and are prey to the gerrymandering of history. In the place of certitude about basic categories—male and female—and assurance that the categories produce natural interest groups interrelated according to the defining features of the categories, practice theory provides only the vague guideline of culturally constructed "sexual" activities (most broadly defined). Clearly the gendered categories may number *more* than two.

The advantage of practice theory is that it can accommodate the issue of internal divisions within categories. Just as class-oriented reproduction theory now faces the challenge of accounting for differences *within* classes, gender theory today faces the challenge of accounting for differences *within* gender. Categorical theories and explanations that posit women as a uniform category—essentially an ideal type—immediately run into a problem. Women from groups other than that presupposed as representative of the ideal type are often offended; the posited ideal type does not resonate with them and denies their experience. Theories based on socially defined gender roles, such as husband and wife, run into similar problems when the presumed form of the family turns out not to be the form familiar to people from different backgrounds. Moreover, categorical theories that simply pit men against women may be unable to encompass adequately political struggles revolving around heterosexuality versus homosexuality, for heterosexual men *and* women may oppose homosexual men *and* women. In Adrienne Rich's (1980) analysis, for example, gender relations in contemporary society should be described as organized not around men versus women, but rather around enforced heterosexuality and homophobia. Categorical theories cannot accommodate such complications, but practice theory can. As conceived by practice theory, different forms of masculinities and femininities are likely to arise, along with different interest groups that stand to gain or lose depending on the ascendancy of one form over another. The categories themselves are at issue as well as the cultural construction of the activities.

As Connell (1987:63) states it, a focus on practice implies that

> structure is not pre-given but historically composed. That
> implies the possibility of different ways of structuring gen-
> der reflecting the dominance of different social interests.
> It also implies different degrees to which the structuring is
> coherent or consistent, reflecting changing levels of contest
> and resistance. Sexual politics is embedded in the structure
> of gender relations at the most basic level. Structures de-
> velop crisis tendencies which materialize in radical sexual
> politics.

The practice-theory approach also allows us to take advantage of
what has been learned in anthropology and sociolinguistics about
language and knowledge as means of signaling social affiliation and
opposition, and perhaps of most importance to our study, best fits the
cases that we will present. Thus we conclude the chapter by addressing production versus practice as the third major conceptual distinction that has emerged in the historical path that began with reproduction theory.

"Production" versus "Practice" Theories of Schooling and Gender

As we have seen, the critics of such class-production
studies as *Learning to Labor*, and especially feminist critics, have complained that while internal class divisions are often described they are
rarely recognized as having theoretical implications (see also Jenkins
1983). A second criticism is that the importance of patriarchy has
been underestimated.

The question of internal divisions is crucial if we are to accept
Willis's assurance that reproduction is not inevitable. It is not ultimately clear that production theory does escape the assumption of
invariant structures and thus, inevitable reproduction. Although Willis himself (1981a, 1981b) constantly denies the inevitability of social
reproduction and reiterates the possibility of structural change, Connell (1983) suspects that Willis remains in the straitjacket of Althusserian structuralism. One can at least agree that Willis worked much
harder to explain working-class boys' apparent acquiescence to their
place in the capitalist system than he did to ferret out the beginnings
of any radically new structure that might have emerged had the boys
refused working-class jobs.

Connell (1987:44) is so convinced that a notion of transhistorical, invariant structures lurks behind the idea of "reproduction" that he counters, "For history to become organic to theory, social structure must be [conceptualized as] constantly *constituted* rather than constantly reproduced." Here Connell is advising that social structures be conceptualized as the impermanent outcome of moment-to-moment processes. To him, reproduction theory wrongly implies that social structures have a permanence. Because of her similar concerns about the concept of reproduction, Arnot (1982) has argued for the use of "hegemony." Both terms convey the weight of social structure, the existence of social constraints, but "reproduction" is flavored by an image of a fait accompli, the successful replication of an already successful status quo, whereas "hegemony" implies that the structure that now exists is held in force (admittedly strong), on a day-to-day basis, against the opposition of time and other forces. Production theory, to the extent that it rests upon taken-for-granted, immutable categories (e.g., class, gender, race) and assumes that its job is to study the conflict between and among these categories and the subcategories formed by their intersection (e.g., black women, white men), is also at risk of the limitations that Connell and Arnot point out for the older theories of social reproduction.

Practice theories attempt to overcome this risk. They focus on the generation of meaning systems by groups in response to structural constraints, as does production theory. But they respond to internal divisions and struggles as well and thus enlarge upon production theory (see also Hebdige 1979). Production theories that ignore the processes of group formation and alliance, in other words, may be considered "categorical"—with the attendant disadvantages. Practice theory, then, though more recent and still in process, has taken yet another step away from "simple" reproduction theory. With incorporation into its theory of internal differences among working-class and other structurally defined categories of youth, a major vestige of the structuralist view, a priori categories and preordained interest groups, is being cast off. Although the importance of regimes of power and privilege has certainly not been erased from the theoretical picture, the spotlight has swung away from the means by which the powerful maintain hegemony. More recently emphasized, both in theory and in research, are the cultural productions of the less powerful. The focus has moved to the production of incipient social movements that could conceivably challenge existing class and gender regimes to the point of crisis and disruption (Connell 1987; Johnson 1986–87; Willis 1981a).[16]

In our own research we began with questions from production theory and previous ethnographic studies of women and schooling, as well as with questions from our previous work on peer groups. As our analysis proceeded, we found it necessary to incorporate practice theory and to pay attention to internal divisions among the women.

4 Questions about Women's Responses to Schooling

In the afterword to the revised edition of *Learning to Labor*, Willis discussed how the concepts of cultural and social reproduction could be extended to gender. He was by then very familiar with feminist critiques of his work and aware of the findings to date on the involvement of girls and young women in counterschool cultures.[1] On the basis of this research—most of which concerned students in their early and middle teens—he advanced the suggestion that, rather like their male counterparts, "at the 'cultural level' girls in schools are involved in forms of resistance and collective identity creation focused on opposition to, and transcendence of both 'official' school gender models and the adult staff themselves, activities which have 'ironic' and partly unintended consequences for the girls' own entrapment in their class and gender destiny" (1981b:209). In other words, reproduction theory, as extended by notions of "cultural production," is relevant to gender as well as to class.

At the time, the research suggested that schoolgirls might be less oppositional in the face of gender oppression than schoolboys are in response to class barriers. Gaskell had pointed out to Willis that schools may be relatively overt about preparing girls for their future roles as housewives and secretaries, that in some sense schools are simply "benignly" accepting of the cultural forms developed by girls from society's notions of femininity (see also Arnot 1982:79, 1984:18; Connell et al. 1982:84–85). Nonetheless, in Willis's opinion, "Either way, we should not underestimate the ways in which the creative cultures of femininity and romance through which girls live might help to direct them into future roles of domesticity and motherhood as well as the double exploitation of periods of dual role oppression: waged work in the lowest skilled, hardest, and least well paid jobs as well

43

as the never-ending domestic burden of 'looking after the family'." In sum, Willis considered that although girls and their schools might seem more in accord about the students' futures than working-class boys and their schools are, the girls are nevertheless just as active as the boys at the cultural level. They too construct meaning systems in response to their collective sense of the societal restrictions they face.

Willis then proposed some ideas about what girls' "forms of resistance and collective identity creation" might turn out to be. He especially cited McRobbie's (1978b) finding that in the classroom girls play off received versions of femininity, sometimes by roughly violating stereotypes to provoke shock or embarrassment, sometimes by "naughtily" exaggerating stereotyped female sexuality. But he also recognized the implications of McRobbie's finding that women's primary path of collective identity creation is to emphasize romance—especially fantasizing about romance—over acceptance of the female student identity proffered by the school: "'Best friend' culture, romance, and particular kinds of femininity do seem to offer a more viable set of cultural opportunities and satisfactions for many working class girls" (1981b:209).

Willis's terse summary foreshadowed some of the snags that would arise in applying production theory to girls and to gender barriers. Subsequent research has thus far discovered no evidence of female equivalents to male groups like Willis's lads (Brake 1980:135–54). The girls and young women that Willis's colleagues were studying did not turn out simply to be "lads" in skirts. The literature instead shows girls' patterns to be quite different and generally attributes the differences to the fact that working-class girls face both class *and* gender hierarchies (Connell et al. 1982; Davies 1983; Kessler et al. 1985; Willis 1981b). More fine-grained analyses have been harder to come by and more subject to debate.[2]

Studies of boys' and young men's subcultures, particularly those of Willis (1981b) and, to a degree, Hebdige (1979), had created a sort of ideal typical version of resistance as collective, overtly countercultural, and antischool. Girls did not fit the ideal type.[3] It became necessary to expand notions of opposition and resistance and to answer a series of questions: What sort of groups were women forming? Could involvement with romance and the cult of femininity be considered a counterculture opposing the sexist ideologies and practices of the school? If not, how *were* women reacting to the gender hierarchy promoted by the schools, and could their reactions even be called "resistance"?

We will first describe issues relating to the groups that women form, their stances toward the school, the debate over romance, and the muddle over the concept of "resistance." In the final section of this chapter we summarize the questions deriving from the literature that guided our approach to the present study.

ISSUES ABOUT GIRLS' COLLECTIVITIES

In a review of the neglected role of girls in British youth subcultures, McRobbie and Garber (1976:219,221) suggested that "the majority of girls find alternative strategies [of resistance] to that of the boys' sub-cultures. The important question, then, may not be the absence or presence of girls in the male subcultures, but the complementary ways in which girls interact among themselves and with each other to form a distinctive culture of their own. . . . [In the case of girls' resistance to sexism] the sub-cultural group may not be the most likely place where those equivalent rituals, responses and negotiations will be located" (see also McRobbie 1980).

McRobbie's important study (1978b) of 14- to 16-year-old girls in a youth club in Birmingham, England, bore out these suspicions. She found small groups comprised of two or three girls who were best friends.[4] Willis's lads participated in a larger, rowdy group of five or six, on the streets, in the school halls, or on the schoolyard; these female pairs or trios of best friends instead went into their bedrooms, closed the door, and listened to records, while talking about boy-friends and feminine things (see also McRobbie and Garber 1976).

More recent work has given a different picture, or at least a more complex picture, of the peer groups that girls and young women form. Some research (e.g., Griffin 1985) confirms the pattern of small groups of close girlfriends, but other studies introduce complications. In the early 1980s Lees and Cowie (see Cowie and Lees 1981; Lees 1986) interviewed 15- to 16-year-old girls in comprehensive schools in London.[5] Their findings describe girls who had a range of friends, including some boys.[6] Although most groups of friends consisted of three or more girls who all knew each other and met regularly, these girls had broader networks than did McRobbie's, and they were less sequestered. They participated in leisure activities outside their homes; they did not simply stay in the privacy of their rooms. Another study shows a decidedly large grouping of girls. In her study of third-year students in a British grammar school for girls, Lambart (1979) found a "sisterhood" with more than a dozen members.

Other studies, of "delinquent" girls, show additional patterns of friendship and activity. Campbell's (1984) study of girls in New York gangs (some coed, some all-girl, but all affiliated with male gangs) and Smith's (1978) study of girls in gangs like the Skinheads and Hell's

Angels report that the girls participated in many activities outside the home, including fighting. Lees's (1986) findings emphasize a pattern in which girls belong to a set of friends—girls and boys—who know each other and do things together. Campbell found a pattern of association, emphasizing by contrast a group of friends in which the main ties are among the boys, with the girls present because they are the boys' girlfriends.

From the pattern Willis describes for the lads or the one McRobbie describes for the girls she studied, it is possible to theorize a same-sex group that collectively generates a cultural meaning system. But associations of girls with other girls *and* with boys, such as those described by Lees, Campbell, and Smith, suggest otherwise. Same-sex groups, like Willis's lads or McRobbie's girls, seem but a limited part of the picture. From the subsequent research, what seems more likely is that many girls (and boys) participate in larger, more diverse peer cultures or student cultures, which are coed. Our study, too, reveals coed student cultures and indicates that these mixed peer groups have great consequences for the women involved.[7] Cowie and Lees (1981) express the effects of mixed groups as creating a "sexual space." Because a girl moved in a "sexual space," she could not roam freely or go out alone, as a boy her age might. Roaming around would have resulted in her being labeled a "slag" or a promiscuous, "easy" girl and possibly in physical assault. Griffin (1985:60) uses the metaphor of a sexual game instead of a space. The girls in her study claimed a preference for going out with girlfriends instead of boyfriends, but found themselves compelled toward the latter. They found themselves in "a game that young women would never win; if you said 'yes' [to sex] you were a slag, and if you said 'no' [and hung around with girls only] you were frigid or a lezzie [lesbian]."

In chapter 3, under the rubric of practice theory, we introduced the issue of struggle over the formation of gendered categories such as "boy" and "girl" and thus, by implication, the struggle over different styles of being feminine and being masculine. Struggles over femininities and masculinities are evident in the testimonies of the girls and young women in both Lees's and Griffin's studies and, as will be seen, in our own study. A "lezzie" in Griffin's study clearly does not stand for a valued type of femininity. Kessler et al. (1985) report explicitly on such struggles in Australian schools and characterize the ascendancy of favored masculinities and femininities as a "gender regime" (see also Connell 1987). Somewhat akin to Arnot's (1982: 80–81) "gender code," a gender regime is defined as "the pattern of practices that constructs various kinds of masculinities and femininities among staff and students, orders them in terms of prestige and power, and constructs a sexual division of labor within the institution" (Kessler et al. 1985:42). In short, as is beginning to emerge from the literature, the important collectivities in the case of gender seem not to be the gender-segregated groups emphasized by Willis or by McRobbie, but rather mixed peer groups and the kind of gender regimes they promote.

WHAT YOUNG WOMEN DO WITH THEIR CRITICISMS OF THE SCHOOLS

Willis's lads dramatically acted out their critical stance toward the school. Although some of the girls in the studies we have reviewed and, as will be seen, in the present study had ideas about school—often negative—that differed from school ideology, they usually did not act out their criticisms.[8]

Some girls do participate in antischool groups and antischool behavior. Thomas (cited by Weiler 1988:42–43 and Arnot 1984:19), who studied antischool girls at two schools in Australia, one middle-class, one working-class, over the course of an academic year, reports aggressively defiant behavior. Like McRobbie (1978b), Thomas mentions an acting out toward teachers (not peers) of an exaggerated aspect of stereotyped femininity—an assertive and sometimes coy sexuality (see also Griffin 1985). McRobbie's (1978b:104) description of this type of behavior is especially cogent:

> One way in which girls combat the class-based and oppressive features of the school is to assert their "femaleness," to introduce into the classroom their physical maturity in such a way as to force the teachers to take notice. A class instinct then finds expression at the level of jettisoning the official ideology for girls in the school (neatness, diligence, compliance, femininity, passivity, etc.) and replacing it with a *more* feminine, even sexual one.

All those involved seem to agree that this tactic is disruptive. Schools do not encourage the acting out of sexual behavior in the classroom. If we may judge from the elementary school in which we conducted our earlier study, school officials would prefer to keep sexual aspects out of gender relations in the classroom and ignore the fact that their charges are becoming sexually mature (Eisenhart and Holland 1983). Generally, in school as elsewhere, women and girls are expected to reveal their femininity but to keep overt sexuality under control (see, e.g., Griffin 1985; Valli 1986). With school adults, but not their peers, girls can subvert this cultural construction of their femininity by aggressively emphasizing their sexuality as a form of resistance. And in the school, as in most workplaces, aggressively used sexuality creates an awkward situation for authorities.[9]

Refraining from joining an actively antischool group or avoiding disruptive displays of sexuality does not necessarily mean that a girl is proschool. The situation is much more complicated. Lees (1986:121) describes a fourfold pattern that she found among the approximately one hundred girls she studied. Being pro- or antischool did not predict whether a girl would be pro- or antilearning. That is, some girls were alienated from the school, but not from learning and getting credentials; others were interested in seeing their friends at school, but were alienated from learning; still others were proschool *and* prolearning; a final group disliked school and was alienated from career and learning as well.

In her study of school girls in Birmingham, Griffin (1985) likewise found a complex picture with no stable pattern of conformity or resistance. It was not possible for her to identify a group of girls who were consistently school "troublemakers" and opposed to academic work and destined for factory jobs; nor was it possible to find "good girls" who were proschool and hoped to go on to college or office jobs. The girls knew various "social scripts" (following Davies 1979), some of which included ways to conform to *and* ways to avoid or contradict school requirements (e.g., embellishing or modifying the school uniform, wearing more makeup or jewelry); to avoid boys (e.g., hiding out in the restrooms); and to express their distinctiveness as women (e.g., smearing menstrual blood around the restrooms). The same girls who sometimes participated in counterhegemonic practices also participated in conformist practices.[10]

Other studies describe girls who are not actively antischool as having fairly pragmatic attitudes toward choice of classes and "future careers" (see Connell et al. 1982; Thomas, cited in Weiler 1988:42–43). These girls do not simply swallow the school's view of their gender-related futures in the home and possibly in the lower rungs of the occupational structure, but rather gear their choices toward an assessment of their own best chances (Fuller 1980, 1983; Gaskell 1985).

Fuller's study, which took place in a London comprehensive school, also reveals that girls have complex reactions to schooling. Her study is particularly interesting because it ranged across ethnic groups to include West Indian and Indo-Pakistani girls as well as white British girls. It turned out that black girls of West Indian or Afro-Caribbean ethnicity were both pragmatic and nonconforming. They were good students in that they worked to pass examinations and did their work in exchange for credentials that they foresaw would further their careers; but they were not conforming or well-behaved in the classroom. They were aware of racial discrimination in the schools and in British society, but saw the schools as a way to increase the odds that their own life situations would be better.

Especially intriguing is that these black girls also saw school credentials as a way to ensure their own independence and autonomy, so that they would be less dependent on men (Fuller 1983:132). This is unquestionable evidence that whatever contradictory messages they may have received, some of the young women nevertheless viewed schools as an opportunity to build a life for themselves—a life freer than otherwise of the constraints imposed by the race and gender hierarchies of British society. Their attitude is reminiscent of Gaskell's (1985) point, made as well by Kessler et al. (1985), that schools have traditionally provided one means by which individual women have been able to build their own intellectual lives and careers.

Willis's lads provided a clearcut case of both rejecting the school's ideology and acting out a critical stance in the school. Most of the young women thus far researched do not fit that pattern. Some did participate in counterschool groups, and some did challenge feminine stereotypes in the classroom by exaggerating those stereotypes in order to embarrass their teachers. But in general, overt collective defiance does not seem to have been their style. Instead the girls seem to have regarded the school individualistically and pragmatically—as a place to engage in the social activities that always go on among students, as a place to obtain a degree for later use, or as both.[11]

And what is to be made of a pragmatic stance like that of the black women reported by Fuller? Can such behavior be defined as resistance, even though the women were clearly thinking of themselves as individuals, working within the system? The knotty topic of what constitutes resistance will be resumed after considering another dispute in the literature: the role of romance and the "cult of femininity."

THE DISPUTED ROLE OF HETEROSEXUAL
RELATIONS AND ROMANCE

We have already cited Willis's (1981b:209) assessment that absorption in best-friend relationships, romance, and the nascent trappings of traditional femininity may create, at least for the working-class girls in the studies he had access to, a "viable set of cultural opportunities and satisfactions." This composite culture of romance, in fact, can be proposed as a cultural production of adolescent girls. McRobbie's girls seemed absorbed in the ideology of romance. Their verbal endorsement of the traditional ideas of femininity and the female domestic role led McRobbie to conclude that they immersed themselves in visions of romance and the cult of femininity as a way of mentally deflecting the possibility that, in the end, their lives would be like those of their mothers—rather difficult and unexciting.

On this basis the argument would be that adolescent girls collectively build and occupy a world—a culturally constructed world—that excludes the grim details of the class system *and* the gender hierarchy that they see enacted in their homes and communities. With the help of the media, such as *Jackie,* Britain's popular magazine for teenage girls (McRobbie 1978a; Sharpe 1976:101–103), they draw upon notions of romantic love to build a world of romance. In that world, men and women have equal importance, the goals are warmth and intimacy, and the dominant emotion is love. Experiencing the world through this meaning system, the argument continues, girls and young women go through school content to come out with lower credentials and lower career potential and are happy to enter fairly soon into heterosexual relations and eventually marriage. They insulate themselves from the tedium of school, but also from the credentials that school has to give. They end up not only untrained for any well-paying jobs but also assured of economic dependence on and a subordinate position to men. Ironically their immersion in romance results—in their own lives anyway—in the continuity of male privilege. (This is essentially a gender-based analogue of the fate of Willis's lads in their resistance to the class system.)

Like the Birmingham working girls of McRobbie's study, Thomas's Australian middle-class girls (less so her working-class girls) engaged in dreaming about, talking about, reading magazines about, and sometimes enacting, heterosexual love. Valli's (1986) study of girls in a co-op program at a comprehensive urban high school in the United States Midwest describes similar fantasies. These girls imagined romance followed by married life, when they could cut back to part-time work.

In Delamont's (1980:70) interpretation of her respondents, romance was not so much an escape or resistance as a straightforward failure to notice the realities of their future lives: "Adolescent girls seem to be blinded to the realities of the labour market by the rosy glow of romance, in ways that boys are not, and schools seem to be failing to dispel that rosy glow."

Romance has thus been interpreted in the literature as an escape— or in Delamont's terms, a blindness—with sad consequences. The conclusion has been that women capitalize on sexual attractiveness to escape, either in fantasy or in marriage, the drudgery of school and the prospect of dead-end employment.[12] It is a resistance or sidestepping of the capitalist world, but one that in the long run "simply embeds them more deeply in the culture of domination and submission, of double work, both waged and nonwaged" (Weiler 1988:45; see also Apple's summary of this argument, 1982:108–14). Unfortunately, the point that romance, at least as it is portrayed in these studies, seems to be a strange *counter*culture has not been thoroughly pursued. Although these girls did create (by selective use and personal adaptation of a popular tradition) a different culturally constructed world, the epithet "counter" does not seem to be justified by the evidence. "Alternative" or "escapist" might be more apt. Giroux (1983a:286) is even more doubtful. He sees the supposed resistance as informed by an oppressive mode of sexism.

In eleventh-century France, where it began, the idea of romantic love was a novel and threatening positioning of women—elite women—vis-a-vis men and a challenge to the hegemony of the church in defining sexual relations (see chapter 7). It has been a fixture of literature and art ever since and long ago entered popular lore. But does it constitute a real-life threat in the twentieth-century countries where the studies we have just reviewed were conducted? Is it a threat to schools, or to men as a group? In these studies romance has been presented more as the source of fantasies than as the basis upon which girls acted counter to the school or toward men. McRobbie (1981: 128), in fact, comes close to equating romantic involvement with pill-popping. And Wexler (1987:176), presumably referring to the same topic, speaks of myth: "With disaffection [from school] the student moves identity work into the mythological realm [of domesticity and sexuality], and seeks to blot out the actual conditions of identity production in the school." How are we to appreciate the world of romance created by adolescents? Is it actually equivalent to a narcotic, used for recreational purposes and escapism?

The questioning of whether girls' and young women's involvement with romance constitutes a counterculture has been pushed even further in the last few years. Is the culture of romance and sexual relations really the girls' attempt to resist their subordination or is it, as implied by Giroux (1983a:286), part of the problem? Lees (1986) and Griffin (1985) have suggested that while women do hope for love and intimacy, their view of heterosexual relations and marriage is not so rosy. And as we shall observe later, on the basis of our own study, premarital heterosexual relations—interpreted as they are through the centuries-old cultural tradition of romantic love—are *not* a constant source of delight and reverie to the young women who engage in them.

The lives of Lees's London girls, both working-class and middle-class, were dominated not by romantic fantasies freely conjured but by the way that heterosexual relationships and sexuality were construed in the social life of the school. All the girls faced a system of heterosexual relationships marked by a double standard and a climate of sexual harassment so commonplace that it was taken for granted. A girl had two choices: she could be totally without intimate relationships and face a life of being on her own, or she could be with boys and risk a ruined reputation as a "slag," especially if she was at all attractive but lacking a steady, exclusive relationship with one boy.

The concept of "slag" applied to girls and women only. For boys and men, going with many women enhanced their reputation among their male peers and was viewed by their female peers as acting out a normal masculinity.[13] In the familiar story of the double standard, it was the girl who decided when and if sexual relations would occur and the girl who was responsible for the damage caused if a man "lost control" and raped or beat her. The victim presumably should have known enough to stay out of risky situations and not permit a man to mistreat her.

From the girls' references to intercourse, Lees concluded that their picture of it might not be so romantic:

> Their description of sex as "jumping on top of her" and as
> a scaring experience is hardly a romantic or informed de-
> piction of sexual love. (1986:151)

Neither was marriage viewed through rose-colored glasses. A contradiction was evident between

> [the] unromantic and stark picture of marriage that
> emerged from the girls' descriptions and their commit-
> ment—if somewhat resigned—to the idea of marriage.
> Most girls saw marriage as inevitable even if it involved
> financial dependency, domestic drudgery, isolation at
> home with young children and, at the extreme, even cru-
> elty. . . .

Their comments were scarcely romantic but depicted
marriage as wasting your life. . . .
What needs to be explained is why the girls wanted to get
married and how they came to terms with or rationalized
the negative aspects of that predicament. . . .
What they seem to be expressing is the rather unlikely
hope that love will save them from the grim reality of most
of the marriages they observe. This does not however explain why girls wholeheartedly endorse the idea that one
day they will get married. Rather than explain this contradiction in terms of romanticism, one might argue that girls
see marriage as the only alternative to a life of ostracism
where an independent existence is an unrealistic choice not
only financially (as few of them will ever be able to attract
a living wage), but socially too in view of the strong constraints on the expression of any independent sexuality.
(Lees 1986:27,89,91,105)

These girls hoped for love in their marriages, but they did not rush
into marriage as a choice. Cowie's and Lees' research does not corroborate the picture of young women rushing into domesticity with
the "sense of a decision freely made, a choice exercised" (Lees 1986:
101). Instead, Lees found that marriage was a virtual financial necessity for the working-class girls and the only choice for those of either
class who did not wish to be alone and on their own.

Yet the lives of their mothers were not appealing. The girls hoped
that love would make their marriages and their lives better. They did
not resist the grim prospects for their future lives by romanticizing
heterosexual relations and marriage, but rather by trying to postpone
marriage (see also Griffin 1985). Their fantasies were not of marriage
but of having fun before marriage, of travel, of seeing the world, and
of excitement (Lees 1986:104).

Lees argues that the working-class girls did not put aside careers
and academic work in favor of a romanticized view of heterosexual
relations and marriage. Rather, their romanticism increased when
hopes for a career were given up. In our study a similar pattern
occurred: as the women became discouraged with schoolwork, they
increasingly turned their interests and identity to the world of romance.

Lees (1986:120), in short, disputes the view of romance given in the
literature:

The fact that much of the pressure towards marriage and
domesticity is to be found in the social life of the school

> rather than in the formal structure of the curriculum
> should not lead to the conclusion that girls end up in mar-
> riage and domestic life because they have constructed a
> "counter-school culture" (as Paul Willis argued with re-
> spect to lower working-class boys) which insulates them
> from the formal equality and achievement orientation of
> the school. It is not the girls who construct sexism as a
> counter-culture. It is there in the social life of the school, in
> the presence of and the interaction with boys and in the
> behaviour of the teachers.

Similarly, referring to the system of sexuality centering around girls'
liability to be socially branded as "slags," she concludes: "This is why,
rather than regarding girls' activities as a resistance, their participation in social life should be seen primarily as a product of gender
subordination" (1986:60–61).[14]

Another point to be gleaned from Lees's study is that the girls'
experience, behavior, and response to school were profoundly shaped
by the sexism they encountered among their fellow students. The
girls in the London schools faced harsh judgment by their peers and
so were more or less herded into exclusive heterosexual relationships
and taught to interpret and possibly distort their sexual feelings in the
terms of romantic love and marriage. Sexism was certainly embedded
in the curriculum, the textbooks, and the practices and policies of the
school officials. But those forms paled beside the sexism in the peer
relations of the school. Willis (1981b:147) suggests that a similar situation existed at Hammertown: "Although there may be institution-
alised sexism in our schools, it is not as strong as the reproduced
sexism at the informal level of its working class male oppositional
culture."[15] In Griffin's (1985) account as well, the girls and young
women were primarily depicted as practically overwhelmed by the
"sexual game," though trying to make the best of a relatively unpleas-
ant situation.

How is production theory to handle this peer-imposed sexism, and
what difference does it make that the sexism is mediated largely by
the peer group and not by school officials?

Is This Resistance?

The girls and young women studied to date simply do not
fit the ideal type of resistance and cultural production exemplified by
the lads of Hammertown. Nonetheless, no one writing in the cultural-
production literature advocates the view that women are simply

passive pawns. Studies of women thus far do not suggest that their predicament can be accounted for by the early social-reproduction theories, even if women's responses to schooling do not precisely match those of working-class males or racial minorities. The few existing studies of women's cultural production in the face of gender domination describe female students—whether in Australia, Britain, or the United States, whether white, black, or Pakistani—as *critical* recipients of the school's ideological messages. In this sense—that female students filter ideological messages and produce their own meaning systems to interpret the schools—production theories can accommodate girls. Young women, like working-class males and racial minority groups, fail fully to internalize the ideologies, promulgated in their schools and homes, that justify male privilege. They tend to see the schools from the perspective of their own goals rather than conceiving of themselves and their goals from the perspective of the schools. As McRobbie and others have argued, there is evidence that young women do create a sort of counterculture. But their responses do not fit the prototype of Willis's lads of Hammertown, and the concept of resistance becomes especially difficult to apply.

Weiler (1988:47–48), for example, questions Fuller's (1983) use of "resistance" to describe the Afro-Caribbean women's response to schooling. The women were aware and critical of the racism and sexism of British society and were specifically critical of the world of school. Yet they worked in school in accord with the promise of the school to exchange work for a credential, and a credential for a better job. They did not act out the model of the good student, but they did do the work to obtain the credential. This pragmatic but individualistic response (echoed in Riley's 1985 research with black Jamaican girls in South London) Weiler (1988:47) believes "might also be viewed as a form of individual accommodation to existing social conditions rather than a collective cultural pattern that can be called resistance."

Fuller (1983) and Anyon (1983), also criticized by Weiler, were both aware that their use of "resistance" went beyond the accepted boundaries of the term. Fuller (1983:140) writes:

> Anyone who bothers to listen knows . . . that the girls' criticism cannot be readily accommodated into a definition of deviance or resistance that relies on the flashy, visible and physically confrontational. . . . Just because girls do not, typically, confront, does not mean they do not have their criticisms of schooling. What it suggests to me is that

the form their criticism takes (and their resistance) is inte-
grally related to and shaped by their having been successfully engendered as feminine.

As it has turned out, Fuller's defense of a broad use of "resistance"
is inadequate. The problems with resistance as a concept are due to
more than a possible "gendrocentric" bias in defining what constitutes
resistance. "Resistance" has been greatly overused, as was thoroughly
argued by Giroux (1983a), for example, in his extensive critique of
the critical educational literature. The reasons for the overuse of
"resistance" are becoming fairly clear. As Lakomski (1984) has
pointed out, once we discard the assumption of perfect socialization
and take note of students' actions, we are likely to notice that all
individuals and groups "resist," in the sense that they try to influence
their own social circumstances (see also Kessler et al. 1985:45). Any
close look at student behavior will show that perhaps the most common response of all students—whether boys or girls, young men or
young women—is neither conformity nor resistance, but what might
be called pragmatism. Connell et al. (1982:90–93) make this point in
their study of a group of Australian students (equally divided between
working-class and upper-middle, "ruling"-class students). The study
showed both the girls and the boys to be pragmatists in school. They
did what they needed to do to get by and kept a low profile in class,
but they questioned the reason for much of the work and other activities. They were as far from conformity to the school's projects as
they were from resistance to them.

The general framework of production theory, deriving as it does
from questions of social reproduction, tries to link lived culture and
on-the-ground social practices to structural features of the society and
ultimately to questions of radical change in those structural features.
As Giroux (1983a) among others has explained, the concept of resistance has a particular meaning in such a framework. He would have
us not use the term for just any sort of oppositionary or pragmatic
student behavior, but rather reserve it for collective action that seriously challenges the status quo.

Obviously Giroux's criteria would greatly restrict the applicability of
the concept of resistance in describing research results. Critical educational studies ultimately have as a research object the same kind of
cultural and social processes that social historians such as E. P.
Thompson identify as producing social movements and even, in the
long run, the formation of whole social classes. Yet their interests are
generally focused on the day-to-day events shaped by these larger

processes. Researchers in critical education do their studies without the dual advantages of the social historian: hindsight and great time depth (Johnson 1986–87:54). Whether student responses in any particular case are those of a collective, or whether student actions will end in fundamentally challenging existing social arrangements, are variable issues that change depending on the historical circumstances. Hence the researcher, using Giroux's criteria in any event, ordinarily would not have the knowledge necessary for correct application of the term "resistance."

The overuse of "resistance" has been not only erroneous but also unfortunate, in that it has misguided researchers' attention. Wexler (1987), even more alarmed than Giroux, devotes a large portion of his book to the misemphasis on "resistance" in the critical educational literature. He claims that it has created a "discursive blockage" (e.g., p. 125), a myopia, that has obscured two extremely important social changes: first, the rightward turn of America as the result of a cultural restorative movement, and the related deschooling of U.S. society by rightist political forces; and second, the emergence of postmodern society and its movement of educative processes away from the schools to the media.

The tedious nature of these discussions corroborate Giroux's and Wexler's cautions that resistance can be a seductive but ultimately infertile concept when promiscuously applied. Wexler's depiction may be overstated; there has not been a total occlusion of vision to the rightward turn of society among those theorists who emphasize student and youth resistance. Nor has the importance of semiotic means in postmodern society gone unremarked (e.g., see Johnson 1986–87 for a lengthy discussion of the latter and a list of references regarding the political right in England). Nonetheless, especially in the United States, a number of critical educational writers, some of whom are named by Wexler (1987), became ensnared in the concept of resistance. They did not proceed to study the processes of cultural production and the potential blossoming of such meaning systems and practices into social movements that could disrupt the status quo. In the vocabulary presented in chapter 3, they failed fully to pursue the major strands of production theory, with its emphasis on the creation of cultural meaning systems. Instead, they stopped with a list of apparent student oppositions to school ideologies and practices.

For issues of gender the overemphasis on resistance has been unfortunate in yet another regard. Not only has the full extent of production theory remained unexplored, but movement to the more sophisticated practice theory has conceivably been retarded as well.

The message of practice theory is that a group's responses to structural barriers are reflective of both its internal and external relations. Hebdige (1979) provides a case in point. The created styles and identities in the youth groups he describes—the Teddy Boys, the Rockers, the Mods, and the Punks—grew both in response to British society's negative attitudes toward the groups *and* in response to the youths' understandings of themselves in relation to Britain's growing black (West Indian) community. When resistance is overemphasized, attention is directed toward the relationship of the nonprivileged to the privileged and away from the relationship between and among the groups that are in roughly comparable structural positions. In studies of schooling, attention is directed toward the relationships of students to school authorities, their practices and policies, and away from relationships among students. An undervaluing of within-category, internal politics, and of their importance for the formation of subjectivities, has been identified as a major limitation of production theory. In the case of women, these internal politics, these struggles involving gender regimes and male peers, are tremendously important.

Thus the work of the last decade or so has severely challenged simplistic notions of schools as agents of perfect, unopposed socialization for either girls or boys. It has also raised cautions about the analysis of students' creative reactions to schooling. Students are not productively analyzed as putty in the hands of teachers and administrators, but neither are students' cultural productions usefully presumed to be resistance in every case. Women and girls do not have to create flamboyant subcultures, as do men and boys, in order to resist patriarchal social arrangements. On the other hand, it is not useful to end study and analysis prematurely by labeling any oppositional behavior as resistance.

The more useful avenue is to continue learning about the response of girls and women to present-day sexism in the schools and in society at large, by comparing and contrasting their positions and responses to those of other structurally disadvantaged groups. Weis (1985), for example, writing about black students in a community college in the northeastern United States, shows the conflicting values that lead the students to revere education as a way to improve their individual economic situations, yet at the same time to recognize, as shown by their chronic absenteeism, education's lack of value for blacks as a group in overcoming white privilege. Is it possible that young women's responses show this same sort of conflicting focus, first on their predicaments as individuals and then on their predicament as members of a structurally disadvantaged group? And why might women's responses differ from those of men in structurally disadvantaged groups?

In short, instead of trying immediately to answer the ultimate questions—whether particular responses constitute resistance and the possible birth of a social movement that will ultimately challenge the status quo—we must instead tack back and forth between our recognition that students are creative and our growing understanding of the shape and content of the gender hierarchies to which girls and women respond. The small but growing body of case studies of women and schooling prompted the set of questions that we took to the present study. They also provide, along with the present study, pieces of what we believe to be an emerging picture of how male privilege is manifested in schools.

QUESTIONS ABOUT UNIVERSITY WOMEN'S RESPONSES TO SCHOOLING

The present study shifts the focus from the middle and secondary schools of earlier studies of schooling and women to the university, and from young women in their early and middle teens to young women in their late teens and early twenties. Although these age groups are not so far apart, the social situation of the women in this study is quite different. Many of the women in the studies reviewed would have moved into jobs and perhaps marriage by their late teens and early twenties. The women in the present study instead entered into a prolonged period of schooling different in two crucial respects from secondary schooling. First, the women could use the university to qualify themselves for higher-paying jobs. Second, university attendance put them into age-segregated living situations, as well as age-segregated classrooms. They were off on their own, away from home, away from any domestic demands of their families, yet not completely independent financially.[16]

Despite the differences from the other studies, we entered into an analysis of the university women's experiences with some overarching questions suggested by production theory:

1. What were the women's responses to the university and to the possible sex discrimination that they perceived at the university and in the society in general?
2. How did their responses oppose, if they did, the patriarchal conditions that they faced?
3. How did their everyday experiences, their "lived culture," enter into the "choices" and "decisions" that they were making about their future careers and domestic arrangements?

From practice theory and from the long record of anthropological research in schools and classrooms, including our own earlier ethnographic study, we brought additional questions about peer groups per se:

4. What role did the peer group play in affecting university women's "choices" and "decisions" about their future lives?

5. What were the important divisions within the peer group and the important issues of "gender politics" within the student body?

As we read and reread the two hundred or so pages of interviews and notes taken over the length of the study for each of the twenty-three women who participated in our in-depth ethnographic research, we became more and more impressed by the importance of the student culture in the women's lives. Like Griffin (1985) and Lees (1986), we found gender relations and the cultural interpretation of gender relations to be extremely important in the women's experiences of and responses to the university. Gender relations were especially salient in the lives of the women who were disassociated from, or who became disassociated from, the learning process.

Part 3 *The Study*

5   Campus Profiles and an Overview of the Study

In the fall of 1979 we handed out flyers and put up posters on the campuses of Bradford University and Southern University (SU).[1] The notices asked freshmen women who wished to participate in our study on women and careers to call us. The National Institute of Education, which was funding the study, wanted to know why women were not entering math- and science-related careers. Our goal was to recruit one set of women oriented to traditional women's majors and another set oriented to nontraditional coursework and majors. The women who contributed their experiences to this book called us in response to these posters; that was our beginning contact with them.

From the hundred or so women who called, we selected twelve from Bradford and eleven from SU. We selected the groups so that approximately half of the women at each school were planning to major in math- or science-related fields.[2] We chose women with records of strong academic performance in high school; all had high-school grade averages of B+ or better and had been in college-preparatory tracks at comprehensive Southern high schools. Each had an expressed serious commitment to pursuing a career in the future and had a range of extracurricular interests and peer networks. They all entered college in the fall immediately after their graduation from high school.

These twenty-three women became the focus of the major part of the study. We followed them closely during their first three semesters of college. About halfway through the ethnographic study we designed a survey and administered it to a random sample of sophomore women on the two campuses. As will be seen, this book draws mostly from the ethnographic study, because it reveals more of the telling day-to-day experiences of the women and the unfolding of their lives. Although the study formally concluded at the end of the women's sophomore year (1981), we conducted telephone follow-up interviews with the women in 1983 (when they should have been about to graduate from college) and again in 1987.

This chapter and the next are devoted to the institutional and historical context of the women's college experiences. The first aim of this chapter is to describe the two universities. We present brief profiles with "facts" akin perhaps to those a high school counselor might list about the two schools. Comments about the women's initial impressions of the two campuses are interspersed. Then, we sketch the components of the study and introduce the group of women who participated in the ethnographic part of it, in comparison with other women students at the two universities.

THE TWO UNIVERSITIES

Bradford University is located in the midst of a Southern city. Although near the central downtown district, Bradford has a large campus. Its red brick buildings are scattered over expansive lawns. The campus is surrounded by black residential areas, several black churches, and business establishments that cater to the college crowd's tastes (fast food franchises, barbecue joints, and small shops). The city of Bradford has a large black community—more than 85 percent of public school students in the district are black—and, for a Southern city, an unusually strong black middle class.

Bradford University was founded in the early twentieth century as an undergraduate school to train blacks for careers in religion and education. Today it offers undergraduate instruction in the arts and sciences and in business and education. A range of graduate programs and professional degrees is now available as well. Bradford's self-designated special mission is to provide academic and nonacademic programs deemed appropriate for the type of student it draws: black, lower-middle-class or low-income, from mostly rural areas of the piedmont South. (The university is officially desegregated, but almost all of the students are black.) In its promotional literature Bradford lists one of its major goals: "to bring the majority of students into the mainstream of American society."

Since its inception, Bradford has had to struggle for money. It has been a publicly financed state school since the early 1920s, but it has never been, and is not presently, either well supported or well endowed. Its libraries, buildings, and grounds are far less extensive than those of SU, and its faculty members are paid considerably less and are not as highly credentialed, on the average.

Bradford is not among the elite of historically black institutions of higher learning. It is less well known and well regarded among the state's black community than are some other predominantly black universities. This is not surprising, as it was founded later than some other black colleges in the state and certainly in the region. It also lacks a strong association with any religious denomination. Many of the students who come to Bradford are the first in their families to attend college.

SU is located on a sprawling campus adjacent to what was once a small, mostly white, college town. The town has grown with the university but until recently has depended on the university for its livelihood and residents. Although the town is now large enough to be considered a small city, it retains (and tries to retain) something of the character of a small town. The community is still predominantly white and upper-middle-class, and its atmosphere is still dominated by events at the university: concerts, plays, sports events, and the various intrigues of university politics. Like Bradford, SU is surrounded by college-oriented businesses and by churches, as well as by some residences, but at SU there is a much greater sense that the local community revolves around the university. As someone (presumably white and middle-class) wrote in SU's promotional materials, "There is a comfortable air of stability and solidarity here."

SU also has a much longer history, as a school and as a comprehensive university. Financially, SU has been well supported for years, both by the state and by the contributions of its alumni. In 1979 SU had about four times as many students as Bradford, but the size of its library collections and the extent of its physical plant were many more times greater. SU also offered a wider range of courses and degree programs, especially at the graduate level. And students or their parents had to pay more to attend SU—about a third more than to attend Bradford.

SU considers itself a strong state-supported university with a regional focus, but able to draw outstanding students and faculty from around the country. Though SU is national in its perspective, most of its undergraduates come from middle- and upper-middle-class white families in the state. Black students comprise only about 10 percent of the student body, and out-of-state students are limited by quota to a small percentage. SU is highly regarded, especially in the state, and is probably the first choice of many of the state's top-ranked high-school students.

At both schools the ratio of women to men was about the same in 1979: 60:40. Also at both places, 50 percent of those who applied were admitted, and 60 percent of those admitted were enrolled.

COLLEGE REQUIREMENTS AND THE
SHIFT TO COLLEGE LIFE

Although different in many ways, the two schools are both public institutions in the same state system. Thus they officially share many admission requirements, attendance policies, and rules and regulations governing campus life. Students were expected to take a general set of required courses during their freshman and sophomore years, to declare a major by the middle of the sophomore year, and to make application to any special degree programs (such as nursing, physical therapy, journalism) during the spring semester of the sophomore year. Most students began specialized study in their major fields during the junior year. During the period of the study SU freshmen were required to live on campus; Bradford women were not, but most did.

Because both Bradford and SU are residential campuses that draw from a dispersed region, students often are a considerable distance away from their families and home communities. When we initially encountered the women in the study, they were experiencing their new lifestyle on campus as a challenge. Many at first tried to maintain close contact with home. They described how often they called home—some as many as three times a day—during their first few weeks of college. A number complained about feeling isolated and unimportant in what was for them a larger, more impersonal, and less familiar environment. One said, "It's so hard to get anything done here . . . there are so many steps. . . . I just went home [one weekend] and cried." Another said, "You come here, you're just a face in the crowd . . . a number . . . it's not easy. . . . It takes [some] close friends to know you're not just a number."

As the semester progressed, the women on both campuses gradually organized their lives around course schedules and requirements, informal dormitory groups and activities, and the need to establish relationships with the many new acquaintances with whom they were living, working, and playing. By their second semester of college, most had settled into some kind of routine. One described a typical day as follows: "I get up, go to class, go to work, go out to dinner with some friends, . . . relax and watch TV [with friends], . . . study." For some, their view of college and themselves in college became more positive. One woman described how she felt about college in February of her freshman year:

> I'm really enjoying college [now] . . . because you get a wider atmosphere [here]. . . . My hometown is so small and narrow. . . . [When I came to college] I realized that you had to allot your time to study, and I got my schedule straight and . . . the one thing that stands out is my ability to do just as well in college as I did in high school. . . . I'm proud of myself for not going astray, because there's so many temptations in college, like parties when you have a test. But I realized that I tackled all these things with determination and will, and I succeeded . . . and I'm really proud of myself.

For a few, however, feelings persisted of being only a face in the crowd or only a number.

Many of the women talked about the "new freedoms" they experienced at college—freedom from parental rules, freedom to make their own decisions. One said, "There's no restrictions on relationships, on what you can and can't do. . . . It's all up to me. . . . It's fun, but scary too."

Also by the beginning of their second semester in college, the women were involved in numerous extracurricular activities and relationships. They went to class and studied, but they also participated in dorm activities, attended sports events, club meetings, and religious services. They went out on dates and traveled off campus to go to restaurants, bars, discos, and shopping centers with friends. And they spent hours just talking and informally "partying" with their girl-friends and boyfriends.

Our monthly interviews and observations of the women began when they had been at college for most of one semester and were beginning to know their way around, to make some college friends, and to understand what it would take for them to be successful in college.

OVERVIEW OF COMPONENTS OF THE STUDY

At the time of the study our research purpose was to find out how women chose and formed a commitment to a major and a future career. We were particularly interested in how peers figured into that process. The ethnographic component of the study was largely oriented to learning the meanings that the women themselves attached to their experiences and to uncovering the student cultures in which the women were immersed. As described in chapter 2, we began with the idea that peers encouraged women to take up traditional careers. Because of the research design, however, we found out that there was a more important and overarching question: How is it that many college women end up with marginalized career identities, no matter what their choice of major?

The Ethnographic Study

We wanted to find out what was important to women at Bradford and SU, what events were big in their eyes, and what they considered to be problems in their college lives. We decided we needed to get to know some individuals well and to follow them over time. We wanted to see how they reacted to their college experiences as those experiences were unfolding.[3]

A crucial feature of the research design was our ongoing attempt to learn what college life meant to the women in our study. To increase our chances of finding out what they were thinking about and feeling, we paired researchers and informants. We expected the same researcher to engage in all the participant observations with an informant and to interview her for the duration of the study. (A fuller account of our research procedures appears in the Appendix.) Black researchers worked at Bradford, white researchers at SU. The researchers were only slightly older than the informants and were or had been students on the campuses at which they worked. We hoped that each researcher and informant would become friends, learning to trust and share openly with each other. In all but two cases (when the researchers left the area), the pairs worked together throughout the study. The following excerpts from the field notes of several of the researchers indicate the nature of the relationships the informants and researchers established and the kinds of things we began to learn about the texture of the women's lives. The notes are from "observations," in which the researcher joined the informant in some activity with her friends.

> I entered Sybil's [a Bradford informant's] room about 6 P.M. I put my coat down on the bed and sat down. Percie [Sybil's roommate] asked me if I knew French. I told her I didn't. At this, she moaned and said that she really needed some help with her French. She continued, saying that she didn't know why she had taken French in the first place. She said that most everyone else was taking Spanish.
>
> I asked Percie what happened to a young man she had been hiding from at the cafeteria. Sybil started laughing

and before Percie could say anything, Sybil started filling me in on Percie's activities. Sybil said that Percie had gone to a show with him and spent all day. Percie said that she had spent *part* of the day with him and that he had been hanging all over her, and she told him that she didn't want to see him anymore. Sybil and I started laughing at this. I said we'd see how long that lasted. Sybil agreed with me.

Percie and Sybil started talking about Willa [a friend who lived across the hall]. They decided that Willa had slept enough—she had slept through dinner tonight—and that she should wake up. Sybil went to wake her. When Willa came in, Sybil started telling her about a girl they had run into in the cafeteria tonight. Sybil and Percie both added some in describing this girl. Willa said she thought she knew the girl. Both Sybil and Percie tried to make it sound like the woman was after Willa's boyfriend. Willa kept trying to find out who the woman was. Sybil said she hadn't described the girl correctly and so she described her again. Sybil continued to tell Willa that she knew the woman. Willa was really getting upset while she talked about this woman. About this time, Sybil and Percie started laughing uncontrollably. At first, Willa just looked at them. Then she suddenly realized that they had been playing a joke on her. Willa started laughing herself at how angry she was getting.

Then Sybil started talking about [another woman] who might be flunking out of school. The others joined in. They seemed to feel that the parents had sacrificed in order for the girl to go to school and that she was only throwing it away. They talked about several other women who were doing the same thing.

Notes from observations at SU show the researcher in similar settings, listening to similar sorts of conversations about men and school-work.

I arrived at Kim's [the informant's] dorm room at 2:40 P.M. [Saturday afternoon]. She offered me a glass of orange juice, and we walked down the hall to the lounge where a group was gathering to watch the school's basketball team on television. Several other women came in, including Debra and Marilyn [two of Kim's close dormmates]. Debra and Marilyn discuss an errand they are to run for another friend during halftime. The friend is going to her pledge formal and had asked them to pick up a boutonniere for her date. In exchange, the friend will loan them her car and take them out for pizza or ice cream whenever they want.

Debra and Kim ask Marilyn if her roommate has found a date [for Marilyn] for the dorm's stranger mixer. [Roommates invite dates for each other; the woman does not know the identity of her date until he shows up.] They tease her about going with some males they all know but don't rate very highly. Marilyn rejects their suggestions. Marilyn and Kim go on to discuss a date for Carol [Kim's roommate]. Kim says that the date she picked is someone that Carol has known for a long time but had previously refused as a blind date.

Attention is drawn back to the television as the announcer introduces the school's basketball players. The women discuss the looks and social skills (dancing ability, conversation) of each player as he comes onto the court. They talk about getting a basketball player as a date for the stranger mixer—seems to be something they would all like but are not very optimistic about. They go on to discuss friends they think would make good cheerleaders. This is interrupted as a substitute enters the game for their team. They all comment on how unattractive he is.

On another occasion, the same group and several others were assembled in Kim's room, discussing courses to take.

Kim asks what's a good humanities course to take. This is addressed to no one in particular. Jill says, "Don't take art history." She doesn't elaborate. Carol says, "Take Drama 15, because [another friend] is." Then Carol says, "Don't take philosophy." She offers no explanation. [Another friend enters the room] and says she missed class today. Carol interjects to Kim, "Don't take Professor _____; he's hard." They all discuss art history some more. Jill says, "There's not much reading but you have to remember all those slides." Kim gets up and looks at her hair in the mirror. "It looks like seaweed." The conversation switches to hair and the group sets to work fixing Kim's hair.

The activities and views of each woman became the focus of our attention during the ethnographic observations and the "talking-diary" interviews. Both the observations and the interviews were conducted once a month while school was in session. The observations were scheduled so as to cover a range of usual activities for each informant. During each interview, the researchers used a standard set of open-ended questions first, but then asked about specific activities in which the informant had been observed. In these ways, we tailored the observations and interviews to the specific and everyday college life of each woman in our study.

The ethnographic study produced about two hundred pages of typewritten notes and transcribed interviews for each woman. Our analysis of this material involved reading through the pages many times to acquire an understanding of each individual woman's orientation and then indexing and summarizing the interviews according to a set of themes, such as friends, schoolwork, and family. The process is described more fully in the Appendix.

The Survey

In 1981, after we had followed the women through one full semester, we developed a survey instrument. The survey, based on a preliminary analysis of the ethnographic data and focused on choice of and commitment to a major, was administered to random samples of sophomore women at each university. The survey investigated changes in women's chosen majors during the freshman and sophomore years and tested a model of factors that we hypothesized, from the ethnographic study, would affect a woman's declared commitment to pursuing training in a chosen major. We surveyed 362 women at the two universities (see Holland and Eisenhart 1981 for a detailed report of the survey).

As might be expected, given our oversampling in the ethnographic study of women interested in math and science careers, a comparison of the college majors and campus activities of the women chosen for the study and the women randomly selected for the survey shows that the ethnographic sample represented a range, but not the full range, of college experiences on the two campuses. Table 2 includes the distribution of entering majors, by general category, for the survey respondents and the ethnographic sample. Table 3 includes the specific major of each woman in the ethnographic sample. Table 2 reveals that some majors, such as education at Bradford, were underrepresented in the ethnographic sample. Other majors, such as biological sciences at SU and business at Bradford were overrepresented.[4]

We intentionally chose women with avowed career aspirations for the ethnographic sample. However, most of the survey respondents also said they were serious about pursuing a career. In the survey at Bradford, 93.3 percent said that they wanted to begin a full-time career after graduating from college. At SU, the figure was 84 percent. In contrast, 48.6 percent of Bradford women and 57.5 percent

TABLE 2. Survey and ethnographic sample: Entering and sophomore-year majors, by university

Major	Bradford (N = 176) (ethnographic [N = 12])[a]		SU (N = 179) (ethnographic [N = 11])	
	Entering	Sophomore	Entering	Sophomore
Applied biology[b]	11.4%	10.2%	21.7%	20.1%
	(16.7%)	(16.7%)	(27.3%)	(9.1%)
Arts/humanities	7.4	6.8	16.1	14.0
	(8.3)	(8.3)	(36.4)	(9.1)
Biological sciences	2.3	2.8	12.2	5.6
	(0.0)	(0.0)	(18.2)	(18.2)
Business	29.0	29.0	14.4	19.6
	(41.7)	(41.7)	(0.0)	(0.0)
Computer science	0.0	0.0	3.9	0.6
	(0.0)	(0.0)	(0.0)	(0.0)
Education	20.5	15.3	3.9	10.6
	(8.3)	(8.3)	(0.0)	(9.1)
Engineering	0.0	0.0	0.0	0.0
	(0.0)	(0.0)	(0.0)	(0.0)
Mathematics	0.0	3.3	1.6	2.6
	(0.0)	(0.0)	(9.1)	(18.2)
Physical sciences	1.7	2.3	10.0	6.2
	(0.0)	(0.0)	(9.1)	(9.1)
Social sciences[c]	19.9	22.2	5.6	14.0
	(25.0)	(33.3)	(9.1)	(27.3)
Other	5.1	9.0	3.9	6.7
	(0.0)	(0.0)	(0.0)	(0.0)
Undecided	2.3	0.0	7.2	0.6
	(0.0)	(0.0)	(0.0)	(0.0)

SOURCE: Adapted from Holland and Eisenhart 1981:72.
NOTES:[a] Top figure, from survey; bottom figure (in parentheses), from ethnographic sample. Percentages for the ethnographic sample total slightly more than 100 because those with double majors were counted twice. Figures rounded to the nearest .1%.
[b] Includes premed, nursing, physical therapy.
[c] Includes "pure" and "applied" areas, e.g., social work, criminal justice.

of SU women said they wanted to be married soon after graduating; only 28.5 percent of Bradford women and 12.8 percent of SU women wanted children soon after graduation (Holland and Eisenhart 1981:49).

The family backgrounds of the Bradford and SU women, in both the ethnographic study and the survey, reflected the differences in student-body characteristics of the two universities. For the most part, the parents of the SU women, especially fathers, had more years of education and better-paying, more career-oriented occupations than the parents of the Bradford women. Also, the women at SU were

TABLE 3. Ethnographic sample: Majors and changes in majors, by interpretation of schoolwork

Name	University	Entering major	Interim	Major at graduation
"Getting over" interpretation				
Cynthia	Bradford	Business	No change	Business
Rosalind	Bradford	Applied biology	Left school	
Cylene	Bradford	Business	Left school	
Phyllis	Bradford	Business	No change	Business
Deidre	Bradford	Social science	Left school	
Charlotte	Bradford	Applied biology	No change	Applied biology
Della	Bradford	Business	No change	Business
Sybil	Bradford	Social science	No change	Social science
Maureen	Bradford	Social science	No change	Social science
Sandy	SU	Arts/humanities	Left school	
"Doing well" interpretation				
Linda	SU	Applied biology	Scaled down	Applied biology
Kelly	SU	Applied biology	Scaled down	Social science
Susan	SU	Physical science	Scaled down	Math
Kim	SU	Biological Science	Scaled down (BS to BA)	Biological science
Paula	SU	Applied Biology	Scaled down	Social science
Natalie	SU	Math	No change	Math
Velma	Bradford	Business	Left school	
"Learning from experts" interpretation				
Valecia	Bradford	Arts/humanities	Switched to something better for her	Business
Aleisha	Bradford	Education	Kept original major and added another	Education and social science
Karla	SU	Arts/humanities	Switched to something better for her	Physical science
Kandace	SU	Social science	No change	Social science
Stephanie	SU	Biological science, arts/humanities	No change	Biological science, arts/humanities
Exception				
Lisa	SU	Arts/humanities	Change spurred by boyfriend	Education

NOTE: "Interim" designation based on the informant's stated or implied view.

more likely than their Bradford counterparts to have lived with both parents while growing up and to have had mothers who did not work full-time while they had young children. These patterns of difference reflect differences in the class backgrounds of the student bodies on the two campuses as well as differences between black and white populations nationally (see, for example, Farley 1984). (Tables 4 and 5 include comparisons of the background characteristics of the women in the ethnographic and survey samples.)

Aside from assisting us in comparing the women in the ethnographic sample to their female classmates, the survey material was less relevant for our present analysis than the ethnographic data. Although the survey's hypothesized predictors of commitment to major were very successful, "explaining" considerably more variance than social science studies usually do, the material in this book is drawn largely from the ethnographic part of the study. Issues of the dynamic of women's opposition to and participation in the reproduction of gender hierarchy are difficult to capture in a survey, especially one composed after only six months of ethnographic study, when the important cultural forms and peer and individual practices are only beginning to emerge. However, the survey is clearly related to the ethnographic materials at points and is useful at those points for assessing the extent to which our findings can be generalized to university women on the two campuses. Where relevant and helpful, we have included findings from the survey.

The Language and Cultural Models Studies

Given the character or basic design of the study—following the lives of individuals—we learned about and observed what anthropologists would call "rituals" (for example, football games) and other important collective events *only* if the individual women took us to them or talked about them in the interviews. The same was true of classes and other points of contact with faculty and administrators. In a perfect world, we would have conducted a simultaneous study of the ritual forms on campus and a more formal study of interactions between the faculty and the students. Because of the constraints of time and money, however, we were not able to do the complementary studies.

We did conduct in-depth studies of the extensive vocabulary of gender-marked terms used on the SU campus (such as "jocks," "pricks," "foxes," "down-to-earth girls") and the cultural models associated with those terms, during the same period as the NIE-funded studies. These associated studies were carried out in 1978, 1980, and

TABLE 4. Ethnographic sample: Summary of background characteristics

Name	Hometown (pop.)	Mother's occupation/ education	Father's occupation/ education	Residence
Bradford				
Cynthia	midstate (under 500)	Factory worker/h.s. grad.	Factory supervisor/ h.s. grad.	With both parents
Valecia	midstate (under 500)	Kindergarten teacher, social worker/coll. grad.	Not clear/some h.s.	With both parents
Velma	coastal (700)	Part-time teacher's aide, factory worker/h.s. grad.	Ret. military; construction/h.s. grad.	With both parents
Rosalind	midstate (150,000)	Factory worker/no info	Ret. military/no info	With mother
Cylene	coastal (5,500)	Telephone operator/h.s. grad.	No info/h.s. grad.	With mother
Phyllis	coastal (55,300)	Part-time work/ gram. sch. or less	No info/gram. sch. or less	With both parents
Deidre	coastal (14,600)	Nurse's aide/no info	Ret. military; cook, textile worker/no info	Mostly with mother
Aleisha	out-of-state/ southern (145,000)	Not clear/no info	Welder (disabled)/ no info	With father's parents
Sybil	midstate (150,000)	No info/some h.s.	Deceased/no info	With mother
Charlotte	midstate (59,500)	H.S. science teacher/grad. degree	Ret. military (disabled)/some post-h.s. training	With both parents
Maureen	out-of-state/ southern (81,400)	Librarian/coll. grad.	Social worker, administrator/ coll. grad.	With grand-parents, then with parents
Della	midstate (75,000)	Nurse (deceased)/ no info	Construction worker/no info	With aunt and uncle
SU				
Linda	midstate (64,100)	Clerical worker/ some post-h.s. training	Salesman/h.s. grad.	With both parents
Karla	midstate (3,000)	Own business/coll. grad.	Engineer/grad. degree	With both parents
Kelly	midstate (2,600)	Insurance coordinator/coll. grad.	Ret. military; dept. manager/some post-h.s. training	With both parents

(*continued*)

TABLE 4. (*continued*)

Name	Hometown (pop.)	Mother's occupation/ education	Father's occupation/ education	Residence
Susan	out-of-state/ southern (66,800)	housewife/no info	Ret. military; own business/no info	With both parents
Lisa	mountains (30,100)	Factory worker/ some h.s.	Ret. military; farmer (deceased)/ gram. sch. or less	With both parents
Kandace	out-of-state/ southern (573,100)	Housewife/coll. grad.	Salesman/some post-coll. courses	With both parents
Kim	midstate (155,700)	Housewife/some grad. school	Orthopedic surgeon/grad. degree	With both parents
Stephanie	out-of-state/ southern (42,500)	Part-time consul- tant/grad. degree	Professor/grad. degree	With both parents
Paula	midstate (155,700)	Part-time accoun- tant/some coll.	Ret. military; dept. manager/some coll.	With both parents
Sandy	out-of-state/ northeastern (4,200)	Part-time secretary/ h.s. grad.	Own business/some grad. school	With both parents
Natalie	midstate (8,600)	Part-time recep- tionist/some coll.	Banker/some post-h.s. training	With both parents

NOTE: The women in both the ethnographic sample and the survey were asked whether their families were "middle-class." The specific question was: "Relative to other families in this country, would you characterize your family as 'middle-income' or 'middle-class'? (Circle yes or no)" In the survey, 77.5% of Bradford women said yes, compared to 42% of the Bradford ethnographic sample; 90.1% of SU women in the survey said yes, compared to 91% of the SU ethnographic sample. In interpreting these results, it is important to note that socioeconomic status as viewed emically versus etically shows greater discrepancies for blacks than for whites. Sociological labeling is oriented toward white labeling. What is viewed in the black community as middle-class would be classified lower in sociological scales.

Another question in the survey provided data about the women's backgrounds (especially about previous experiences with working women) and about the differences between the experiences of the ethnographic and survey samples. The question was: "While you were growing up and living at home, how much did your mother (or female who raised you) work, excluding housework? (Circle one: Did not work most of the time; Worked part-time; Worked full-time)" Among the surveyed group at Bradford, 16.2% said their mothers had not worked most of the time; 64.2% said their mothers had worked full-time (as compared to 0 and 66% respectively among the Bradford ethnographic sample). Among the surveyed group at SU, 44.8% said their mothers had not worked most of the time; 30.6% said their mothers had worked full-time (compared to 27% and 36% respectively among the SU ethnographic sample). See Holland and Eisenhart (1981:51).

TABLE 5. Survey and ethnographic sample: Highest level of education of parents or guardians

	Bradford				SU			
	Survey (N = 179)		Ethnographic (N = 12)		Survey (N = 183)		Ethnographic (N = 11)	
Level of education completed	Mother	Father	Mother	Father	Mother	Father	Mother	Father
Grammar school or less	8.5%	20.5%	8.0%	8.0%	1.1%	1.6%	0.0%	9.0%
Some high school	30.5	26.0	8.0	8.0	5.0	3.8	9.0	0
High-school graduate	26.1	28.3	25.0	25.0	25.0	15.4	9.0	9.0
Post–high-school (not 4-year college)	9.0	7.8	0	8.0	13.7	8.2	9.0	18.0
Some college	8.5	6.6	0	0	18.6	13.7	18.0	9.0
College degree	10.2	5.4	17.0	8.0	21.3	24.7	27.0	0
Some grad. or prof. school	2.3	1.2	0	0	2.7	3.3	9.0	18.0
Grad. of prof. degree	4.5	4.2	8.0	0	13.1	29.1	9.0	27.0
No information	1.0	0.0	33.0	42.0	0	1.0	9.0	9.0

NOTE: Survey figures are rounded to the nearest .1%; ethnographic figures, to the nearest 1%.

1983. They provided us with implicit cultural knowledge about romance that informed many of the conversations among peers, as well as the women's accounts of their experiences in the talking-diary interviews. Relevant portions of that work are reported in detail in Holland and Skinner (1983, 1987).

Although we did not do a similar study at Bradford and we know that some terms used there were different, our analyses of the Bradford women's talk during our ethnographic interviews and observations suggest that the terms used there labeled gender types and distinguished kinds of gender relationships similar to those at SU. We will discuss the important differences that did exist at Bradford.

The Follow-up Interviews

In 1983, when members of the ethnographic sample were due to graduate from college, and again in 1987, attempts were made to recontact the women and to learn about their current activities and plans. Nineteen of our twenty-three informants were contacted in 1983. Seventeen informants were contacted in 1987. Information on the graduation status of all the women was obtained from each university in 1987.

In essence, then, we followed the lives of the women for eight years. The intensive part of the study took place in the first two years of their college careers. The follow-up interviews provided a chronicle of their subsequent life events, a glimpse of their current plans and visions of themselves, and some retrospective views of their college experiences.

On the basis of our analysis of the interviews and all the material from the other parts of the study, we have become more and more convinced of the centrality of the peer group in mediating gender relations and the women's participation in the gender hierarchy. Guided by the importance of the peer group, we begin the rest of the book with a historical presentation of campus cultures in the United States. In Part 4, we turn to the culturally constructed world of romance and attractiveness and to the women's responses to pressure to participate in that world. At that point the reader will begin to meet the women as individuals. Because classes and studies were overshadowed in the women's lives by the pressure of romance, description of academic demands and the women's responses to schoolwork is postponed until the nature of gender relations in the peer group has been described.

Campus Life:
The Past and the Present

Officially, American schools exist for the purpose of education. The word "education" usually conjures up an
image of a teacher standing in front of a classroom lecturing, while students, textbooks stowed nearby, sit and
listen, trying to absorb the information. But in the minds
of students, school is also a world of agemates or peers.
College students are like high-school and elementary-
school students in this regard. Although they do go to
classes and think about their studies, they spend a lot of
time with their friends and concern themselves to a large
degree with student-run activities. The women in our
study were no exception. For them, if we may judge by
our interviews and observations, what went on outside the
classroom was of much more interest and concern than
what went on inside.

As it turned out—and as has been true on U.S. college
campuses since the 1920s—gender relations dominated
student culture and activities at both Bradford and SU.
Thus, male/female relationships and interactions, sexual
activities, and sexualities and their cultural interpretations dominated in women's experience of and response
to the university. Their centrality in the women's lives and
university experiences dictates that we begin with descriptions of student, or campus, culture and of gender relations within this culture.[1] We describe characteristics of
student cultures in general and their history on U.S. college campuses in particular. The second part of the chapter is devoted to an overview of campus life at Bradford
and SU at the time of our study.

STUDENT CULTURES

By the time the women in the study became students at
Bradford or SU, they had probably spent a great deal of
their lives participating in student cultures; at least their

79

accounts of their high-school experiences indicated that they had. If our mid-1970s study of an elementary school in Bradford can be taken as an indication, they had been part of thriving student cultures in their elementary schools as well.

Vital student cultures seem to be a ubiquitous element, if not an unavoidable consequence, of age-segregated schools. Colleta (1976), for example, in an anthropological study of South Pacific Ponapean children, watched a student culture develop in a newly introduced Western-style school system. Colleta describes the discrepancy that existed between the multi-age groupings of the everyday life of the Ponapean children and the narrow age cohorts of the Western schools that they attended. In the schools, children developed among themselves a social order different from that directly encouraged by school adults and different from their previous ways of associating with one another. According to Colleta, the new order began to appear as early as the third or fourth grade and was exercised through mechanisms of control, shame, and ridicule adapted from adult Ponapean society to fit the school context. By the seventh and eighth grades, the solidarity of the peer group had been achieved to the point that it could collectively oppose or resist the formal authority of the school.

Opposition, as noted in chapters 3 and 4, is a frequent characteristic of student cultures. They are often oppositional to official school ideology and adult-approved practices. Possibly because these peer cultures develop in part in response to strict age hierarchies, in which privileges are dispensed by age and students are forbidden "adult" privileges, dissident student cultures are likely to incorporate denied adult roles and privileges. From older siblings, parents, and young adults in their communities, students adopt behaviors they associate with being older than they are and with being more up-to-date than those of their teachers. Willis's lads of Hammertown created a cultural form in which the roles and ranks were constituted from working-class adult behaviors (such as drinking, boasting of sexual exploits, and "having a laff") and from attitudes (such as irreverence for formal authority, valuation of manual, as opposed to mental, labor) that the students observed among the adults they knew outside of school (see also Brake 1980:166; Gallimore et al. 1974). Willis (1977:19) writes:

> In a very typical conjunction of school-based and outside meanings cigarette smoking for "the lads" is valorised as an act of insurrection before the school by its association with adult values and practices. The adult world . . . is turned to as a source of material for resistance and exclusion.

As well as inducing a "nice" effect, drinking is undertaken openly [in school] because it is the most decisive signal . . . that the individual is separate from the school and
has a presence in an alternative, superior and more mature
mode of social being.

In our work with fifth- and sixth-graders at the Bradford elementary school, we found informal peer groups that promptly segregated
themselves by gender whenever possible and that emphasized cross-
gender relationships, despite the school's careful efforts to downplay
or ignore the emerging sexualities of their students (Eisenhart and
Holland 1983). The students worked out the meaning of their cross-
gender relationships by appropriating interests, relationships, and
styles of appearance and clothing characteristic of their older peers
and siblings.

Given what we know about student cultures, it is scarcely surprising
that student peer cultures are an important part of residential college
life. Residential colleges provide an even more age-segregated community than do schools for younger students. Students leave home
and find themselves surrounded by peers in classes *and* dorms. They
spend almost all of their time with peers. At the same time their
connections to families and home communities are significantly decreased and often experienced only long-distance. Visits home are
relatively infrequent and limited to weekends, vacations, or the telephone. Student cultures flourish in such situations, and in fact
campus cultures have a long history.

HISTORICAL BACKGROUND OF CAMPUS LIFE IN THE UNITED STATES

In *Campus Life* (1987), Helen Horowitz argues that for
most American college students from the late eighteenth century until
the 1970s, a campus peer system, organized in opposition to the academic values of the faculty, dominated student life. It "forged a peer
consciousness sharply at odds with that of the faculty . . . dating from
the late eighteenth century. . . . classes [were] the price one had to pay
for college life . . . 'a little space of time where the young made a world
to suit themselves'" (Horowitz 1987:11–12). Although in Horowitz's
view, the strength of this college peer culture declined in the late
1970s and early 1980s, we found continuities with the earlier culture.
Her account helps us to put the patterns we found in historical perspective.[2] (For unfamiliar terms in what follows, see the glossary.)

According to Horowitz, peer culture at American universities

developed in the late eighteenth century, when elite men in some
numbers began attending college. The freedoms and pleasures that
had been enjoyed by the men before arriving on campus were strictly
curtailed by the faculty and administration, in hopes of encouraging
attention to academic matters. To young elite men these restrictions
appeared harsh, and a peer culture that opposed the academic values
of the faculty soon emerged. The men organized clubs and sporting
activities that were consistent with their genteel upbringing and that
became a "collective form of covert protest and escape" (Horowitz
1987:118) from the academic life the faculty sought to impose.

In this campus culture, several themes emerged and have persisted:
a strict social distance between teachers and students; a devaluation of
academic work; a peer-culture definition of a "reasonable" amount of
schoolwork; and a valuation of athletics and social graces. After 1920,
when coeds became numerous on college campuses, an emphasis on
"style" (physical appearance, dress, walk) and sexual play was added:

> College dating created and confirmed the system of pres-
> tige on campus. Students . . . chose [partners] . . . of the
> opposite sex . . . in ways that established and strengthened
> their social position. . . . The Greek system established the
> ranking order . . . the group prestige they lent made the
> individual a worthy candidate for a potential date. Men
> from the top-ranked fraternities therefore could pick from
> among the coeds. . . . Fraternities . . . defined and . . .
> control[led] the major social events of the college year: the
> proms, the student plays, . . . elections, . . . and sports.
> (Horowitz 1987:128, 131)

Freshman students were immediately exposed to the peer culture
when they arrived on campuses, and many were drawn to it. Based on
her own and others' research, Horowitz reports that within seven
weeks of college matriculation a large number of highly motivated,
academically oriented students had lost the "grade orientation" they
brought to college and replaced it with interests associated with the
peer culture. Those who embraced the campus peer culture—Horowitz labels them "college men" and "college women"—sought approval from their peers, not from their teachers. (See also Smucker
1947:163–68; Wallace 1966.)

Horowitz is careful to point out that not all students entered equally
into campus life. Some retained serious academic interests. They
came to do the schoolwork necessary to become professionals such as

ministers and lawyers. In her view they remained within the "culture of their parents" throughout college, sought approval from their teachers, and ignored or withdrew from the peer culture.

There was also another type of student, who either came to college with a cynical attitude toward the campus culture or was at first enthusiastic about participating in the campus culture but later experienced its "foolishness" and dropped out of it. These students tended to band together into a group, the "rebels," that actively opposed the dominant peer culture and the accepted academic culture. Although the rebels often outnumbered those who embraced the peer culture, Horowitz contends that peer culture was hegemonic on college campuses until the 1960s—that is, it tended significantly to dominate the ethos of college life for students. (See also Clark and Trow 1966: 17–18.)

According to Horowitz, the first women college students were few in number, often from elite families, and intent on academic work in preparation for professional careers. By the 1920s, however, the picture had changed. Middle-class women were being attracted to college campuses in large numbers. These women, in contrast to the earlier ones, expected college to be fun, and they expected to find husbands there. They did not go to college to prepare for a career.

Because men's clubs and sports, the preserve of "college men," usually excluded women, coeds developed their own equivalents, although their groups did not attain, and still have not attained, the campus status of the men's groups. In contrast, women gained status primarily by dating.

> As dating entered the college scene, . . . it established the key way that women gained status. . . . College women gained their positions indirectly by being asked out by the right man. Their primary contests became those of beauty and popularity, won not because of what they did, but because of how and to whom they appealed. By the 1920s, the conventional college woman was becoming the consort of the college man. Coeds glowed in reflected light. . . . In the balance of trade, she exchanged her carefully studied appearance for an evening's entertainment with a man. (Horowitz 1987:208, 211)

Wallace (1966:32) describes the campus coed of that day in similar terms: women's "striving for success . . . consists chiefly in manipulating people and in eliciting their personal affect, and the relevant skills are therefore 'personal appeal' and 'attractiveness'" (see also Rothman 1984). Horowitz is careful to point out that in the dating arrangement, men were expected to carry the economic burden. Women were expected to spend money making themselves more attractive to men; men were to pay for the dating activity itself and any additional costs, such as flowers and food, associated with it.

After the 1920s, the major developments in campus life occurred during the 1960s and early 1970s. In the 1960s the dominant character of the peer culture changed markedly. Campus rebels prevailed, until they were demoralized and disorganized by the killings of students at Kent State, South Carolina State, and Jackson State. The student deaths, plus the assassinations of Martin Luther King, Jr., and other national figures, combined with the end of the Viet Nam War and with increased competition for jobs to drastically change the mood on college campuses. In place of the ethos of the rebels of the 1960s and early 1970s, according to Horowitz, a dominant ethos of "making good grades" in order to achieve future occupational success has emerged. (See also Becker, Geer, and Hughes, 1968.) The "good grades" ethos is oppositional too, but in a more benign sense: it does not involve the quality of commitment to academic learning that faculty want students to have, but instead emphasizes doing whatever is necessary to make good grades (Horowitz 1987:249). This opposition is certainly less overtly challenging, though possibly just as frustrating, to the faculty's orientation than the pre-1960s campus peer cultures were.

Today, student oppositional culture may be less overt for an additional reason. During the campus upheavals of the 1960s, colleges withdrew their longstanding oversight of student manners and morals, thus removing one of the main targets of student opposition. College peer culture was left opposing some adult standards concerning drinking, drugs, and permissive sexuality, but its response was not as distinctive or as compelling as it once had been. "[With a few exceptions] college [today] neither provides an alternative world of its own nor promises one in the future. Since [most of the students] aspire to imitate their parents, [they] struggle in college to maintain [most of] the standards of home" (Horowitz 1987:271).

The students at SU and Bradford in 1979, 1980, and 1981—the dates of our study—showed signs of the good-grades ethos described by Horowitz, but our research revealed that many remnants of the older college peer cultures persisted, especially in the area of gender relations.[3]

CAMPUS LIFE AT BRADFORD AND SU

Peer cultures at Bradford and SU absorbed a great deal of the students' time and energy, as they had for the students' historical counterparts. Peer-organized activities went on continually; peers were in constant attendance, day and night. For most of the women in our study, like the "college men and women" described by Horowitz, the academic aspects of college life paled by comparison with the peer culture. Although academic pursuits took time—sometimes large portions of the women's time—they did not capture the women's interest and attention nearly as much as the peer system did.

We also found evidence of another cultural theme that Horowitz attributed to the college peer culture: the great emphasis on cross-gender romantic relationships. When the women came to Bradford and SU, they entered into a peer culture built around an ethos of romantic heterosexual relationships. The peer-ranking systems at both schools were intimately tied to gender relations interpreted in terms of attractiveness and romance. As a consequence, for the women in our study other kinds of relationships, as well as academic interests, became hard to establish or maintain. In particular, we found that in the ethos of the student culture, women's relationships with other women, like their interest in schoolwork, tended to be pushed aside.

We argue at some length in later chapters that the peer culture was very important in the formation of the women's romantic identities and indirectly important in the erosion of their career identities. The peer system promoted neither their relationships with other women nor their academic or career-related identities. Thus the peer culture was important ultimately in constructing women's economic marginality and their subordination to men.

Although similar in broad outline, the peer cultures at the two universities were not identical. Romance and attractiveness were prominent aspects of peer culture, as Horowitz describes, on both campuses, but only at SU were they the major organizing principles of women's social world. At Bradford, reminiscent of Fuller's description of West Indian women in London, principles of female self-reliance also applied. The differences between Bradford and SU are more fully elaborated in chapter 8.

The Pursuit of Romance

In the world of peers encountered by the women in our study, the most exciting and popular activities included opportunities to meet men or to enact romantic relationships. The women devoted considerable time and energy to going places (bars, mixers, parties, pools) where they hoped to be noticed by men, to taking care of male friends by cleaning their apartments or cooking for them, to assisting at fraternity activities as "sweethearts" or "little sisters," and to supporting men's sports (as spectators, cheerleaders, flag girls, majorettes, and managers). In addition, their conversations frequently concerned men and romantic relationships. Women spent hours, in the dorm, in the library, on the way to class, discussing who was attractive and why, who was "going with" whom, who wanted to go out with whom, what couples were doing when they went out, how well-matched members of a couple were, what was needed to become more attractive, and so forth.

In contrast, relatively few peer-group activities or conversations had much to do with academic work or career-related matters. In preparing to formulate questions for the survey, we scoured the notes and interviews for different kinds of campus activities that the women engaged in. The fifty-five activities we identified and the importance the surveyed women attributed to them provide a profile of the women's interests at college (see table 6). Less than 25 percent (thirteen) of the activities were directly related to schoolwork or career; more than 40 percent (twenty-four) were peer-dominated. As part of the survey, we asked respondents to rate the importance to them of each of the activities. We found that many of the peer-dominated ones, including socializing, friendships, and romantic relationships, were rated equally important as or more important than schoolwork or job-related activities.

In other words, the survey results corroborate what we found ethnographically: that academics exist alongside and sometimes in the shadow of peer-centered activities. Further, the survey results indirectly suggest a relatively marginal interest in finding peers who share educational aims and interests. Table 7 presents the academic and career-related activities in slightly more detail. Individual-centered academic interests and activities were rated as more important than peer-related ones. The ethnographic interviews and observations gave a much more definitive picture of the tangential quality of academics in the peer culture.

When asked about the majors or career interests of their peers, most of the women in the ethnographic study said they knew little or nothing about them. We have made some reference to academics in this chapter precisely in order to reveal its relative lack of importance in the peer culture and thus to explain why academics fails to take the

TABLE 6. Survey: Importance of activities and relationships, by university

	Bradford	SU
Friendships	59.8%[a]	91.3%
Girlfriends	3.47[b]	4.16
New women friends	2.59	3.31
Male friends	2.89	3.60
New male friends	2.76	3.40
Romantic relationships	71.5%	65.6%
Steady boyfriend	3.51	2.73
New steady/main boyfriend	1.76	1.98
Lots of dates	1.40	2.05
Hometown activities and family	92.7%	89.6%
Family connections—own sake	4.53	4.31
Family connections—their sake	4.58	4.37
Hometown activities	2.83	2.36
Socializing	54.7%	90.2%
Having parties to go to	2.55	3.28
Having friends who party	2.21	2.83
Getting together with friends	3.15	4.04
Going out with boyfriends	3.38	3.70
Sororities	18.4%	19.1%
Being in a sorority	1.64	1.25
Present participation in a sorority	0.85	0.81
Contact with others interested in sororities	1.42	1.26
Sports activities	33.5%	48.6%
Following university teams	2.68	2.80
Doing some sports activity on a regular basis	2.66	2.92
Being in a sports club	1.68	1.69
Present participation in a sports club	1.63	1.73
Contact with others interested in sports	2.20	2.13
Performing groups	34.6%	23.5%
Attending performances	2.93	2.23
Being in a performing group	2.20	1.75
Developing skills in a performing art	2.63	2.37
Contact with others interested in performing arts	2.70	2.25
Religious activities	71.5%	63.4%
Following own religious beliefs	3.89	3.66
Attending services regularly	3.45	2.76
Participating in religious groups	3.34	2.74
Political activities	71.5%	49.7%
Being knowledgeable about local campus issues	3.42	2.89
Participating in campus groups	2.80	1.43
Being knowledgeable about special-interest issues	3.28	2.85
Participating in special-interest groups	3.16	1.28
Contact with others who share interests	3.24	1.68
Being knowledgeable about state/national political issues	3.31	3.31
Working with policy or electoral groups	2.60	1.58
Contact with others interested in state/national politics	2.66	1.93

(continued)

TABLE 6. (*continued*)

	Bradford	SU
Travel	53.1%	53.6%
Travel during next vacation	3.50	3.41
Contact with others interested in travel	3.24	3.17
Other special interests	44.1%	21.3%
Participating in other special-interest clubs	2.53	1.82
Achieving recognition in special interest	2.85	1.76
Contact with others who share special interest	2.69	1.94
Academics	98.9%	98.4%
Maintaining good grades	4.57	4.28
Getting an academic award	3.66	2.57
Contact with others who want to do well	3.73	3.33
Doing well in major	4.78	4.48
Participating in a group related to major	3.29	1.93
Achieving special recognition related to major	3.64	2.63
Contact with others who share same academic interests	3.54	3.30
Acquiring a good education	4.68	4.51
Contact with others who want a good education	3.84	3.62
Job/volunteer work	81.0%	85.8%
Having a job during school year	3.22	2.50
Doing well in current job	2.94	2.23
Contact with people who share same job concerns	2.90	2.00
Having a job for the summer	3.93	4.04

SOURCE: Adapted from Holland and Eisenhart 1981:24–26.
NOTES:[a]The main categories (subheadings) are listed with the percentage of the sample that rated one or more of the items as one of the most or one of the more important things in their lives right now.
[b]Students were asked to rate the activities on a scale of 0 ("not part of my life right now") to 5 ("one of the most important things in my life right now"). The figures are the mean for each sample.

center stage that one might expect in a book about college experiences. The secondary place of academics for most of our informants is described in detail in chapter 12.

Although the women's conversations about boyfriends and about their favorite activities included references to other women, women and their relationships with each other were not a primary focus of attention. Relationships with women (as described in chapter 8), although valued and enjoyed, almost always revolved around relationships with men.

Campus and community political activity also failed to interest the women very much. Vestiges of campus radicalism remained, but attracted little attention. The one woman in our ethnographic study who was deeply interested in political causes gave this description of a protest march she tried to organize at Bradford: "When we had that

TABLE 7. Survey: Average importance associated with individual versus peer-oriented academic and career activities, by university

Activities		Bradford	SU
Individual activities	Average	3.93	3.41
	s.d.	.69	1.0
Doing well in major		4.78	4.48
Acquiring a good education		4.68	4.51
Maintaining good grades		4.57	4.28
Having a job for the summer		3.93	4.04
Getting an academic award		3.66	2.57
Achieving special recognition in major		3.64	2.63
Having a job during the school year		3.22	2.50
Doing well in current job		2.94	2.23
Peer-oriented activities	Average	3.46	2.84
	s.d.	.38	.81
Keeping in contact with others who want a good education		3.84	3.62
Keeping in contact with others who want to do well in school		3.73	3.33
Keeping in contact with others who share same interests and concerns about major		3.54	3.30
Participating in special-interest clubs related to major		3.29	1.93
Keeping in contact with people who share same job interests and concerns		2.90	2.00

SOURCE: Adapted from Holland and Eisenhart 1981:32.
NOTE: Students were asked to rate the activities on a scale of 0 ("not part of my life right now") to 5 ("one of the most important things in my life right now"). The figures are the mean for each sample.

march, we had a measure of students, but the majority were down there at the step show. . . . We marched right through them, and they looked at us like they didn't even know what was going on. It was very upsetting . . . and it was kind of embarrassing for the university, because we had all the news coverage here and . . . nine-tenths of the university in the middle of stepping and clapping and carrying on."

As for the women's movement, although there was some administrative support and campus activity—more at SU than at Bradford—the women in the study were not much engaged by either the activities or the available courses on women's issues. An officially designated program of women's studies was in place at SU and had been for several years.[4] A major in women's studies was possible through an umbrella program that permitted interdisciplinary courses of study; during the period of the study, women's studies courses began to be listed as such in the course catalog for undergraduates. There were feminist organizations on campus that held meetings and events and sponsored speakers, but we did not hear much about them from the members of our study. The same virtual silence was true for the Bradford women. They had far fewer campus resources than the SU women. A few relevant courses were listed in Bradford's catalog during the 1980–81 school year, but no courses addressed exclusively to topics in women's studies were featured until 1983–84. There was no official program in women's studies at Bradford at the time of the study.

In short—judging from the interests we heard about in the interviews or saw in the observations—the women had few engaging alternatives to the peer group and its emphasis on gender relations. An initial answer to the question of why the women did not see past the peer culture to feminist alternatives can be found in the way women's prestige is defined by the peer group. Horowitz suggests that women on college campuses in the past devoted so much time to the peer system, with its emphasis on romantic relationships with men, because women could gain prestige only by making themselves attractive to men and by dating attractive men. The women described in the research Horowitz reviewed could not gain prestige from academic successes, organized extracurricular activities, participation in political causes, or relationships with other women. At Bradford and especially at SU, we found the same pattern.

Part 4 *Gender Relations*

7 Gender Relations Culturally Construed: Romance and Attractiveness

In chapter 6 we depicted college life at Bradford and SU as centering around gender relations. Consistent with a pattern dating back to the 1920s, Bradford and SU students culturally celebrated sexual attraction as a dominant theme of campus culture. Drawing upon a much older tradition, they interpreted a world of gender relations according to the cultural idiom of romance and attractiveness. In this chapter we describe these cultural notions of romantic attraction, the link made by the students between sexual attraction and marriage, and the manner in which definitions of attractiveness constrain women.

ROMANCE AND ATTRACTIVENESS: A CULTURAL MODEL

Romantic love is a cultural construction of sexuality that defines a world of gendered persons and their relationships. Historians date the beginning of modern conceptions of romantic love in the West to eleventh-century France and to the twelfth-century court of Eleanor of Aquitaine (Heer 1962; Lewis 1936). At first perhaps in the spirit of play, members of the court adopted a metaphor from feudal society to describe a new form of gender relations. In courtly love the woman, who was usually of higher birth than the knight who "courted" her, became the lord, and the knight became her vassal. He paid his respects to her and won her favorable regard by carrying out her wishes (Capellanus [c.1180]). She in turn granted him small intimacies as tokens of her esteem, admiration, and affection. Permitted and perhaps encouraged by Eleanor (Heer 1962; Parry 1941; see also Kelly 1937), the ideas and rituals of courtly love grew and prospered, much to the consternation of church officials, who saw them as threatening the church's teachings about the subordinate position of women (Painter 1940).

Although its popularity and celebration have waxed and waned, romantic love over the centuries has gradually been transformed from a courtly indulgence of French aristocrats to the ideal of sexual relations in the West for aristocrat and commoner alike (Reilly 1980; Rougemont 1940). Its basic outlines can be discerned in the way in which gender relations were interpreted in the peer cultures of Bradford and of SU.

As with courtly love in medieval France, the cultural interpretation of gender relations at Bradford and SU seems to give an equal if not superior position to women. Yet, as will be seen, this "cultural model of romance" has implications for women that differ from those for men. Campus standards of attractiveness were not conceived in the same manner for women as for men, and the different standards constrained women's lives more than men's.

The Cultural Model of Romance

A year or so before the start of the NIE-funded study, Holland became intrigued by the hundreds of gender-marked terms like "jerk," "hunk," "nerd," "doll," "bitch," that students at SU used to talk about one another. Holland and Skinner (1987) began a series of "ethnosemantic" studies (described in the Appendix) to trace the meaning and use of those words.[1] Their studies were augmented by interviews and observations for the NIE study. In the interviews and the peer-activity observations, the women frequently used gender-marked terms to refer to the men in their lives. From an analysis of those segments of the NIE interviews and from the researchers' notes on occasions of use of the terms, as well as from additional consideration of the ethnosemantic studies, Holland and Skinner arrived at a cultural model of romance.

The model predicates a taken-for-granted world in which gendered persons—men and women—are attracted to one another and act out that attraction. The main points of the model, summarized from longer discussions in Holland and Skinner (1987:89–90, 101–2), follow:

> An attractive man ("guy") and an attractive woman ("girl") are attracted to one another.
>
> The man learns and appreciates the woman's qualities and uniqueness as a person. Sensitive to her desires he shows his attraction by treating her well: for example, he pays attention to her, he buys things for her, takes her places

> she likes, and shows that he appreciates her special quali-
> ties.
>
> She in turn shows her admiration and care for him and
> allows the relationship to become more intimate.

The model also implies the motives for such relationships:

> The relationship provides intimacy—both emotional and
> physical.
>
> It also provides prestige. The relationship demonstrates
> that the woman is attractive—she has attracted a man—and
> vice versa.

In addition, the model provides a way to compensate for unequal attractiveness and thus a means for calculating relative attractiveness:

> If the woman is more attractive than the man, he can com-
> pensate by treating her especially well. The man's treat-
> ment of the woman is a sign of (his assessment of) her
> attractiveness relative to his.
>
> If the woman's attractiveness is the lesser of the two, she
> compensates by lowering her expectations for good treat-
> ment. The woman's expectations of the man are a sign of
> (her assessment of) his attractiveness relative to hers.

The model is interlocked with the meanings of gender-marked terms. To understand how "dumb broads," "jocks," and other gender types are conceptualized, one must understand that the types are relevant characters in the world of romance and attractiveness as constructed by the model. Most of the pejorative terms refer to types of men or types of women who cause the taken-for-granted unfolding of a romantic attraction to go awry. Further, the model helps to unveil the complexities of the cultural construct of attractiveness as both an essence of a person *and* an effect on others and to make sense of the importance of attractiveness as an idiom of ranking in the peer culture.[2]

It should be noted that the cultural model of romance is first and foremost an interpretive structure, a meaning system, not a set of prescriptive rules. Actual relationships are not dictated or determined by the model, but rather experience is anticipated, interpreted, and evaluated in light of it. Most of the hundreds of named male types, like "jerks," "pricks," "assholes," "playboys," and the hundreds of named female types, like "bitches," "dogs," "dykes," "prudes," turn out to be troublemakers. The existence of so many labels is testimony to the seemingly unending need to talk about all the ways that gender relations can veer off the path proposed by the model.[3]

The cultural model of romance interprets sexual attraction or, as we shall put it later, establishes "attractiveness," as the commodity of value in an ongoing "sexual auction." (See also Griffin 1985:187, who describes a "sexual marketplace" where women are valued according to their perceived attractiveness to men.)[4] Romance and attraction as described by the model can lead to marriage, but the sexual auction and the "marriage market" are not completely interlinked. As we will ultimately argue, the women in our study sometimes managed to escape continuing exposure on the sexual auction block through marriage or at least a steady relationship, but they could not totally elude its shadows in the classroom and the workplace.

SEXUAL INTIMACY AND THE CULTURAL MODEL OF ROMANCE

As interpreted by the cultural model described above, romantic relationships begin with attraction. Closeness between the couple develops as the man treats the woman well and as she in turn reveals her attraction to and affection for him and permits the relationship to become more emotionally and physically intimate. Interpreted in this fashion, sexual activities—physical contact, kissing, intercourse—are an integral component.[5] In the most simple interpretation, sexual activities are a natural outcome of such a relationship; they are a natural part of attraction. But their meaning is much more complicated because they are also something else. In echo of courtly love, intimacies are a sign that the man has won the woman's affection. It is the woman who allows the relationship to become more intimate. Their relative attractiveness to one another, then, is testified to by the kind of treatment that he gives her in relation to the kind of intimacies she permits. In such a system, for example, a woman who permits intercourse despite bad treatment by the man is providing testimony to her own low status. Her demands for and expectations of good treatment are claims about her own attractiveness. Correspondingly, the man's demands for physical intimacy relative to the kind and quality of attention that he pays to the woman are claims about his own attractiveness (see also Holland and Skinner 1987:100–1).

SERIOUS RELATIONSHIPS LEAD TO MARRIAGE

Returning to the eleventh century, we find that courtly love seldom led to marriage. Marriage was not in fact a part of the scenario of romantic love. For one thing, the parties were usually already married to other people. For another, romantic love was not seen as a viable framework for conducting relations between a husband and wife. Over the intervening centuries romantic love has come to apply to unmarried parties and to be seen as the precursor to marriage and the framework of relations within marriage. Nonetheless, even now the step from romance (or perhaps to put it more precisely, romanticized sexual attraction) to marriage is not taken for granted, and the idea of a close connection between the two has been discarded by various groups, including, for example, the hippie counterculture of the 1960s.

In the student cultures of Bradford and SU in the early 1980s, romance and marriage were conceptualized as *potentially* linked stages in a relationship. The development could be arrested at any stage by either party's "breaking it off." As interpreted from the perspective of the women in the study, there is a sequence to a romantic relationship, beginning with a search for an attractive partner. A woman's activities during this stage are focused on making herself physically appealing to men and getting herself into settings where she can be seen by and meet men. In the words of SU women in the study, some (white) women spend "every minute not in class" beside the pool, "working on their tans." Women diet, exercise, go shopping, and trade clothes, with an eye toward making themselves "look good" to men. They "dress up" to go almost everywhere, including the lounges of their dorms, because "there might be some guys in there." In addition, women who are searching for men organize groups of women to go together to mixers, clubs, bars, restaurants, and sports events to meet attractive men. As a result of her efforts, a woman hopes to find an attractive man who is interested in her.[6]

The second stage involves increasingly regular, frequent, and close contact between a man and a woman who are attracted to each other, often culminating at SU in "going steady," or at Bradford in "talking to" and sometimes becoming "engaged to" a particular man. The relationship becomes a more exclusive one, in which the partners are not "seriously" dating anyone else.[7] As this stage develops, partners are expected to want to spend more and more time together. Women speak of couples who want to be together twenty-four hours a day, of those who exchange extravagant gifts, and of those who write to, call, and see each other every day.

As this stage continues, especially if it develops into an exclusive relationship, the woman begins to arrange her life to be available to her boyfriend, to do things to help and support her boyfriend, and to participate in social activities chosen by her boyfriend. Women with steady relationships do things like scheduling their classes on Tuesdays and Thursdays so as to be able to spend long weekends with their boyfriends, keeping weekend nights free in case their boyfriends want to go out, and deciding not to look seriously for a job after graduation because their boyfriends are not ready to leave the area. In general (especially at SU), the woman in the relationship is expected to make arrangements to visit an off-campus boyfriend, to forgo her own activities in order to serve as a little sister in his fraternity "because [the fraternity is] so important to him," or to set aside her time to make him study "because he won't do it on his own." Women also find time to wash their boyfriends' clothes, buy their food, clean their apartments, and work out refunds or repairs for defective purchases. In exchange for their efforts, women hope that their boyfriends will provide them with attention, gifts, and emotional closeness.

There is a third, more "serious" stage, in which a romantic relationship leads to marriage and a family. This stage gives some form to the women's thinking about their futures. When a woman has had a steady relationship for some time, she begins to consider this third stage. One said, "[My boyfriend] and I have been together so long, it's inconceivable that we wouldn't have talked about marriage." Another said, "We're getting engaged [soon]. . . . I'm sure I'm gonna marry him . . . probably in the next one to two years."[8]

Attractiveness in the Sexual Auction and Ranking in the Student Culture

The cultural model of romance not only describes a sequence of events that may lead to the establishment of an intimate sexual relationship and perhaps in the long run to marriage, but also places sexual relations within a calculus of attractiveness. We found that this calculus of attractiveness extended to peer rankings and to some male/female relationships outside the peer system.[9] Being attractive was an extremely important quality to have at SU and Bradford. It was believed to be a necessary commodity for marriage and, although in a less explicit way, for all male/female relationships.

For the women in our study the importance of attractiveness could be easily discerned in its consequences: the kind of men they could attract, and the treatment they received from them. Following the cultural model, a woman's attractiveness and prestige were validated, to a major extent, by her relations with men who were her (potential) romantic partners. For a woman, having a man interested in her as a romantic partner was a sign of her attractiveness. One of the women put it this way: "All [the girls] wanted a date on Saturday night. That was the most important thing, 'cause now somebody else was interested in you. They found you attractive." A male romantic partner made a woman feel attractive and prestigious. Reflecting this dependence on men for feelings of social worth, another woman said about her boyfriend: "I depend on [him] for attention. . . . He makes me feel good, he compliments me . . . he's attentive to me and sensitive to the things that I feel."

The idea that equals attract meant that the women expected attractive men to pair up with attractive women; conversely, low-ranking women deserved low-ranking men. Good-looking men deserved good-looking women, or as one woman put it, speaking about the same system in high school, "The boys wanted to date a pretty girl, [not] a girl that the group considered not as attractive as someone else."

Women proudly proclaimed that they were going out with men who were "popular" on campus, known as sports figures, residents of the "best" men's dorm, or "outstanding" in their fields of study. Women were also proud to have it known that they dated men with the correlates or signs of prestige and attractiveness, a lot of money or especially nice clothes, apartments, or cars. In contrast, they were uncomfortable when their dates or boyfriends were described by others as low-status, as "jerks" or "creeps." If a high-status man was interested in a woman thought to be average, her prestige among her peers would be raised. Correspondingly, if a "good-looking" woman was involved with an "average" man who didn't compensate by treating her especially well, her prestige tended to decline. According to the model, the best "finds" were the attractive men, the ones who had prestige on campus, the ones who were sensitive to a woman's needs and respected her viewpoints and interests.

Besides ordaining that attractive men will be attracted to attractive women, the model of romance also implies that attractive women will be well treated—a sign of their attractiveness—and correspondingly, that unattractive women will be badly treated. By treating a woman well, by giving her gifts, sending her cards and flowers, calling long-distance, doing what she wants, a man attests to the woman's attractiveness. He appreciates her special qualities as a woman and a person and is responsive to her concerns. One woman described "every girl's dream" as follows: "He is really cute . . . something special. I've never gotten so many flowers and stuff in my life . . . and gifts. He'd do anything that I wanted."

The opposite treatment implies that a woman is not attractive, or at least is less attractive than the man. The following account, given by a roommate of one of the SU women, reveals the acute embarrassment that a friend felt for a woman who exposed herself to bad treatment (Holland and Skinner 1987:94–95):

> A friend of mine [Annette] invited us . . . to a party in the dorm. And, she told us that there'd be . . . a couple of people there that she really liked a lot: guys, that is . . . and . . . when we got there . . . the main one she wanted to see . . . I mean . . . he didn't even hardly acknowledge her presence. He practically didn't even speak to her. . . . And it just sort of messed up the whole party—mainly for her, and because of that, it messed it up for all of us. I expected . . . some real nice guys. I thought they'd be really glad to see her. But they [weren't] . . . the one she wanted to see acted real stuck-up, as if she wasn't even there. . . . He ignored her. . . . She'd be standing practically beside him, and he wouldn't say anything.

Later the interviewer asked why the man had acted the way he did:

> I don't know . . . maybe she just had it in her head that he liked her . . . and he was just trying to talk to this other girl or something. But he did act, he acted sort of too good for her, you know?

Annette continued to be upset about the incident, and Karen, the woman describing her plight, explained that Annette was trying to reason out why the man had acted as he did:

INTERVIEWER: What were some of the ways she reasoned it out?
KAREN: Um, well, she thought at first maybe because he was with that girl, he didn't want to talk to anybody else. And, but then, he was talking to other girls that were walking by, and um, then she was thinking, maybe he was mad at her, but she didn't know why, you know, she was just thinking of different stuff like that.
INTERVIEWER: Did you think of any things like that too?
KAREN: Uh, not really, I, I, it's gonna sound terrible. I thought, well he just didn't want to, didn't want to see her at all, 'cause he just didn't, I don't know, what I thought was that, he was like I said before, he was some big jock on campus, you know, and he just wanted the real, just certain girls around him, you know.
INTERVIEWER: What . . . what kinds?
KAREN: Really pretty.

In her friend's eyes, Annette was treated badly. The man she was interested in did not even acknowledge her presence. The situation was so embarrassing because Annette had publicly revealed her attraction to him and he had ignored her. She was shown to be less attractive, to have less prestige than he, in front of her friends.

Bad treatment means being treated as though one does not exist, or is simply a sexual object without any special characteristics, or is simply one woman among many others. Bad treatment from a male is an indicator of a woman's low status. If a man treats a woman badly by not paying much attention to her, by not giving her things, or by disregarding her and her feelings, his action can be taken as a sign that she is lower in status than he is. If the woman has no particular attractiveness relative to the man's prestige and attractiveness, then she cannot expect to be well treated. She is expected to reveal her good feelings about the man, provide services to him, support him, and allow the relationship to become more emotionally and physically intimate, without concomitant attention and special treatment from him.

In the cultural interpretation of sexual relations provided by the model of romance and attractiveness, rape is an ultimate form of bad treatment. The man disregards the woman's feelings completely. He treats her as though she deserves nothing or, worse yet, abuse. In the logic of the culture of romance and attractiveness, he claims physical intimacy from her with nothing given in return. In effect, he states with his act that her prestige is so low that he does not need to win her affection at all. And, because attractiveness is attested to by the treatment women receive from men, rape *creates* the victim's low prestige (see also Sanders 1980).

In the logic of this system women who "accept" bad treatment, who, for example, "invite" themselves to be treated solely as sex objects, deserve bad treatment and unattractive men: "The hall slut deserves the dullest guy around." This aspect of the culture of romance and attractiveness, the notion of *deserved* bad treatment, was much more elaborated in the peer culture of the London comprehensive schools described by Lees than it was at Bradford or SU. In the London schools women were dichotomized into two types: those without prestige who deserved bad treatment—the "slags"—and those with prestige who deserved good treatment: "It is almost as though there are two kinds of sexuality, one that is without emotional feeling and treats women ["slags"] as dirty and provocative, and the other that involves strong feelings of sensuality and compassion; and that these two concepts of sexuality are inextricably linked to the concepts of the virgin and the whore" (Lees 1986:149–50). Although Lees does not relate this complex of bad treatment/good treatment to the culture of romance and attractiveness, she ends with a conclusion similar to ours: "Rape and violence [against women] cannot be explained as the behaviour of psychopathic sex maniacs but rather as actions which are the extension of the normal oppressive structure of sexual relations" (pp. 149–50).[10]

ATTRACTIVENESS AS SYMBOLIC CAPITAL

In order to fathom the logic of the cultural model of romance, it is useful to realize that attractiveness is spoken of both as an *essence* of a person and as an *effect* on another person. At one level, attraction occurs because of something in the other person. A man is attracted to a woman because she is in essence attractive. Something about her—her looks, the way she talks, the way she acts—is attractive to him. On another level, a person's attractiveness is judged by the behavior he or she elicits from others (see also Holland 1988b).

The idea of attractiveness as a quality or characteristic or essence of a person is extremely important. Particularly with regard to physical appearance, the cosmetic and fashion industries make great profits by convincing Americans that they can make themselves more attractive by purchasing and using certain products.[11] The SU and Bradford women certainly subscribed to the idea, for they worked, some very hard, to become like the examples of attractive women—the beauty queens, the models in glossy advertisements, the "after" example in the "before" and "after" pictures accompanying diet plans—that were constantly presented to them in the media and were pointed out by the men and women in their lives.

Although attractiveness is often talked about as strictly an essential or inherent quality that can be perceived at a glance, in actuality one's attractiveness is also appraised by how one is treated. When a man, especially one who is considered by others to be attractive, is attentive to a woman and treats her well, he is attesting to her attractiveness. His attention is taken by others as a sign that she is attractive. Although the media and other institutions promote certain standards of beauty, a hegemonic attractiveness, there is no accepted authority that certifies the extent to which an individual possesses such a quality.[12] Hence the interpersonal signs of attractiveness are important; one gains or loses attractiveness depending on the attractiveness of those whom one attracts and the treatment that one receives from them.

Another way to state this point is to say that having attracted one man a woman is more likely to attract another, because the first man is symbolic testimony that she is attractive. Correspondingly, once having been badly treated by a man, a woman is more likely to be badly treated by another man. Thus attractiveness is self-reinforcing. It becomes what has been called "symbolic capital." Bourdieu (1977b) has applied this term to honor in Kabylia: a Kabyle man who is thought to have a lot of honor today will be given the benefit of the doubt in the interpretation of his actions tomorrow. He can trade upon his reputation in ways that a man who is without honor cannot, and thus he can further his honor in ways that a man without honor cannot. (See also Bourdieu and Passeron 1977, on intelligence in France.) Along much the same lines, under the cultural model of romance, women who have a reputation for being attractive, as attested by the men who find them attractive and worthy of good treatment, are given the benefit of the doubt. What they do, say, and wear tends to be considered attractive, and thus they become more attractive.

Waller (1937:730), writing about similar topics as observed on college campuses in the 1930s, also noted the self-reinforcing characteristic of attractiveness. He pointed out that women's attractiveness and prestige depended upon having good clothes, a smooth line, ability to dance well, and popularity as a date. "The most important of these factors," he added, "is the last, for the girl's prestige depends upon dating more than anything else; here as nowhere else nothing succeeds like success. Therefore the clever coed contrives to give the impression of being much sought after even if she is not."

Some forty years after Waller's research, the ploy of boosting one's attractiveness by being or appearing to be the recipient of positive attention from more than one man was reported in the present interviews. A woman at SU spoke of "keeping the upper hand" as a means of making sure a man treated her well. As was the case for validating one's honor in Kabylia, the timing of responses to male interest was used in making claims about relative attractiveness:

> I didn't want him [a man she had just started to go out with] to think that I was really crazy about him and that he could just use me, you know, maybe if he knew I'd want to go out with him and stuff like that. So that's why I just sort of let him, in fact, I was trying to get it with him, you know, get the upper hand with him, but it didn't work. He's the same way. . . .

The interviewer asked how she tried to get the upper hand.

> He'd say something about going out and I'd say, "Well just
> . . . we probably will, but it's a little early right now." I'd do
> stuff like that, and he'd ask me, he asked me if I had . . . a
> boyfriend back home and I didn't say anything, and he
> says, "Well, I figured you did."

She went on to explain other ways in which she tried to give the man
the impression that she had other boyfriends, including such subter-
fuges as leaving the dorm when she thought he was going to call.

In sum, although attractiveness is frequently talked about as an
essential quality of a person, it is, in fact, also a function or outcome
of the way in which one is treated. For women, good treatment from
attractive men provides prestige and status. Likewise bad treatment,
or potential bad treatment, from men is taken as a sign of unattrac-
tiveness and low prestige (Lees 1986:21, 41). The essence and the
treatment become merged, and treatment becomes proof of essence.
By such logic, women deserve whatever treatment they receive from
men.[13]

ATTRACTIVENESS: ANOTHER FACE OF THE
DOUBLE STANDARD

On the surface, the culture of romance is based upon
equality: the woman and the man are equally attractive and their
exchange involves intimacy and prestige for both. The hidden inequality is revealed, however, when the different bases of attractiveness
are examined. Men's prestige and correlated attractiveness come
from the attention they receive from women *and* from success at
sports, in school politics, and in other arenas. Women's prestige and
correlated attractiveness come *only* from the attention they receive
from men.[14]

This way of seeing things was illustrated by one woman's description of how another women tried to insult her: "She told me, '[You]
may be able to do calculus, but I'm dating a football player.'" Both
women were well aware that dating a football player was "the big
thing" at SU.

This sort of gender-differentiated prestige system is described by
Horowitz (1987:208) as beginning on college campuses in the earlier
part of the century:

> As dating entered the college scene, it fundamentally re-
> shaped the college lives of coeds. . . . It established the key
> way that women gained status. College men vied for posi-
> tions on the [sports] field or in the newsroom; college

women gained their positions indirectly by being asked out by the right man. Their primary contests became those of beauty and popularity, won not because of what they did, but because of how and to whom they appealed.

In the context of a ranking system in which self-worth and prestige were validated primarily by the prestige of male romantic partners, the Bradford and SU women's concerns about appealing to men become more understandable:

> [When I'm with my girlfriends,] we always talk about our boyfriends, or how we wish we had boyfriends, or how fat we are—we all say that. . . . None of us have to lose weight, but we just want to be thinner. . . . I'm gonna lose weight and clear up my face and [grow] my hair out, so I'll be all beautiful this summer. . . . When we did anything with the guys, we always asked them, "What do guys like in girls?"

In the longer passage from which the preceding quote comes, the women's quest seems comical, because they pester the men about what guys like in girls so much that the men get bored and go away. However, Bartky (1982) believes that this self-absorption is not so funny. She argues that women are indeed taught at an early age to focus on themselves as viewed by others, especially by men. The result is an arrested narcissism that absorbs them and blocks their recognition of the ill effects of the ranking system. Men, on the other hand, are not so constrained. They can gain prestige and attractiveness in other ways.[15]

Romance and Attractiveness and the Interpretation of Gendered Sexualities

Another entailment of the model of romance and attractiveness concerns the sexualities of men and women. In the model of romance and attractiveness, women's sexuality is cast as something different from men's sexuality. A woman and a man who are sexually attracted to one another both desire intimacy, according to the model, but when a woman acts upon her sexual attraction to a man, she permits intimacy. That is, physical intimacy is something the woman gives and the man gets. "Good treatment" (primarily being respected and valued as a unique person) is what the man gives and the woman gets.

Of course, both men and women can lose prestige in the system. A woman may permit intimacy, yet be badly treated. A man may spend a lot of time, money, and attention on a woman, yet never receive any signs of affection from her.[16] But the point remains: male and female sexuality is differently interpreted, and the outcome is that female sexuality is more constrained. Female sexuality is interpreted in the framework of how the man treats the woman in return for her "sexual favors"; male sexuality is subjected to no such interpretation.[17]

SUMMARY

In this chapter we have presented what we found to be a central focus of the student cultures at both Bradford and SU: gender relations interpreted according to a cultural model of romance and attractiveness. This model provides the framework in which sexual relations are interpreted and evaluated. It defines the terms of what might be called the "sexual auction" and thus organizes a major ranking system within the student culture.

For most of the women we studied, romance and attractiveness seemed to be thought of strictly as routes to having boyfriends and possibly getting married in the future. Nonetheless, some were beginning to realize that the sexual auction could be carried over into the workplace and the classroom. That is, they were beginning to realize or suspect that men whom they did not even remotely regard as potential romantic or marital partners might evaluate and perhaps treat them in accord with their sexual attractiveness (see chapter 14).

It is important to note that the model of romance and attractiveness was also used to interpret nonsexual friendships between men and women at the two universities. These friendships were like romantic relationships, but without the sex. Women gained prestige from their male friends as well as from their boyfriends and appreciated good treatment from them as well.

The reasons why romance and attractiveness were so important in the women's lives should be coming into clear relief by this point. The women's prestige or lack of it came from their appeal to men. The cultural model of romantic relationships set men up as the judges of women's claims to prestige in the peer system. The kind of treatment women received from men determined their prestige. Thus the women's allocation of a lot of time and energy to staging occasions for, talking about, and working on romantic relationships is not hard to understand. Spending time and money to make oneself physically attractive, to hear from others about romantic endeavors, to plan for activities in which romantic possibilities can be exercised, and even to give up one's own interests, activities or plans, all make sense when viewed from the perspective of the model of romantic relationships and the route to prestige it prescribes for women.

Although the ideas of romance and attractiveness seem on the surface to place men and women on equal footing, with different though equally valuable qualities and experiences to offer one another, a deeper look reveals a different picture. Men's prestige and attractiveness can derive from success in other domains. Admirers and lovers certainly attest to a man's prestige and give him more prestige, but are not necessary to attaining prestige. A woman's prestige, in contrast, comes solely from her appeal to men. In the student cultures at SU and Bradford, being a basketball star made a college man attractive—but not a college woman. Standards of women's attractiveness are determined by men, but the reverse does not hold. Further, the model constrains women's sexuality in a way that it does not constrain men's.

In chapter 4, we noted that the behavior of the London women described by Lees (1986) was strongly affected both in and out of school by the way in which sexual relations were culturally interpreted within their peer culture. The two cultural interpretations—described by Lees and described here—are similar, which is not surprising since they draw upon the same cultural tradition of romantic love, found and commercially exploited in both England and the United States. Although elaborated in different ways, the two interpretations of sexual relations lead to somewhat similar results: the sexuality of the women was more constrained and the women's focus on gender relations more all-encompassing than was the case for the men.[18] Both sets of women attempted to escape their vulnerable position in the sexual auction. The women in the London high schools tended to end up in exclusive heterosexual relationships; so did the women at Bradford and SU. Moreover, ranking by attractiveness and its associated constraints followed the women into the classroom and was likely to follow them into the workplace.

8 Girlfriends: Fragile Ties with Other Women

Whereas heterosexual attraction was interpreted in romantic terms, the women talked about their attraction to and relationships with other women, as well as with some men, in terms of friendship.[1] At both schools, friendship included going places together, helping each other out, sharing personal information, and giving advice and emotional support. The women responded to their shared vulnerability to the sexual auction block not by teaming up to oppose it, but rather by, at best, helping one another to fare as well as possible. At both schools, supportive friendships were vulnerable to problems with and demands of boyfriends. The primacy of heterosexual relations in the peer cultures shaped women's friendships at both schools, but in different ways.

GIRLFRIENDS AT SU: ON THE MARGINS OF ROMANCE

In their discussion of the personal style valued by the high-school women they studied, Schwartz and Merten (1968:1128) make the following observations about attractiveness and other valued characteristics among the high-status group, the sorority girls, who were referred to as "socies":

> One of the essential elements of a socie identity depends upon a girl's ability to manage relationships with others so that her circle of friends and acquaintances is as wide as possible, and she must impress others as vivacious and genuinely interested in them. This sort of role performance is thought to rest partly on inherited characteristics, a girl's physical attractiveness. Socies believe that there is a high though not perfect correlation between coolness and cuteness.[2]

At SU, the valued personality type for women to some degree fit with Schwartz and Merten's description of "socies." However, at the point in their college careers that we interviewed them, the women were much more concerned about impressing men than they were about impressing women. Most considered other women somewhat peripheral.

At SU, the main problem was finding a man and letting people know when a suitable one had been found. The women's efforts sometimes had an urgent air because of two themes the women emphasized. The first was that attractive men or "good boyfriends" were hard to find. The women at SU tried to find "Mr. Right," but Mr. Right was difficult to find. The second theme was lack of success in attracting men: "I see a lot of cute guys, but I never end up with them." The SU women seemed to believe that, in general, their attractiveness and prestige was lower than that of the men they found attractive. Thus, attracting a desirable man could take time and concentrated effort.

In this atmosphere of urgency, alliances and affiliations among and between women often had to do with the pursuit of romantic relationships. Women friends tended to be turned into a support group for orchestrating the main activities—activities with men. Women often sought out one another's company, but their activities together were frequently directed toward being with male romantic partners. For example, in response to a question about what she had been doing since the last interview, Kelly said, "Going to [a bar] with a bunch of girls; we were all hoping we'd run into somebody interesting"—that is, a man. She went on to describe the elaborate preparations she and some of her girlfriends had made to hold a mixer in their dorm. Later, at the mixer itself, she decried the fact that no men were in attendance. When some finally showed up, she exclaimed, "Now the excitement begins."

Once an SU woman "fell in love" or "found the right person," she became embroiled in the highs and lows of the relationship itself. At this point girlfriends were enlisted for support. Linda, for example, described the tremendous burden she and her roommate, who was also her best friend, placed on one another: "I subjected Lee to a lot. [She'd] try to bear my problems and burdens [of my relationship with Donny]. . . . She was going bananas. Donny was giving me such a hard time." When Linda came to feel that she could no longer burden her roommate with her problems with Donny nor commiserate with her roommate's problems, the two of them decided to go their separate ways in search of new friends and new roommates—women with whom such information could more freely be shared.

Most of the women we interviewed initially came to SU with a range of concerns and interests, from doing well in their schoolwork, to finding a group of friends with whom to share an orientation to life, to having fun. However, as these women moved through their freshman and sophomore years, they tended to become more focused on men. Karla, unusual in our sample because of her sustained emotional investment in her academic work, described several women's passages into situations in which their day-to-day and life plans revolved around men. She noted with amazement how hard her roommate was working to make an A average in college while at the same time devoting hours and hours to maintaining her relationship with her steady boyfriend. The roommate planned to marry the boyfriend, and the boyfriend did not want her to work once they married: "She's really working hard. . . . It seems so illogical for her to be working so hard on certain things and obviously planning to do things [i.e., get married] that will forbid her from ever utilizing these things." Karla described how her roommate wrote to her boyfriend every day, talked to him on the phone at least once a day, and usually saw him every day. Karla was astonished that they could spend so much time together and wondered what they found to talk about during all that time. She described her encounter with her roommate as "a real education" in the ways of conducting romantic relationships.

Karla was also astonished to learn what had happened to her best friend from high school when she got to college. Karla's friend fell in love during her first semester of college, permitted her grades to drop, and had to quit school. Karla was shocked at this turn of events because she considered her old friend "ambitious"; the woman had had serious plans to become a physician. To Karla, the friend seemed to change completely and somewhat inexplicably: "She fell madly in love . . . spent all her time with him . . . let her grades fall . . . and just forgot about everything else." The change in her friend hit Karla particularly hard because they had once been close and, at least from Karla's point of view, had understood each other well. "We used to be so much alike. . . . [We've] always been so high on a career . . . so ambitious . . . and not letting our personal relationships keep us from attaining our ambitions. Now I don't think she even wants to share those recent events with me. . . . It's kind of sad, you know."

Losing a woman friend to a boyfriend was not uncommon. Linda, too, lost her best friend from high school when romance intervened. Linda said about her friend, "She never does anything with [us] any-

more . . . she's found the only thing she wants [a steady boyfriend]."
(Griffin 1985:61 reports a similar finding, as does earlier research in
the United States. See Henry 1963:180–81.)

In summary, at SU the peer culture made finding and keeping an
attractive man as a romantic partner a paramount concern for
women. The fact that attractive men were viewed as scarce height-
ened the concern and encouraged a woman to do everything in her
power to find and keep a good man. Even women who came to SU
with other interests and intentions found themselves surrounded by a
peer culture that encouraged them toward romance. Especially for
those who had negative academic experiences, coursework, extracurricular activities, and relationships with other women were gradually
overwhelmed by the ethos of romance in the peer culture. Even those
like Karla who did not succumb were affected through the loss of
girlfriends who did.

Girlfriends at Bradford: Avoiding Interpersonal Manipulation and Controlling Damaging Information

Like the women at SU, the women at Bradford tended to
have their strong relationships with male romantic partners and to
have weak relationships with other women on campus. However, the
texture of and the reasons for women's alliances and affiliations, particularly with other women, were different at Bradford.

At Bradford women formed friendships using kin metaphors,
mainly "cousin." "Cousin" indicated a close friend tied by a kinlike
connection. The women also had a conception of "home girls" and
"home boys," people to whom they were connected through networks
in their hometowns. Home girls were women from whom one could
expect a little special consideration. (The white women at SU also
talked about close friends and other girls from their hometowns, but
for them this friendship tie seemed to be thought of more as a type of
voluntary association.) Yet despite the additional cultural idioms for
conceiving friendship, female solidarity at Bradford was in the long
run no stronger than at SU.

There were strains on Bradford women's solidarity with one another from a practice that was much more evident there than at SU.
At Bradford, friends and dormmates used each others' things—
books, clothes, food—to a great extent. This practice of "sharing" was
sometimes abused. Some women were regarded as liabilities because
they took things that they did not really intend to return or replace.
It was taken for granted that each woman would protect her personal

belongings, especially ones she valued, according to her cleverness at seeing what was going on. An analogous pattern held with regard to information about each other's personal affairs and with regard to control over personal business. Individuals were expected to protect themselves from some people, often wome., who learned others' "business" and treated others' feelings and affairs in a careless fashion.

As a result of this taken-for-granted system of self-protection, avoiding interpersonal exploitation, having a strong sense of self and being a "together person" were extremely important in the Bradford women's evaluations of themselves and of one another. The emphasis on ability to avoid exploitation affected relationships among and between women and articulated with the pursuit of romantic relationships.

At Bradford the peer culture encouraged women to evaluate one another and themselves according to ability to avoid manipulation. To an important extent, women gained standing in the peer community by demonstrating that they were following their own chosen course of action and were not susceptible to the negative and self-diverting pressures of others. Hence, avoiding manipulation was a central issue in forming and participating in relationships with others. It was something that not everyone knew how to do. One student, Rosalind, described what freshmen women faced in the dorms at Bradford:

> When freshmen get here, everyone [the upperclasswomen] just crowds around, laughing and having a good time . . . trying to see what we got . . . and then slowly but surely [they] ease into a personal spot. Everything starts to get personal. . . . [One freshman] said she was a virgin. And [the upperclasswomen] said, "Next semester you won't be." And now this girl is the hottest thing on the floor. She's the good-time girl.

In Rosalind's depiction, the new woman allowed herself to be influenced by the crowd of girls. They were not necessarily looking out for her welfare; they were having a good time. Rosalind did not blame the crowd for making fun of an inexperienced younger woman or for getting to her "personal spots." And she was not critical of the men who enjoyed the younger woman's company. Rosalind's negative evaluation was aimed at the younger woman, because the woman had demonstrated by fulfilling the expectations of the upperclasswomen that she could not defend herself against others' attempts to manipulate her. In Rosalind's eyes, she appeared weak.

At Bradford the premium for women was on maintaining one's own course. Friends encouraged one another to avoid being exploited and to stay away from people such as older, more experienced men whom they had not yet learned how to handle. There was also lots of talk about situations in which one might be duped. Rosalind provided an example:

> A guy hates a dumb chick, but they will take advantage of you. Who cares how dumb you are as long as the lights are out and the time is right? That's the kind of attitude guys take. . . . They don't care anything about you; they're just out for a one-night stand.

Along the same lines, she talked about how some men enjoyed sex with women on campus even though they were really serious about someone at home.

> I have heard a lot of guys . . . say, "I'm just messing with her because I'm up here. I got my own lady at home, and she's doing me right. . . . She wants to wait till marriage."

Note that here again, Rosalind did not really condemn the men. Her point was more that women must be aware that a relationship might not be what it seemed and that women must be careful to assess others' intentions correctly.

Cylene told a similar story about her friend Bea and a would-be boyfriend:

> [Bea] didn't really want him, she didn't want him at all. She couldn't stand him. And he wanted her, you know, and she just gave in to him because she likes somebody [making a fuss] over her, and he would send her all this nice stuff and everybody said, "You ought to [tell him]." She was gonna tell him when we were home for Christmas, but she just didn't. And he bought her a ring, [a] pretty ring, so she said . . . "I'll tell him when we go home for spring break." [Then] she said, "No, I'm gonna tell him when we go home for Easter." [Laughter.] So, when we went home she told him. And I know it broke his little heart, but he shouldn't have been so stupid.

It is evident in both Rosalind and Cylene's stories that each party was responsible for ascertaining what others were really up to. Rosalind provided another example. She regularly went out with men other than one she planned to marry. One of them, Kenneth, became serious about her and wanted to marry her. He even went so far as to buy her an engagement ring. She was stunned when he presented her with it. Because she knew that she was planning to marry Tyrone, she could not understand why Kenneth would buy her a ring. She said that Kenneth should have figured out that she was only going out with him to have some fun while she was away from Tyrone. Rosalind said, "It's not my fault . . . if he didn't know, he should have talked to me about it." In her view, it was his responsibility to figure out what she was doing.

A woman at Bradford lost control of her affairs when others talked about her behind her back. It paid to keep personal information about oneself hidden from others, particularly information about one's boyfriends. Cylene, in talking about her women friends back home, said,

> Like one of my friends, I go over to her house, whole time I'm over there it's just continuously so-and-so, so-and-so, so-and-so this, you know, and I say, "Wow! Did she?" . . . It really is some wacky stuff, it's hard for me to believe they did. . . . They know too much about each other, they know about their boyfriends.

On another occasion Rosalind said, "It's [bad] to go broadcasting your private business like 'a man up in the bed,'" and Cynthia contributed, "Girls are better off if they don't talk about their business to other girls . . . if [others] know, they can boss you." In other words, information about one's personal life is dangerous in the hands of other people, especially women, because it can be used for purposes of manipulation.

Emotional commitments were also seen as a problem in maintaining respect. Emotions, like personal information, made people vulnerable to losing control of themselves and thus to being manipulated. The women cited cases in which women in love even seemed to stop caring about themselves. Cylene recounted what had happened when her friend Roxanne let her emotions get out of control. In Cylene's eyes, Roxanne lost respect for two reasons: she let another woman influence her, and she became too emotionally involved with a man, and an unattractive man at that:

> She started hanging around with this other girl . . . and she was sort of letting this girl influence her. . . . And she met this guy. If me and her had been together, we would never have paid any attention [to him because] he was like older than us and he wasn't that nice looking . . . he was just

> somebody that would never attract her, us; but she just
> started dating him. . . . She was pretty hung up on him too.

Roxanne apparently did not realize how vulnerable she was becoming
to manipulation, not only by her lover but also by the other woman:

> She really didn't know what she was getting into. It was all
> going too fast . . . and her [girl]friend slept with the guy. . . .
> And then when [he and Roxanne] broke up . . . that
> changed her whole life. She has just totally changed. . . .
> She acts like a person that doesn't care, that just doesn't
> care anymore. . . . She didn't try to cool off . . . or stick it
> out, or nothing. . . . [And] she used to care about herself
> and care about who she was with, and care about her name.

As Cylene's example shows, romantic relationships with men were
a special source of vulnerability for Bradford women attempting to
avoid manipulation. Romantic relationships were considered to be a
natural and enjoyable part of life for women of this age, and male
romantic partners were envisioned as important for having a family in
the future, a strongly desired goal. However, romantic relationships
involved the women in emotional attachments that made it difficult to
control, or sometimes even to recognize, manipulative attempts by
men. Being involved in a romantic relationship with a man not only
made a woman vulnerable to sexual exploitation, but also provided
fuel to other women who might want to discredit her for some reason.
For example, the Bradford women believed that other women might
try to steal someone's boyfriend by telling the man about his girlfriend's personal business or by directly attacking the girlfriend in the
man's presence.[3] Rosalind provided a vivid example of what women
sometimes did to each other:

> That girl would do anything in her power to spite me. . . .
> She's always trying to get something against me. She'll do
> things right in front of my face to make me mad.

The researcher asked what the girl would do.

> Well, to start off she likes [my boyfriend]. And she'll tell
> him things [lies] about me. . . . And she'll come over to [my
> neighbor's] room. You can hear right through the walls.
> She'll even open the door . . . and she'll strike up a con-
> versation about me. She calls me every name in the book
> . . . trying to provoke me into fighting her . . . and trying
> to make [my boyfriend] think that I'm lying to him. . . .
> [She'll be] telling him that some [other] man paged me . . .

> or came and picked me up . . . [when] no guy called me that
> morning . . . or picked me up.

The danger lay not so much in what one actually did with a man but
in how whatever was done might be presented detrimentally by other
women, if they found out about it. The special way in which romantic
relationships made women vulnerable to loss of respect, especially
among other women, led them to be especially vigilant to control what
other people knew about their romantic relationships.

In sum, the women at Bradford considered it better not to allow
their personal business, especially their romantic and sexual activities,
to be known and talked about. They feared that such information
might be used to manipulate their feelings and their reputation with
others and could interfere with their ability to defend themselves
against exploitation.

Allowing oneself to be exploited in interpersonal relationships, especially in male/female relationships, was viewed as a failure of character and upbringing, or, in some cases, as having let love and passion
overwhelm one's good sense. Such failures did not entitle the "victim"
to pity but rather to contempt and ridicule.

Thus the ranking system at Bradford was based in part upon women's strength of character and "caring" for themselves. Attractiveness to males and attention from males were important in and of
themselves, but so were the ways a woman conducted herself and
handled attacks on her character. Ability to manage romantic relationships without losing control of oneself or of personal information
about the relationship was a major way in which strength was shown.

The perception of the need to avoid manipulation and the emphasis on maintaining respect seemed to inhibit the Bradford women's
solidarity with other women. There was a collective assumption that
others—even some who posed as friends—might use information
against a woman and take advantage of her if they could. Cylene said
about a friend of hers:

> Colleen's real sweet, but she lets her personality change . . .
> she's influenced easily. . . . If any friend has a date, she
> wants to like go with them. . . . [They'll ask her to go
> places.] She can't say no, and she goes. . . . [Bea will get her
> to do things], and then after she does it, Bea'll be talking
> about her and laughing at her, you know. And then she
> [does] . . . a lot of stuff that she just wouldn't do, she ends
> up doing it because she'll be trying to fit in—trying to fol-
> low the crowd all the time—a lot of things she'd be sorry
> for afterwards.

The more respected a woman was, the less likely others were to think that they could made fun of her or to try to take advantage of her. (The same was true of men.) One had to protect oneself. Much energy went into maintaining respect and into controlling information about personal relationships and emotional investments. Because the women lived in close proximity to each other in the dorms, they tended to maintain their distance from each other. Enduring trust of others, especially of other women, was not easy to achieve. In such a climate, closeness, even for women who desired close friendships, was hard to maintain. No matter how "tight" two women might seem, or how intense their relationship was, the friendship might disappear tomorrow.

Lest it seem that the women at Bradford were more concerned about their reputation among other women than about romantic relationships with men, it is important to stress that they, like the SU women, put relationships with men before those with women and expected their women friends to do the same. One Bradford woman explained her relationship with her "best girlfriend" to the researcher:

> He is her boyfriend. He sorta comes before us [her girlfriends]. . . . I understand that he is more important to her than [I am]. I feel the same: I wouldn't stay with her if [my boyfriend] wanted me [to do something]. No big deal. They have a good relationship. They shouldn't mess it up [by her spending too much time with me].

Summary

As might have been expected, the texture of women's relationships at Bradford and SU differed. The black women were drawing upon different cultural traditions and faced different sets of social constraints than the white women did. At Bradford, the student culture emphasized protecting oneself from manipulation, albeit in an indirect way (see also Folb 1980; Heath 1983). At SU the student culture more clearly revolved around romance and attractiveness. At Bradford romance and attractiveness were important to women but less explicitly emphasized. No doubt because of the premium on self-protection, Bradford women were simply less likely to talk to each other about men. Their reluctance applied to the interviews as well. In several cases months passed before the women told the interviewers about their serious romantic relationships.

Despite these very marked differences between the two campus cultures, the outcome was in one major respect the same: weak and secondary relationships among women. The women at Bradford emphasized maintaining control over their personal affairs to the point that it was difficult for them to achieve trusting relationships with women. The women at SU relied on their female friends to support them in their efforts to find and keep desirable men, but once romantic partners were found, they tended to spend time with female friends only when the boyfriends were unavailable.[4]

At both Bradford and SU, the peer culture established an ethos for women that emphasized romantic relationships with men as a major route to self-worth and prestige. At both schools the women spent their time surrounded by peers. Although they may have expected something else at college, they could not ignore the peer culture and its standards for assessing self-worth and prestige. They had to learn to deal with the peer system somehow.

9 *Getting into the World of Romance and Attractiveness*

College was not, of course, the first place the women had encountered a peer culture, nor was it their first encounter with a peer culture focused on romance. However, life at a residential college elevates the prominence of peers and peer culture. At Bradford and SU the pressure to become involved with romance was constant. The women were continually supplied with interpretations of themselves as romantic types and urged to enact those interpretations.

Rosalind's depiction of the virgin who was teased by a group of female dormmates (in chapter 8) illustrates that some women were confronted with pressures to undertake romantic activities in ways they might not have chosen or even imagined if acting alone. In the interview Rosalind attributed the virgin's transformation into a "good-time girl" to the urgings of the women in the dorm—their barrage of innuendos and suggestive talk—and to the woman's underdeveloped sense of herself. Of course, Rosalind might have been wrong about this particular woman, but her image of the women crowding around the newcomer and bombarding her with encouragement to participate in romantic activities captures the sense of our findings. Figuratively speaking, the women were mobbed by romance.

In this chapter and the next, we further illustrate the pressure to participate in the world of romance and attractiveness, we describe in some detail how individuals responded to this pressure, how they tried to cope with the peer-defined system of romance, and we describe how individuals sometimes managed to circumvent or resist the system urged on them by their peers.

SOCIAL PRESSURES TO PARTICIPATE IN THE
WORLD OF ROMANCE

The women faced an immense array of subtle and not-so-subtle pressures to participate in the peer-defined system of romance. They were continually being invited to or asked to help organize parties, mixers, and dances. They were invited or encouraged to make arrangements to visit bars, attend sports events, join clubs, take certain courses, go away for the weekend, and even go to the library in order to meet men.

The "stranger mixer," held in almost every women's dorm at SU, was an especially good example of the pressure to participate in romance. The idea of the stranger mixer was to have every woman in the dorm find a date to escort her roommate to the mixer. Preferably the date was someone known and thought attractive by the matchmaker but not known, or not known well, by the roommate. Ideally the roommate was not to discover her date's identity until he arrived to pick her up for the mixer. The women prided themselves on being able to find high-status dates, like athletes, for their roommates, and they looked forward both eagerly and anxiously to learning the identity of their own dates. Since the mixer was a dormitory activity, sponsored, promoted, and organized by friends, full participation by the women in the dorm was expected. Planning for the mixer and speculation about it went on for several weeks prior to the event. Almost every woman we interviewed at SU talked about it to us. Even women who had steady boyfriends were expected to participate, "for the fun of it." Those who were uncomfortable with the idea of the mixer or with their own ability to find a suitable date got help and encouragement from their friends.

The themes of male/female relationships dominated the vocabulary that the students used to talk about each other and thus further encouraged them to think about themselves and others as romantic types. The women knew or learned literally hundreds of words for types of men: "jerk," "jock," "cowboy," "frattybagger," "prick," "hunk." Most of the terms made reference to ways that men acted out romantic, or potentially romantic, relationships with women. The women also knew many words for feminine styles of enacting gender relations: "nice girl," "sweetheart," "dumb blonde," "lesbian," "prick-teaser," "slut," "bitch."

People were expected to know about these types and the markers that cued them. Linda expressed the taken-for-granted nature of this knowledge. She was describing a skit she had devised that featured

some of the campus types, like "frattybaggers" and "sorority susies."
When the interviewer asked for definitions of these types, Linda finally stopped in exasperation:

LINDA: . . . I can't believe we're talking about this!
INTERVIEWER: Why?
LINDA: I don't know. You just don't sit around talking about it
    that much with anybody. It's just kind of there.
INTERVIEWER: So it's not the sort of thing you'd sit around in
    your dorm room and talk about to your roommates?
LINDA: No, you allude to it more than anything else.
INTERVIEWER: What do you mean, allude?
LINDA: You know, little things, like, "Oh, you're wearing your
    add-a-beads today." Things like that.
INTERVIEWERS: And that's all you have to say?
LINDA: Yeah, it's understood.

Romance also figured in the semiotics of clothing and personal
adornment. A comment on clothing, or even a knowing look, was
sufficient to communicate a romantic interpretation. The "add-
a-beads" that Linda referred to was an item of jewelry associated with
sorority women, and indirectly with their particular way of relating to
men (Holland and Skinner 1987).

In conversation the women often indirectly identified themselves
and others as romantic types. One woman from Bradford, when
asked what she was majoring in, answered perhaps somewhat face-
tiously, "men." Woven into discussions were numerous themes from
the peer-defined world of romance and attractiveness. As earlier
quoted in chapter 7, one of the women at SU described the focus on
becoming more attractive:

> [When I'm with my girlfriends,] we always talk about our
> boyfriends, or how we wish we had boyfriends, or how fat
> we are—we all say that. . . . None of us have to lose weight,
> but we just want to be thinner. . . . I'm gonna lose weight
> and clear up my face and [grow] my hair out, so I'll be all
> beautiful this summer.

And a Bradford woman described a long and detailed conversation
she had with her girlfriends about which of several suitors was the
most attractive:

> I came back [to school] and there was actually a list of five
> [guys]. . . . It just accumulated. . . . All of them are so hard
> to choose from. . . . Me and my girlfriends were sitting in
> the room and I am telling them this, and they said, "All

right, who's got the most money?" "Who's got the most
prestige?" "Who's the nicest?" "Who's the best-looking?"
We just debated it back and forth.

Not only were the women expected to know about the culture of
romance, they were also constantly exposed to model-based interpretations of their own behavior; their goals, intentions, and qualities
were likely to be assessed by others according to the model of gender
relationships. They were cast by their peers, and sometimes by their
professors, as actors in the romantic world.

In chapter 5 we included some excerpts in which both the researcher and the informant construed other women's behavior as
romance-related. When the researcher (who was there as a partici-
pant-observer) asked about the man Sybil's roommate was hiding
from in the cafeteria, and when Sybil and her roommate teased a
dormmate about a girl who was trying to steal her boyfriend, they
were relying on shared understandings of romantic behavior to establish rapport (in the first case) and to make a joke (in the second
case). In both cases they were construing the world of gender relations and the women around them as participants in this world.

Professors sometimes interpreted the women's behavior in terms of
gender relations as well. Della, a Bradford woman, gave the following
account:

> And I sit in front . . . of the class, and my teacher says,
> "What's this? What's this? Della, where's she at?" . . . and he
> said, "Oh, there's Della." He looked my legs up and down,
> up and down, and the whole class [was] looking at him. He
> said, "Oh, oh, I see. I see Della. I see. Oh, oh." . . . I was so
> embarrassed; the whole class was looking at me.

Della and others were embarrassed and offended by being cast into
the world of gender relations in inappropriate situations, by men, like
the professor, whom they considered inappropriate partners.[1] But by
and large they did not take amiss interpretations of themselves as
romantic types. The women talked and acted as though everyone
wanted to, and did, participate in romance as described by the model.
Even women like Susan, who for some time kept romantic possibilities
at bay and was somewhat uncomfortable with the whole idea of the
romantic world, behaved as if it was important to participate. Susan
talked about Howard, who never appeared on campus, when she was
involved in conversations about romance, referring to him as her
"boyfriend" and making statements about wanting to be with him,
though she scarcely ever made plans to see him.

The women we encountered tended to regard romance as a "natural" activity that most people found irresistible and compelling and that most people their age engaged in at a reasonable level of competence. Although there were various levels of knowledge and expertise among them, no one talked of romance and romantic relationships as something at which one was good or bad, expert or inexpert (Holland n.d.). There was little talk of lack of interest or lack of competence. In the peer culture, knowledge of romantic relationships and interest in them was largely taken for granted.[2]

INDIVIDUAL RESPONSES

Given the constant interpretation of themselves as romantic types, as acting in the world of romance, the women had to come up with new routines, or fall back upon old ones, for handling invitations to participate. They all had to have a way to deal with the emphasis on romance in the peer culture. They did not all respond in the same way. Romantic relationships promised valued rewards, but not all the women found such pursuits engaging or fun.

Some of the women were very much at home with gender relations as interpreted romantically. They had no trouble seeing themselves in this world; in fact, they enjoyed it. They accepted the motive of prestige as defined by the model, they had a sense of themselves as romantic types, and they cared about their success or lack of success in romantic relationships. Aleisha, the Bradford woman who told of debating the pros and cons of her suitors with her dormmates, was one who enjoyed participating in romantic relationships, was proud of her ability to attract interesting men, and reveled in discussing and choosing among them. She commented to the researcher, with obvious delight, that after the debate about her suitors, her roommates told her that she had better treat the chosen man "right" or they would try to take him away from her. The roommates' comments indicated their recognition of Aleisha's ability to attract a very desirable man and therefore, her attractiveness.

Karla at SU was another who enjoyed romance. She had a boyfriend, but her interest was piqued by a "new guy" who did things like showing up at her door with outlandish gifts and dressing in creative and outrageous costumes to charm her. She seemed to be enjoying the situation: "I must say, he fascinates me, he fascinates me more than anyone I've ever known and furthermore he's making the most interesting efforts to get me."

Other women felt much more ambivalent. Aleisha and Karla found romance compelling, but some of the others found themselves propelled into it by peers and family. They had no clear sense of themselves or confidence in themselves, as being a romantic type or as having a romantic self—either a self to avoid or a self to realize.

Susan had a clearly unsettled identification with romance. Her ambivalence showed itself in a number of ways. In one of her interviews she talked about being out west and about its being a beautiful place for romance, but said that she had not gotten involved in a romance because it was "too much trouble." During the study, she claimed Howard as a boyfriend back home, but he never came to visit her on campus and rarely contacted her. He seemed more of a convenience than a reality, mostly someone for her to refer to in conversation with her friends. Further, she explicitly criticized one motive for romantic relationships, the idea that a boyfriend should be a source of prestige. At one point, she purposefully took the researcher into the lounge of her dorm to show her the couples lying on couches and the floor. She told the researcher that "girls bring their boyfriends [to the dorm] to show them off." She said she thought that was dumb. She did not have to show off her boyfriend—she didn't think boyfriends were for showing off.

During most of the study, Susan seemed to be going through a process of deciding what sort of lifestyle she wanted to have. She thought in terms of "socialites" versus "hippies" and was inclined to disavow the upwardly mobile, upper-middle-class lifestyle that she felt pressured—perhaps by her family—to embrace. This struggle, which occupied a lot of her time and effort, related to her ambivalence about romantic relationships. Reliance upon boyfriends as a source of prestige, as emphasized in the student culture, seemed to remind her of socialite women in her hometown, who frequented the country club and talked about their rich husbands. Her feelings about socialites, and her distaste when she thought about herself as one, made it difficult for her to identify with the world of romance as constructed in the SU peer culture.

Despite her ambivalence, Susan seemed to feel called upon to handle the issue of having a boyfriend. Howard came in handy. She could talk about him as her boyfriend if necessary, although she felt awkward when she was actually with him. Eventually, by her sophomore year, she had given up the absent Howard and turned in earnest to finding a local boyfriend. She pursued this goal even though, as she told her interviewer, it was painful for her:

> You just scope out the crowd first . . . see, I found this guy that I'm interested in. . . . But I never see this guy, so that makes it difficult. . . . I get all nervous and paranoid, so I can't ever talk to him. It's pretty funny. All my friends are

like, "Go talk to the guy, Susan. Let's go talk to him." I JUST
CAN'T.

The situation the individual women faced is analogous to that described by Fordham and Ogbu (1986) in a high school in Washington,
D.C. There, the peer culture emphasized being black. Compliance
with school authorities and orientation toward academic achievement
were construed as signs of misguided identification with the white
world. Turning in assignments, working to do well on exams, and
reading required materials were all interpreted in the meaning system
created by the peer culture as "acting white." Although the focus here
is on a different issue—participation in the world of romance—the
situations are similar in that individual students in both cases had to
deal with peer systems, regardless of their own personal proclivities.
In the Washington, D.C., high school some of the students wholeheartedly embraced and internalized the ideological stance that succeeding in school was an attempt to join the white world and that
joining the white world was bad. Others, who did not totally identify
with the peer system and who were oriented toward school achievement, had to cope with peer interpretation of their behavior as acting
white. The solution was to use various strategies for achieving in
school, but hiding achievement from peers. Similarly, although all of
the college women we studied had to deal in some way with the peer
emphasis on romance, and all spent much time and energy doing so
while we were following them, they did not all respond in the same
way.

We next describe the women who more or less accepted and identified with the world of gender relations as defined by the model of
romance and attractiveness. Those individuals who participated
wholeheartedly in romance faced one of two situations: looking for a
boyfriend or dealing with a boyfriend.

LOOKING FOR A BOYFRIEND

The search for a boyfriend was particularly evident at SU
for several reasons. First, most of the women there wanted to find one
man with whom to have a romantic relationship. Although they enjoyed the mixers, dances, and trips to bars where they met numerous
men, they were, for the most part, looking for "Mr. Right" among
their male peers. They believed that attractive men were scarce and
therefore hard to find. At Bradford, in contrast, there seemed to be
less concern about the scarcity of men. The Bradford women did not
worry so much about finding dates and boyfriends, perhaps because
to a much greater extent than at SU they were introduced to and went

out with men from places other than the college: from their home-towns, military bases in the area, and the local community.

Most of the women at both schools had established romantic rela-tionships with men when they came to college, but those at SU were more likely to look for new boyfriends once they got to campus. At SU, nine of the eleven women in the ethnographic study gave up their hometown boyfriends during their first year of college and started looking for another. Most of the nine were able to find dates fairly easily, but not necessarily attractive steady partners. One of the nine eventually returned to her high-school boyfriend.

At Bradford only five of the twelve women we studied searched for new boyfriends during their first year of college, and those were not so anxious to settle on a steady partner. Aleisha, for example, thought she might eventually like to date several of the men she was consid-ering during her conversations with her dormmates.

Seven of the twelve Bradford women had boyfriends from home whom they said they planned to marry. In contrast to the women at SU, the Bradford women maintained their steady relationships long distance, calling and visiting frequently men who lived and worked many miles away.

For those who were wholeheartedly and earnestly looking for boy-friends, the search was sometimes fun but often exasperating and anxiety-provoking. The women at both Bradford and SU complained about the would-be romantic partners they were meeting on their respective campuses. The men pushed for sexual intimacy too soon and denigrated the women if they refused. One woman at SU said:

> When I first came here during orientation . . . I met these two guys. They were going to show me around campus . . . and then one came up to me and said, "Why don't you come over to my house . . . come by yourself." He wanted to start, just to jump right into, a real serious relationship. I told him no, I didn't think that would be a good idea and then he told me I was silly. . . . And then this guy got all upset and he wouldn't talk to me the whole school term . . . just [because I said] that I won't ball with him. I guess that hurt his feelings. But, it was orientation!

Another woman said she didn't like to go out with new guys because:

> They're full of hot air . . . like to run from bedpost to bedpost . . . I know what's going on . . . I don't want any part of that.

Kelly, who fit the campus standards of attractiveness better than most of the women in the study, expressed her excitement about a high-status football player she hoped to date more regularly:

> I've never been with anybody like this . . . he knows every-body . . . [usually] I kind of feel in-the-woodwork, but he's introduced me to everybody . . . it's really nice . . . he's sincere about going out with me.

He was an exception; most of the time, she implied, she did not feel that way with her dates. She and others were left feeling used, as Paula lamented:

> We go out, and see the same guys, and talk, but they're not even sincere anymore . . . we know the way they are. . . . They'll come up and flirt with you all night long, and they really don't care—just as long as they're seen talking to a girl.

Paula put herself through a lot of agony trying to improve her chances of finding a man. She tried dieting, improving the condition of her hair, and clearing up her complexion. Later, soon after she did start dating one man, she found out that he was going out with one of her friends.

> While we were dating, he asked her out, so that was the end of that. . . . I wasn't going to go out with him, and he dating her at the same time. . . . His last line to me was, "Well, you'll make somebody a good wife someday." Oh gee, thanks! I can't wait. . . . Now I'm back to [only] wishing I had a boyfriend . . . wondering when Mr. Right will come along.

Paula and others worried about how long the search for a partner was taking. Still without a boyfriend by the middle of her sophomore year, Paula said,

> A lot of people get married their senior year in college . . . but if things don't change drastically, it's not gonna happen for [me]. I'm not even dating anybody.

For some others, even making the move toward gender relations was anxiety-producing. It appeared that Susan's efforts to find a boy-friend were spurred by her desire to participate in the same activities and talk that her friends did. But she had a great deal of difficulty getting started. Like some others in the study, Susan felt both pushed away from and pulled toward romantic experiences. On one occasion she had an opportunity to go out with an older man who had called her dorm in search of a woman who had previously lived there. Susan happened to answer the phone, they began to talk, and he asked her out. First she put him off by saying that she had homework to do, and eventually she told him that she had a boyfriend back home—Howard. The man was not so easily put off. He got her to admit that she had gone out with men other than Howard, and almost persuaded her. In the end she returned to the boyfriend-back-home position and refused to go out with the man. In the next interview it was clear that she was still debating whether she should have taken the chance and gone. "I guess I should meet him, you know; he seems like a pretty interesting person to meet." On another occasion, she expressed some relief about discovering that a potential boyfriend was "homosexual." She said, "[I'm] glad not to have to worry about that [sex] with him anymore."

Getting hurt was another possibility. Sandy had had a particularly tough time with a boy she liked in high school, and as a consequence she expressed some hesitancy about pursuing new romantic relationships in college:

> There was someone that I've liked a lot for five or six years. It was a bad situation because, first of all, there were three years between us and as soon as one moved on to the next thing, the next one was there but the other one was gone. . . . And he was the brother of one of my dearest friends who . . . always thought that her [female] friends only liked her as a way to get to her brother, so I had to tread lightly because of that. . . . And I walked away from that with a lot of half-said things and came to college. . . . And since then, I've found out that he [didn't really feel the same about me] . . . but, he did care. . . . The situation went on for so many years, and I cried every night and had all these traumas . . . but I still love him to death . . . and as long as I've been down here, I really haven't met anyone I'd like to date. I just expect that I'll always love him.

Sandy felt dismayed and hurt when she discovered later that the man was dating someone else seriously.

Embarrassment was a real possibility, if a woman approached a man more attractive than she was. This situation is clearly illustrated in the story about Annette (in chapter 7), who was totally ignored by the athlete she was attracted to.[3]

In short, being on the sexual auction block exposed the women to various risks. They often received messages, tacit or outright, that they were not very attractive—that they expected too much, that they should be willing to engage in sex sooner than they wanted to, or that they did not appeal to the men who appealed to them. Their chief overt way of responding to these risks was not to condemn the system of romance and attractiveness in toto, but rather to see particular men as arrogant, or "full of hot air," or unlikable. The way out was to find "Mr. Right."

We suspect that most of the women had a good idea of their own value on the auction block and hence did not publicly approach men who were considerably more attractive—according to peer standards—than they. They, like the woman who told Annette's story, would not risk being embarrassed like she was.

The tendency of the women at Bradford to keep their feelings and romantic activities to themselves seemed to be another strategy for avoiding embarrassment. Claims to being loved and admired by a man could be easily turned to ashes by reports that he was seeing someone else or revealing his true feelings to others. In another case, a Bradford woman's boyfriend apparently went around campus saying that he had a job as her gigolo. Because men were so important to women as validators of prestige and attractiveness, these slights were humiliating.

DEALING WITH BOYFRIENDS

Once a woman found a potential "Mr. Right," or at least someone she liked going out with, the problems were different, but not over. A boyfriend, especially an attractive one, validated a woman's attractiveness, provided intimacy, and if she desired, relieved her from further searching and potential rejection. But there were problems that the women experienced within relationships.

Once an intimate relationship was established, a woman faced her boyfriend's expectations for continuing intimacy, continuing attention and admiration, and continuing support, just as the boyfriend faced the woman's expectations for continuing intimacy and good treatment as a sign of his attraction to her. The woman often became dissatisfied with the treatment she received as the relationship progressed and with what it signified about her attractiveness and worth.

At Bradford, women were vulnerable to their boyfriends' talking about them around other women, thus supplying the other women with weapons to destroy their claims to status. Another problem developed when a man started dating more than one woman, throwing the women into competition for signs of his romantic interest and their attractiveness to him. Della, who experienced both problems at once with the same man, had this to say:

> I can't stand him now. . . . I hate him. I could beat him up
> . . . he just humiliated me so bad . . . running his mouth
> when it's all . . . made up. . . . See, . . . he was in the
> cafeteria, talking about me, saying this week, he's the gig-
> olo. Well, he had made it all up. . . . And then he tried to
> [apologize]; he gave me a shirt and a decal [gifts she
> thought inadequate] he got from some convention he went
> to, and I said, "Well! I've had enough. I've had it up to
> here. I don't want to talk to you no more." So later he tries
> to call me, and so I told him, "I've got a present for you,
> and I want you to come over and get it." And so he came
> over, and I just gave him that shirt back. . . . And he says,
> "Why'd you do that?" So I told him: "I saw you with two
> different girls . . . explain that to me . . . I want some
> answers." But he couldn't explain. So, I said to myself,
> that's a boy; no man would play those childish games.

Della still liked the man, and so did her friends. She decided, after a short time, to continue dating him.

Some of the Bradford women tried to get the things they wanted from men by seeing several men at once: if one man did not treat a woman right, she could switch to another. At one point Della described how she managed this:

> He's all right, like, he told me that he was gonna take me
> somewhere tonight, and he's gonna buy me what I
> want. . . . He gives me everything I want. . . . I told him I
> wanted me some blue shoes, and I said I ain't been to no
> steak house lately, "You gonna take me?" And he says,
> "Sure." But, he ain't my type, you know.

When the interviewer asked why she had the man do so many things for her, Della said, "Don't have nobody else right now. My other honey's at work. My other one, he probably [left school] already."

Although seeing two or more men could be a way to get things, it could also be hard to manage, because a man might complain about the woman's spending time with and accepting gifts from someone else. Further, such behavior made it more difficult to keep one's personal business from getting out and around.

Once a relationship became more established and moved into a "serious" or more committed phase, women were often in the position of having to deal with what seemed to them like stifling demands on their appearance, as well as on their time. Kim and her boyfriend had "gone steady" since her junior year of high school, when he was a college freshman. She joined him at SU after she graduated from high school. During her first semester of college, Kim said about the relationship: "Most of my time is always with [him]. Since the beginning of this year, I have become more and more dependent on [him], and doing more and more of what he likes." During her second semester of college, with the support of her dormmates, Kim began to experiment with her clothing styles and her makeup. Her boyfriend was not happy with these changes and told her so.

One day during her freshman year, a representative of a modeling agency came to campus and picked Kim out of a crowd in the dining hall. The agent promised her a beauty "makeover" and the chance to model for a fashion magazine. Without her boyfriend's knowledge, Kim had her hair cut and restyled and her makeup done by the agency's expert. She viewed this experience as fun and exciting, but when her boyfriend saw her, "he just went crazy . . . he hated it . . . and he told me, if my picture came out, he'd never look at it."

Kim did not really object to her boyfriend's assumed "right" to make decisions about what she should do. She interpreted the problems between them as a lack of shared interests. When she couldn't change his mind, she decided not to pursue modeling, even though she enjoyed it. She wanted to avoid further "hassles."

Another SU woman, Lisa, had been "going with" her boyfriend since she was a high-school sophomore and he, a senior. She chose her university in order to be close to him and fully intended to marry him sometime in the future. Their families were friends and were pleased about the relationship. Throughout the period of the study, she dated him steadily and looked up to him, relying on him to give her advice about her coursework and counting on him to give direction to their social life and future. Once when she expressed an interest in the same subject he was majoring in, he discouraged her, and she accepted his advice. "He told me that I just wasn't cut out for that . . . that I probably wouldn't like it at all in the long run."

Lisa was one of the two at SU who maintained her steady relationship through college, and she eventually did marry the man. But points of discomfort remained in her relationship with him. She once mentioned in an interview that she would like to have more time to spend with her dormmates, but that she ended up spending most of her time at her boyfriend's apartment with his friends. During her second semester at SU he temporarily moved to a distant city. Although she visited him frequently, she also participated actively in campus mixers and parties, accepting and enjoying other dates while making it known that he was her "steady." She revealed some discontent with the constraints of her exclusive relationship when she said about the semester when her boyfriend was away, "I was having a great time!" Later, after his return, she commented, "I really had more fun last semester when he was gone."

Lisa seemed at times to be ignored by her boyfriend, although she never commented on this to her interviewer. He had little knowledge of some of her positions and interests. She told her interviewer, for example, that she opposed the Equal Rights Amendment: although she was for equal pay for equal work, she said, she was "old-fashioned" because she liked men to pay for dates and open the door for her. Later in the study her boyfriend told the interviewer that he was in favor of ERA. He said he knew that many women were opposed, but he didn't know why. Lisa was not present at the time and thus was not available to comment on his remarks. He did not appear aware that she held a different opinion. In a later conversation he brought up the women's movement again. This time Lisa was present, but his comments were directed to the interviewer, and Lisa made no response. At another time Lisa expressed interest in working for a presidential campaign and went to two organizational meetings. According to her, when she told her boyfriend and her family which candidate she was working for, "everyone made fun of me," and she decided not to work for that campaign and to rethink her presidential choice.

Our final example concerns Linda and her relationship with Donny, also an older boyfriend, whom she had dated for almost three years before coming to college. Besides the rewards of the attention she got from him, Linda seemed really to enjoy the many social events (football games, fraternity parties) that she and Donny attended together, and she happily did many things for him (baking cookies, washing his clothes). On the other hand, he made many demands on her time: asking her to meet him at his campus (which was nearby but a difficult trip for Linda, who did not have a car), asking her to go out when she felt like studying, and calling her unexpectedly to "test" her explanations of how she spent her time. At one point Linda's dormmates overheard a telephone conversation between Linda and Donny. When she was finished, they accused him of upsetting her and called him a "jerk." Linda seemed to acknowledge that Donny was not always the perfect boyfriend, but she was convinced, with the backing of their parents, that he was the "right person" for her. When asked to account for her continued interest in him, despite his bad treatment of her, she responded, "It must be love." Linda did eventually marry Donny, but by the time of our second follow-up interview, they were divorced.

It is important to note that at least for some women, struggles with a future husband over what the woman would do, how she would act, who she would be, or what she would become began relatively early. All of the women who had steady boyfriends at the beginning of college had already dated those men for at least a year and had chosen a college, at least in part, in order to be able to continue their relationships. Of these women, we know that at least three married their boyfriends after graduating from college. Thus at the time of marriage, the relationships and their implications for the women had been developing for at least five years.

Reinforced by the peer culture of romance and their uncomfortable experiences on the sexual auction block, some women seemed to find an uneasy refuge in acquiescence rather than struggle. We encountered several cases, like Linda's, in which friends thought the women were being mistreated by their steady boyfriends. Despite the pleas of friends, most of these women left the relationships only after much time or not at all. This outcome led us to believe that the women had learned to put up with mistreatment from early in the relationships.

SUMMARY

Along with their fellow students, the women created and constructed the world of romance, attractiveness, and attraction. They pushed and were pushed into this world. Meeting new men could be exciting, partially because of the possibility of finding men they really liked who really liked them, but it was also risky. Their attractiveness—their ability to attract men—was on the line. Some of the women had a strong sense of themselves in the world of romance, felt comfortable in meeting new men, and enjoyed the process of forming romantic relationships. Others were more dubious about romance and more frightened. Our informants at SU especially seemed to want to find a man and get off the sexual auction block quickly.

Like Fordham and Ogbu's black students in an urban high school (1986), who responded variously to the student culture, the women in our study variously accepted pieces or parts of the prevailing peer culture and tried to live out the script as best they could. Like Fordham and Ogbu, we observed some strategic responses and ways of circumventing the system, as well as some resistance to the cultural interpretation itself. We met some women who at least temporarily altogether dropped out of the peer group and its emphasis on romance. This range of alternatives, from working within the system to abandoning it entirely, is our next subject.

10 Strategic Moves: Postponing, Feigning, and Dropping Out of Romance

Not all the women we studied were rushing headlong into intimate heterosexual relationships. Not all agreed to the terms of the peer culture. Some had discarded pieces of the cultural interpretation of love, romance, and marriage. Others spoke of a sense of discrepancy between their feelings and their actions, and some revealed oppositional or heretical views about romance. One dropped out of the romantic scene altogether.

POSTPONING

Women at both universities engaged in various practices that led to limiting involvement in heterosexual romantic relationships. They did this in different ways and for different reasons, attempting to postpone the requirements or demands of romantic relationships as one way to limit involvement. For those who tried to postpone, the object was usually to balance the demands of a romantic relationship with other interests.

Karla was one who was keen on romantic relationships but also cared a lot about her studies. She seemed to enjoy her social life and to consider herself attractive and an expert in managing romantic relationships. However, she preferred men who were involved in their own work, because they did not demand so much of her time:

> [My boyfriend] is my favorite date. He's very busy . . . he can usually get free for only one night a week, he's a workaholic. . . . We have . . . a really good relationship. . . . He allows me as much freedom as I want. . . . My main complaint about [another man she had dated, who wanted to see her more] is that he is continually calling me . . . wants to take up all my time. . . . [With him] I feel like a dog trying to take a walk with this slow little human dragging behind.

Because of dating someone who was so busy, Karla did not have to face nearly as many demands as someone involved in a full-time romantic relationship. She began to see herself as different from her fellow women students. We have already mentioned Karla's perplexed response to her roommate's constant contact with her boyfriend and to her efforts to make good grades despite her upcoming marriage to someone who did not want her to work: "It seems so illogical for her to be working so hard on certain things and . . . obviously planning to do things that will forbid her from ever utilizing these things." We have also heard Karla express her sadness and sense of confusion regarding her best friend from high school, who had begun college committed to a career but had "fallen in love" and let her grades fall to a point that obliged her to leave school.

Karla was not so perplexed or uncomfortable that she avoided romantic relationships. She participated in them with obvious enjoyment, but she thought about and conducted her relationships differently from most of the other women in our study. Although Karla did not explicitly talk about her choices as a means of postponing marriage or any other demanding relationship, she did avoid relationships that would have required her to meet the kinds of demands that her roommate or her former best friend faced.

Valecia, at Bradford, was quite explicit about wanting to postpone what she seemed to consider the inevitable demands of romantic involvements. She had had a boyfriend in the past but did not want to continue the relationship, and she had a foreboding that getting too involved in romance would deflect her from her academic goals:

> [He] used to be my boyfriend . . . maybe later, not now. . . .
> I'm too young to get involved. . . . When we both get settled
> and our life is straightened out, then we can have this
> mutual relationship . . . [but right now] I want to further
> my education. I've got this goal . . . and when I have a
> boyfriend, I feel clustered in, like somebody at any time
> could just stop my life completely.

Kandace, like Karla and Valecia, had some clear ideas about what she wanted to accomplish in college. When Kandace came to SU, she found herself in a place where she could learn answers to some questions that had troubled her for years. She had grown up with a relative who abused drugs. She thought about her coursework and her social life in terms of discovering more about drug addiction and about herself. In this context she did not actually reject romantic relationships, but she had not been particularly attracted to them in high school, nor was she in college:

> [In high school] it was not important to me . . . to go out
> and get drunk or to flirt. I just thought that was the dumb-
> est thing that ever came along . . . and [yet] that was very
> much the accepted thing. . . . It just seemed like you got so
> bent out of shape if you had to have a date every Friday
> night. It just didn't seem worth it to me. . . . I think I was
> more preoccupied with what was going on in my family.

To an extent, Kandace rejected some aspects of the romantic for-
mula provided by the cultural model. She made it clear that she
believed that men who acted "macho" and that "girls who joined
sororities" and constantly worried about their appearance were not
"sure of who they are." In contrast, she saw men "who act almost
feminine" and women who were not so concerned about "how they
look" as people "who must be sure of who they are." Perhaps because
Kandace was concerned about discovering her own interests and talents during college, she seemed more attracted to those who "were
sure of who they were" than to those who participated wholeheartedly
in the peer system. She saw herself and her friends as atypical of the
people at SU: "I know girls who basically came here for their 'Mrs.'
degree . . . but not the people [who are my friends]. . . . They're not
your typical student at all."

Kandace found support for her interests in Christian organizations.
In fact, when she talked of her first experiences with a Christian
group, in high school, she suggested that she had joined at least in
part because she had found there a more acceptable formulation of
male/female relations than among her high-school peer group.

> All of a sudden it was easier for me to be myself, like I
> wanted to be for a long time. . . . The Bible . . . talks about
> the role of the wife and husband. . . . The husband is the
> head of the household and the wife is submissive. . . . It is
> not that they are not equal, it's just that there is a head of
> the household, and it should be the husband. . . . That
> would suit me fine. To have a passive husband who lets the
> wife run the house doesn't work, especially with the chil-
> dren because the roles aren't straight. . . . Whoever I marry
> had better not be passive, because I have a tendency to take
> over.

When asked directly about her plans for marriage, Kandace said
she would like to marry and expected she would, but she was not
interested in it right now. She had a lot of other things to learn first.
And she did not need marriage for self-confidence:

A lot of my self-esteem comes from handl[ing] myself and communicating with people who are on a different plane than I am. I mean they're older, have positions, Ph.D.s, and all that kind of stuff.

Even some women who were heavily involved in heterosexual relationships tried to use postponement as a means of limiting the demands of the relationship. Rosalind, for example, explained that she "broke up" with her boyfriend, whom she fully intended to marry, so that she could get away from some of the pressures she felt as his girlfriend:

He's not really my boyfriend anymore. I broke up with him. . . . [Now] I can do what I want to do without answering to him . . . [like] sometimes I'm too tired to call him back and then he gets upset because he thinks I'm with someone else. I got tired of that. . . . I feel like I'm being watched . . . his friends report on me.

Nonetheless, Rosalind was the person this man called when he got into trouble and when he wanted to get a message to his parents. Likewise, he was the person she dated most consistently, whose ailing mother she attended, and whom she planned to marry. In "breaking up" she was not ending the relationship; she was merely putting off in some ways his demands for exclusivity and for her constant availability.

In chapter 9 we described how Kim's budding career as a model was challenged by her boyfriend. On numerous occasions she tried to explain her interest in modeling to him in such a way as to suggest that the differences between them were minor. By doing so she hoped to ensure that he would not press his case further. At one point she decided to give up modeling because it was too bothersome to deal with his objections. Eventually she decided that they could not get along, that she was too seriously affected by their fights, and she left the relationship.

Lisa, the woman whose boyfriend was uninformed about her views on ERA, planned to marry him and eventually did. But at the time of the study, she was not always enthusiastic about the idea:

I'll probably end up getting married, like when he gets done with [graduate] school. . . . I know it sounds bad to say it, but I'd rather not think about it; I'd rather go out and travel . . . just go all over the place and enjoy it . . . until I'm twenty-eight or so, and then settle down. That's what I would like to do, but I don't think he would like that too

much. Sometimes he even talks about [marriage] now, and
I don't want to. There's no way I would even consider it
now.

Another woman who was in a longstanding relationship that she
expected would turn into marriage, although sooner than she really
wanted it to, put it this way:

We are planning on getting married in at least two to two-
and-a-half years . . . [but] as far as I'm concerned, I'd let
marriage hang in the air. . . . It's not that marriage isn't
important to me because of course someday I do want to
get married so I'll have a family. He would rather get married this year. . . . But we both decided it was just best that
he complete school. . . . He gave me my limit, you know:
two to two-and-a half. I asked for three to four, trying to be
greedy, but he gave me my limit.

These last two women were deeply involved in steady romantic
relationships, and they expected these relationships to continue. At
the same time, they seemed to have some forebodings about the relationships, particularly about marriage. They tried to handle their
misgivings by postponement.

Strategic Enactments

Some of the women were aware that they were enacting
relationships halfheartedly. They sensed a discrepancy between how
they felt and how they acted.

Della, at Bradford, became more strategic with her boyfriend as
time passed. When she first began to talk about the relationship, she
expected him to propose to her soon. She explained that earlier in the
year she had asked him not to buy her anything for Christmas but to
get her an engagement ring instead. At Christmas he had agreed and
told her he could have the ring for her by March. On March 1 he had
it, and his father took it for safekeeping. Della in turn agreed that
they would be officially engaged in May. Her views in March were
these:

Me and my boyfriend have an understanding: you don't
have any such thing as friends; nowhere in the world do
you have another thing as a friend. He has me as a friend,
and I have him as a friend. When it comes to him having
other women friends, or I having male friends, we don't
have any use for that kind of people. He says, "You never
can be a friend to anybody, because it always leads to some-

thing else." See, both me and him have been out there. We know.

Later, when her boyfriend told her that he had seen another woman, she said:

> I told him that he'd better practice what he preaches. . . .
> He's got an attitude with me and we argued. . . . I fussed
> with him just as long as he fussed with me. He knows now
> that I'm a woman who sticks up for her rights.

Things had not worked out as Della originally had planned. Her thoughts about her boyfriend had changed. Even so, she still wanted him to give her the ring. One day before they were to become engaged, she said:

> The way I see it, once you show a man that you love him,
> he'll stop [caring so much for you]. Then you start not
> caring about him . . . giving him the attitude that you don't
> care. Then he'll start caring more for you, and that's what
> [I did] to [my boyfriend]. . . . We'll be officially engaged
> [tomorrow] . . . but I don't know. . . . I can't be tied
> down. . . . Seems like he's closer to me that I am to him . . .
> seems like I've been in the dark for a while . . . and it's
> almost too late. . . . I feel like I'm just playing a role. . . . It
> took him too long to come around; like he wouldn't half
> listen to what I said . . . and now he's trying to play [that]
> everything I say is important. . . . I'll just get that ring and
> take it to the store and see how much it's worth. He's not
> gonna get it back. I'll pawn it; I believe in revenge. . . . I
> don't have no feelings for him no more.

Della expected to replace her boyfriend immediately with a man who reportedly did everything she asked, bought her whatever she wanted, and took her wherever she wanted to go:

> Really now, to be truthful about [her about-to-be ex-
> boyfriend], laying it right down on the line, . . . [he] cannot
> accept the responsibilities of me as a woman. He knows
> that he cannot satisfy me as a woman, because he knows I
> don't want anything but the best. . . . He can't give me
> everything I want.

Another Bradford woman reported "always getting mad" at a man she was quite attracted to. Getting mad at him seemed to be a way to get him to treat her better and also, a way for her to control her emotional involvement with him:

> I met him in the summer. And ever since then, he'd come
> over . . . and we'd go out to dinner and stuff. . . . And [now]
> I get mad at that man all the time. I got mad at that man
> because he was supposed to come over to my house . . . but
> of course he didn't, and he said he was playing tennis, but
> we know he wasn't . . . and he said he was working, but he
> doesn't work then. . . . He's been giving me a hard time. . . .
> He hurt my feelings and . . . after I got so mad, then he
> came over and apologized, but you know, he's just wild . . .
> says how all these girls used to like him, try to hit on him,
> try to get close to him . . . and I would say, "Hey, I don't
> even care." He would make me so mad . . . he's telling his
> business to everybody . . . and starts talking to somebody
> else . . . and me standing right there! I was hating him then
> . . . [but] I really like this guy. I'm gonna give it some time,
> but I ain't gonna wait long, you know.

The reasons varied for these strategic enactments—acts, such as pretended anger, carried out for their effect on others—by the women at Bradford. For some, the reasons seemed to be tied to the desire to salvage something from a long-term but spent relationship. Della seemed to be saying that the struggle to get her boyfriend to treat her properly had exhausted her involvement with him. But she continued to play the role in order to get something out of the relationship—the engagement ring.

Other women wanted gifts and attentions from men when these were offered but also wanted to maintain their emotional distance, because they did not find the men particularly attractive. About such a relationship, one Bradford woman said:

> He's always liked me . . . anything he could do with me, he
> would. . . . He likes to do a lot of nice things for me—he
> takes me to lunch . . . lets me borrow his car . . . last year
> he gave me a calculator for Christmas—and I am not doing
> anything nice for him. . . . I told him, you know, I don't feel
> the same. I like him as a simple friend, but he wants to be
> more than that. So, I've been trying to avoid him because
> of that.

Others wanted to limit their emotional involvement with attractive men because they knew the men were dating other women at the same time.

There was another reason for strategic enactments at Bradford. Some of the women wanted to avoid the possibility that information about their romantic affairs would become public knowledge, and thus fuel for rumor and innuendo that could be used to manipulate their emotions. These women were motivated less by genuine "romantic involvement" than by desire to protect themselves against damaging talk within the peer system. Cylene talked about how she had had a steady boyfriend in high school; looking back, she realized that she probably had kept him as a steady, not because she was particularly attached to him and did not want to date other men, but because she was worried about people "talking." Since knowledge about one's behavior and feelings could be used by others to manipulate, having a steady boyfriend—as opposed to going out with a number of boyfriends—was a strategy for controlling information. We have some evidence that Cylene continued the same practice at Bradford with the men she met there. At least she seemed to use the strategy of concealing her interest in men other than the one from home.

In a similar way Rosalind managed information about herself by what she called "keeping one name up front." That is, even though she rather freely dated other men after "breaking up" with her boyfriend (the one she still intended to marry), she talked only about this one man and thus encouraged her women friends and acquaintances to believe that she only had one boyfriend.

At SU, Susan was one of the clearest in revealing her sense of discrepancy between her feelings and her actions. Some of the other women had absentee boyfriends who also seemed like useful excuses not to go out with other men, but Susan's way of talking about her absentee boyfriend explicitly revealed her limited involvement in the relationship. She talked about her discomfort when she and Howard did see each other and about their awkwardness with one another. She made statements about him that could have come from grade-B movies in tones of voice that indicated she was not serious about the relationship. In describing her feelings about Howard's decision to attend a university two thousand miles away, she said: "I don't know exactly when he's going but, I'm sure I'll see him sometime. So . . . heartbreak, sob and everything like that!" In another instance, after an older man tried to persuade her to go out with him, she told the interviewer: "I mean I'm eighteen years old. I don't want to go out with someone who's thirty. It's not that bad, but shucks, I don't want to go out with anybody but Howard. He's worth the wait."

Susan's reason for having an absentee boyfriend seemed to be that he offered her a way of avoiding invitations from other men. He also supplied a convenient way to appear to be a participant in the romantic world "like everyone else," without actually having much involvement. Susan had some reservations about romance as interpreted by the peer group, and for a while Howard provided a cover for her while she tried to work out these doubts.

One of the other women at SU, Natalie, also had a strategy for maintaining appearances while avoiding romantic involvements. She led a very active social life, attending numerous mixers and parties and frequently accompanying her girlfriends to bars and to other places where they met men. She talked the part of someone quite involved in the peer system. She said things like "I'm going to the library for the first time in ages . . . [pause] to pass out beer to everybody," to convey the impression that she did not study much (although she did study quite a bit) and that she was quite committed to the peer system (although she was not).

Natalie did not, however, form romantic attachments, and from her interviews it was evident that she did not find them particularly important. Although Natalie said she expected to marry in the future, she was in no hurry. She had rejected part of the view of marriage that she had formed as a young girl. She described her earlier view, which she believed was generally shared:

> "Marrying rich" is just a term for marrying the whole ideal guy . . . that's just a thing that most everybody thinks about . . . a good-looking rich man who loves me very much and won't let me cook . . . and lives in a big house.

As Natalie watched her older sister become disillusioned with marriage, her own view changed:

> She got married right out of high school. . . . They had a nice relationship—wasn't always fights like some young marriages—but the guy couldn't hold down a job very long. He'd work for a while and then quit and look for something else. She stayed with him for five years, and then she couldn't take it anymore and told him to get out.

Natalie credited her father with convincing her that as a woman majoring in math, she could "write her own paycheck." With her sister's experience in mind and her own chances of supporting herself fairly assured, she rejected the notion of economic dependence on a future husband. "So, I've decided I'm going to make my own money and not worry about the financial status of whoever I marry." She also made it clear that she did not intend to go bankrupt supporting someone else.

Like many of the others at SU, Natalie held a view of marriage that was generally positive, if vague. Unlike the others, she rejected a piece of the cultural model—economic dependence on men. In sum, Natalie did not seem very much interested in romantic involvements, but worked fairly hard to avoid any negative evaluation from her peers. She socialized cheerfully and emphasized an orientation toward the peer culture when she was around her friends.

HERETICAL VIEWS AND OPPOSITION

Some of the women were cynical about romance and used the system to manipulate men rather than be manipulated by men. Their views and the strategies they used might be described as heretical, because they challenged parts of the ideology of romance as portrayed in the cultural model. Natalie's view of men as untrustworthy sources of economic support was heretical in the sense that it countered an orientation she had learned earlier and appeared to differ from the views of other women at SU, though not at Bradford (see chapter 13).

Susan's position was perhaps the most heretical or oppositional. At times, she clearly opposed a central principle of the cultural model of romance. When she took the interviewer to observe the women in the dorm lounge "showing off" their boyfriends, and when she distinguished herself from the socialites of her hometown, she was opposing one of the tenets of the cultural model: the prestige associated with having an attractive boyfriend.

DROPPING OUT

In general the women's friendships with each other tended to be shaped by and in the shadow of women's romantic relationships. One of the few who went against the grain and emphasized friendships with women was Kandace. Since high school she had much preferred having conversations with friends to flirting or getting drunk, which she associated with the peer system:

> If you didn't flirt [in high school], it was weird; they didn't know how to take you. I wanted to get into deep conversations, and I wanted to find out who people were, and they were just kind of . . . "let's have a beer." . . . Having friendships was more important to me than having boyfriends.

Kandace went on to explain why friendships, particularly with women, were so important to her.

> [Friendships were important] for acknowledging my existence . . . showing me that I had a purpose because I had

an effect on their lives, and they had an effect on mine. . . . They were important helping me to find out who "me" was and helping to create who "me" is. . . . From ninth to eleventh grade, guys just were not capable of having a regular friendship with a girl. . . . If you're nice to a guy, it's like, "Oh gosh, she wants to go out with me." They didn't know how to handle it any other way. Senior year, things started to change. So, for the most part, my relationships with girls were more important.

About a new friendship with an older woman, Kandace said:

I asked her one time, "Why did you all of a sudden get so serious on me?" And she said, "I think it's just such a waste of time to do all that small talk and not get anywhere." And that makes a lot of sense to me. That's the way I am too. Maybe that's one of the reasons I have so much trouble with people who are my own age. So much of the time they're just on a surface level.

Kandace's friendships with women continued in college. She was one of the women who was postponing romantic relationships. Thus her friendships with women never met direct competition from romantic involvements with men.

Sandy, on the other hand, began her university career talking the line of the peer group: "You can have the blonds, I get the dark-haired . . . cute ones." Eventually, however, she chose female friendships over romance and dropped out of the world of heterosexual romance, at least for a while. Although some of the other women had some experiences and feelings similar to Sandy's, the trajectory of her life during our study was on the whole quite distinctive. For this reason, we tell Sandy's story in some detail here.

During the early part of the study Sandy mentioned having had "a crush" on the brother of a high-school girlfriend but having been unwilling to pursue the relationship for fear of offending her friend. She described another experience that occurred in college: when a male "friend" kissed her, she worried that a female friend who was present was made uncomfortable by the romantic gesture. Like Natalie, Sandy seemed to be somewhat disillusioned about the way romantic relationships often worked out:

I did not date as much or as frequently or as seriously as my [high school] friends did. I was more into male friends. The guys I liked, I saw them, but they weren't by any stretch of the imagination, beaus. . . . My theory was you had to have a friendship first and then you could have a relationship, whereas some of my friends were just hot to trot, and they wanted the relationship and forget the friendship, and a lot of times, it [the relationship] didn't work out.

Apparently, Sandy's close female friends at college had also experienced hurts from failed relationships, and they often confided to Sandy about incidents that had left them scarred and insecure. When bad things happened to her friends, Sandy said she tried "to pour strength into [them] to make them feel secure with me." Apparently some of her female friends were able to do the same for her, especially after she discovered that her old flame from high school had fallen in love with another woman.

At the beginning of the study, Sandy seemed interested, like her dormmates, in finding a male romantic partner. But she seemed to have trouble finding the kind of relationship she wanted with the men at college. At the same time, she began to feel that she did not fit in with the peer culture at SU:

In my hometown, I was pretty much respected in the community and accepted for what I am, or was, in that community. [I was] basically your nonconformist, and I dressed to suit me. But when I came down here I . . . got the impression that here I was a sloppy little girl and I didn't have any class or I didn't have any style. . . . I have some preppie clothes, and sometimes I wear them but I don't feel that what you wear puts you in a certain circle, and all of a sudden I felt that I was put either to one side or to the other side, . . . and I didn't have a choice because it was all around me . . . and I didn't like that. . . . And it really really bothered me.

Sandy went on to say that the same forces made her feel that she was not a "lady" because she cursed when she got angry, and that she was an "intellectual snob" if she liked to have "deep conversations" with people.[1] Perhaps as a consequence of her discomfort, she felt very strongly about her friendships with women:

Friendships were . . . and probably still are one of the most important things to me. They were important to me not so very much socially. They were important to me as a person. If you have a friendship, you can have them with a lot of people that know each other, but you have to keep that certain thing that makes your friendship different from

the next friendship all by itself. You have to keep the material of that friendship to yourself. You just don't carry
news from one to the next. . . . You don't do rotten things
to your friends. . . . I have a high sense of that. . . . I pride
myself in my friendships.

Not all of Sandy's friendships were at the same level of closeness. As
the study progressed, she developed a very special friendship with
one woman, Leslie.

I have a lot of good friends, but they couldn't help with the
deep things. [They] are afraid to be that deep . . . and you
can't have a friend that is unwilling to give some of their
area just because they might get hurt. You can never reach
someone that way. And so consequently I turned to Leslie
. . . and Leslie and I have become very close.

Soon Sandy's other friends became jealous of the time she and Leslie
spent together, but Sandy felt that her friendship with Leslie was too
precious to jeopardize. She said that she wanted to spend as much
time as possible with Leslie:

Our relationship is terrific . . . I just would like to spend
more time . . . [so far] it's all been crammed into one semester . . . there's probably not gonna be another time in
my life when I can just sit down and just be friends.

Sandy's relationship with Leslie is unusual in our data. It is the only
example of such a special bond being formed between two women.
This relationship became the major focus of Sandy's activities during
the remainder of the ethnographic study. She and Leslie became
virtually inseparable and rarely interacted with others.

Natalie and Susan, although they rejected, or in Susan's case at first
seemed to reject, an aspect of the system of romantic relationships,
did not turn entirely away from it. Only Sandy seemed to abandon
completely the pursuit of a romantic relationship with a man. She
received little encouragement for her actions; her former female
friends were jealous, and her parents complained that she was missing
out on many opportunities by spending so much time in one exclusive
relationship. Apparently she and Leslie found no support group for
the kind of relationship they wanted to have and simply retreated into
their own private world. Before the ethnographic study ended, Sandy
had stopped going to class and had moved into an apartment with
Leslie, who had dropped out of school, and was working to support
the two of them.

We are not certain of all the important experiences Sandy had during the years between the time she left college and our last contact with her in 1987. At that time, it appeared that she had suffered through a difficult separation from Leslie and had been in and out of work. But she was cheerful about a romantic relationship that she had found, which she described as "someone in my life . . . and I'd like him to be in it permanently." In reflecting on her time at SU, she had some very negative things to say about her experiences at the university. She again expressed her feeling of not fitting in there, particularly with the peer culture:

> I never fit in with the stereotypical college social life as far as being involved in the dorms or being involved in mixers or being involved on campus. . . . I really didn't make many friends and I didn't really socialize. . . . I'm the kind of person that does not generally like parties or mixers or bars, and I never went to any of those places.

She went on to attribute her difficulties at SU to her "emotional immaturity" and to her tendency to rely too much on the few close friends she had. She thought that perhaps she could handle going back now, because she felt more "independent," more able to take care of herself.

It appears that Sandy simply could not force herself to participate in the peer culture that she found at SU. She took refuge in her close friendships and away from the university. After several years of working and living more independently, she found something that she had said she wanted when she first arrived at college: a romantic relationship with a man.

Summary

The discussion of the collective peer system in chapters 7 and 8, together with the description of individual responses to that system in chapters 9 and 10, reveals the danger of presenting the peer culture as though it describes or could describe the individual experiences of those who participate in it or are affected by it. The peer system is part of an individual's environment. An individual may be closely affiliated with the dominant view on campus and may sense no discrepancy between her own view and the view she attributes to the other students. Several of the women in our study fit this description. On the other hand, even with much pressure and a variety of encouragements to become romantic actors, some women did not act in accord with the peer culture.

In this chapter we have presented various ways in which the women dealt with the peer culture's invitation to romance without succumbing to it. Two of these stances—postponement and strategic enactment, or "strategic complicance" to use Lacey's term (1977:67–73)—deflected the peer culture's encouragement of heterosexual relationships. The other two—heretical views and dropping out—were more serious challenges to the peer group's enticement of women into traditional romantic and marriage relationships. Of what relevance are these findings to our questions about women's responses to schooling and the reproduction of patriarchy?

On the bases of the women's own emphases and concerns and the emphases in their peer groups, we must conclude that romantic relationships consume an enormous amount of time and energy. The women are faced with a peer group organized around romance, to which they must respond. Our question has become: What role does this emphasis on romance and the women's response to it play in the reproduction of the gender status quo?

Adrienne Rich (1980) has argued that "the institution of heterosexuality itself [is] a beachhead of male dominance," or that, at least, it should be seriously considered as such. She argues that although the common assumption, even among feminists, is that women are "naturally" oriented to heterosexual relationships, there is a great deal of social pressure upon women to look to men for fulfillment of their sexuality, their emotional needs, and their economic support. In other words, she argues that an orientation toward heterosexual relations may not be natural, but rather culturally constructed and that the reproduction of this orientation is essential to patriarchy.

Rich further argues that social pressures lead women to heterosexual relationships of marriage and to unequal relationships within marriage:

> A woman seeking to escape such casual violations [e.g., sexual harassment] along with economic disadvantage may well turn to marriage as a form of hoped-for protection, while bringing into marriage neither social or economic power, thus entering that institution also from a disadvantaged position. (1980: 643)

In chapter 13 we will discuss the possibility that Rich's thesis about marriage may not as clearly apply to the Bradford women as to the SU women, because most of the Bradford women did not expect to be economically supported by men. However, our research does reveal a great deal of pressure on Bradford and SU women alike from their peer groups, as well as from their families, to join into heterosexual relationships.

Rich's questioning of the naturalness of heterosexual orientations may or may not turn out to be valid. It is useful here for alerting us to the way in which women are encouraged to orient their lives toward men and to the way in which they respond to this encouragement. What we see is not women acting from some sort of overwhelming natural orientation or motivation to exclusive heterosexual relationships, but rather women adapting to the culturally constructed world of romance and attractiveness. However much the women in the study might have liked men as friends or potential romantic partners, they also faced peer pressure. It seems to us that the women sometimes got into long-term relationships to escape the uncomfortable aspects of being on the sexual auction block. The situation described by Lees (1986) is more overt and clear-cut: the London women were practically driven into exclusive heterosexual relationships for fear of being branded slags. But the situation at Bradford and SU was risky for women as well. The unattached women had many tense experiences of being told, explicitly or implicitly, that they were relatively unattractive. And then, once into relationships, the women found that they had to manage many demands and, in some cases, what they perceived to be mistreatment.

The situation is reminiscent of Horowitz's (1987) description of what happened to women who were virgins on the sexually uninhibited campuses of the 1970s. It was important for a woman to shed her status as a virgin as soon as possible after beginning college; later she would have time to worry about what the sexual act meant or implied for her as an individual. At Bradford and SU, everybody had to deal with the peer culture and with being discussed, evaluated, and ranked in terms of attractiveness to men. Even the potential "marriage resisters" that we found—especially Sandy—appear to have been motivated by rejection of and by the peer group.

Despite the considerable pressure to enter into heterosexual relationships and to orient to men, we saw hesitation in a variety of guises among the women in our study. Some responded to the peer culture by trying to postpone the course of their relationships; others behaved strategically in an attempt to get the best out of the situation; a few actively challenged the peer system of romantic relationships. Surprisingly, these responses of avoidance, circumvention, challenge, and rejection occurred in the absence of any dependence on collective support for such strategies. The challenges were, for the most part, idiosyncratic.

Potential resources were available at SU. There was an officially established women's studies program, and there were small but active support organizations on çampus for women students, for gay students, and for abortion rights. There were also articles and debates in the student newspaper on national and state issues related to the Equal Rights Amendment and to job discrimination. The student newspaper carried frequent commentary on local gender-related issues, which included an alarming number of rapes and attempted rapes, charges of sex discrimination in cases of tenure denial, the appropriateness of using student fees to fund gay student organizations, and the breaking of university ties with a fraternity whose members had assaulted women at one of their parties. Notwithstanding these sources of information and support, very little awareness of gender-related issues was reflected in the SU women's talking-diary interviews or in our observations. We heard no mention of any campus lesbian groups, no mention of the homosexual rights movement, and no mention of any feminist group that the women even considered joining. There were a few references to the incidence of rapes, and one of the women attended a meeting about the volunteer safety-escort service that had been organized on the SU campus.

At Bradford, potential support in the form of women's studies courses or student groups was much less: the college had no formal women's studies program nor any recognized organizations addressed to women's issues or to gay or lesbian concerns. The Bradford student paper, which was published much less frequently than the SU student paper, had very few articles on women's issues and events. Some relevant letters were sent to the editor, however, and debates did occur. One letter, written by a male, criticized black women as becoming too independent and threatened that black men would eventually become gay or turn to women of other races. Responses to this letter, as well as other letters that appeared in later issues, extolled black women's independence and strength. Another letter criticized the overly sexual behavior of the cheerleaders, and a third letter complained about males "gossiping" about their sexual conquests.

Regardless of differences between the two campuses in the frequency or content of newspaper articles, or in the level of support for women's studies programs, the women in the study rarely became involved. On neither campus, in other words, did the women turn to established organizations to help them identify and refine their discontents and responses to them; neither did they form their own.[2]

Susan is one who might have been affected by joining such a group.

When she arrived at SU, she was searching for a group, but she cast her interests in terms of finding an acceptable lifestyle. She interpreted her criticism of the cultural model of romance not as a women's issue but as an issue of choosing between a hippie or socialite lifestyle. Eventually she found a group to be with, but its members pushed her back into the peer system. She gave up Howard, her absentee boyfriend, and with the help and encouragement of her new friends began to pursue a new boyfriend. She eventually resolved her crisis about boyfriends and lifestyle: when we contacted her in 1987, her biggest piece of news was that she finally had a boyfriend.

Sandy might also have been affected. She was especially bereft of support from her peers. Her friends did not encourage her intense relationship with Leslie. Instead, they and her parents tried hard to discourage it. Like Susan, she did not interpret her discomforts as having to do with women's issues. Rather, she saw them as resulting from not sharing her peers' tastes and preferences for activities and ways of acting and dressing.

Thus, in effect, there was no organized support to help any of the women identify and redefine their discontents and responses to them.

11   *Gender Politics and Peer Divisions*

In this chapter we move from the level of individual coping and interpersonal politics to the level of emergent collectivities and intergroup politics. First, we summarize aspects of interpersonal politics alluded to but not explicitly discussed in chapters 9 and 10. Then we discuss the sorts of struggles that were going on within the peer groups over valued styles of gender relations and attractiveness and the way in which the women in the study were involved with these struggles.

INDIVIDUAL WOMEN AND THE INTERPERSONAL POLITICS OF GENDER RELATIONS

In the process of establishing romantic relationships women exposed themselves to the sexual auction block. On it they faced the possibility of, and in fact often experienced, having their social worth—their attractiveness—impugned. They encountered men who wanted physical intimacy too soon, who made them feel that they were only sex objects, who paid too little attention to them, who let it be known that they were taken for granted, and who spread their attention around to many women and thus cheapened the value of their attention as a sign of worth. In the code of romance, bad treatment was a sign that a woman was unattractive. Since women's prestige was tied to the world of romance, bad treatment was a sign that a woman was of low social worth.

In chapters 9 and 10 we presented the ways in which the women in our study tried to improve their chances of having their attractiveness validated and avoid having it denied. The main strategy at SU was to find and form an exclusive relationship with a "Mr. Right" who was attractive and treated one well. At Bradford the main strategy was to control and manage information about the men in one's life. Both of these strategies could be seen as ways the women could protect their claims to social worth from possible denigration on the sexual auction block. We also found that even when they were looking for men they tried to protect themselves. We suspect that at some level both the SU and the Bradford women had a fairly good idea of their own attractiveness and avoided trying to attract men who were too different from them in prestige. Aleisha, at Bradford, was explicit about who could get whom and about the situational factors that affected attractiveness:

> At this school, it's about six girls to one guy . . . so the ugly [guys] . . . think they look like heaven and will try to [talk to you] all the time. It's really sick. And then the ones that you think are cute, know they're cute, or they're cute and dumb. You never get a good combination. . . . Some of these guys have the cutest girlfriends, and I don't know how they got them. . . . He must have the money. That's the reason why an ugly guy could get a fairly decent-looking girl. He has one of two things: a car or he's got money. . . . And most of the guys here that look good, they're real dumb and . . . as far as holding a conversation, just forget it; I'd rather talk to a wall. . . . But with so many girls to one guy, he's gonna get somebody regardless of how he acts.

Besides the general strategies and the specific strategies developed for covertly avoiding romantic relationships (such as Natalie's limited involvement in student activities), the women also developed particular strategies to try to affect their standing with individual men. Although attractiveness was often talked about as an essence of an individual, it was demonstrated by its effect on others. The system of romance and attractiveness at Bradford and SU was one of ranking and of action, maintained interpersonally in face-to-face relations (like the system of honor practiced in Kabylia, Bourdieu 1977; see chapter 7). Thus it invited various forms of individual maneuvering.

The women in the study, especially those who were more experienced, tried to boost their own attractiveness in a relationship by letting it be known that they were attractive to others, by not seeming to be desperately available, and by giving the impression that they expected to be well treated. The women also went on the offensive at times and tried to reduce a particular man's attractiveness by calling him names and pointing out his inadequacies. They employed a wide variety of insulting terms for men to imply that the men were in various ways not very attractive and unlikely to be able to make up for their lack of attractiveness by treating a woman especially well. Women tried to warn other women away from such a man by saying something like "He's an asshole!" Pushed by anger, they sometimes insulted men to their faces using these terms.[1]

The same devices were used by men in the interpersonal politics of the romantic world. Men tried to affect the prestige of individual women by using names such as "bitch," "dog," or "dyke" that meant a woman was ugly or too demanding relative to her value. To the same ends, women used derogatory terms to impugn other women, and men used similarly derogatory terms for other men (Holland and Skinner 1987).

INTRAGROUP POLITICS

At times the students went further still. They tried to condemn the behavior not only of individuals, but also of whole categories of their fellows whose styles of enacting gender relations they disapproved of. The peer culture was not monolithic. We have described individual women encountering and responding to the peer culture, but until now we have not mentioned the students' ways of defining and disputing the different *styles* of gender relations they encountered—and thus the different masculinities and femininities whose values were current in their world. As pointed out in the chapter 3 discussion of practice theory, intragroup divisions and tensions are important determinants of people's response to socially imposed disadvantage. Within-group divisions affect the content and style of any oppositionary or countercultural groups that may emerge.

Although there existed small student groups at SU that promoted gay and women's rights, the women in our study were not involved with them and did not talk about them. But at both universities the women were affected by, and contributed to, the ambient tensions that linked or polarized much more vaguely defined, less organized groups. The peer culture recognized different styles of enacting gender relations, and the relative value of these styles was a subject of contention and a basis for the formation of friendships.

Intragroup differences were most clearly mediated through language. Alongside the general-purpose terms of insult that implied a man or woman was unattractive, there were also terms that referred to alternative styles of and stances toward gender relations and attractiveness: "Southern belle" and "sorority Susie" and their male counterparts, "Southern gentleman" and "frattybagger," and an array of terms referring to sexual preferences, such as "gay," "queer," and "homosexual."

It is useful briefly to compare these competing views of attraction and attractiveness with the system Lees (1986) described for the London schools. In that system there were evidently two primary constructions of feminine sexuality—a virgin/whore dichotomy.[2] Although the whore types, the slags, supposedly were so labeled because they were sexually promiscuous, Lees makes it clear that girls were labeled slags on circumstantial evidence, such as going out with a number of different boys, wearing certain kinds of clothes, behaving in certain ways, and going to certain places, and not on concrete evidence that they were in fact sexually promiscuous. "Slag," in other words, signified a cultural construction of a specific type of woman, in which looks, general demeanor, and practices regarding sexual intercourse were construed as inherently interrelated.

Evidently there was no contest in the London schools over the value and social standing of these two forms of femininity, only over to whom the negative label could be applied. Bradford and SU differed from the London schools in that the university student cultures offered a plethora of femininities and masculinities and of disagreements as to their relative value.

The disagreements were evident from the names used at Bradford and SU to refer to different types of students. Students knew and made up negative labels to discredit styles of enacting gender relations that they disliked and from which they wanted to distance themselves. In one of the ethnosemantic interviews, a woman used the term "female chauvinist pig." She made up the name in order to refer to negatively and to characterize women who complained about men and called them insulting names.

Choice of label was considered an indicator of whether one was for a particular style of gender relations or against it. The labels "libber" and "feminist" both referred to women involved in or sympathetic to the women's movement, yet one label conveyed a negative valuation of such women and the other, a more positive evaluation. The students regarded "libber" as a pejorative label and considered use of the word to imply an unfavorable view of the women's movement; use of "feminist" implied the opposite.

Clothing styles also served as markers of particular stances toward gender relations and attractiveness. "Add-a-bead" necklaces had become markers of sorority women and later of "preppie" types in general. Sarcastic comments about "add-a-beads" had become evaluative allusions to sorority women and their male counterparts. In short, style of dress, place of residence (at SU), and intragroup labels for outsiders and other subgroups were all treated by the students as markers or indices of one another's style of gender relations.

In theoretical terms, what we are describing here are ill-defined groups, emergent collectivities, that were forming and reforming on the two campuses around ways of enacting gender relations. Although much less well defined or organized than the type of flamboyant counterculture groups described in chapters 3 and 4, or than the small pro-gay and pro-women's organizations that existed on the SU campus, these emergent groups, and the tensions among them, did figure in the ways that the women in our study imagined and responded to gender relations. Before discussing exactly how the women were involved in these intergroup struggles over masculinities and femininities, a brief description is in order of these sorts of emergent collectivities and the way they were in evidence on the two campuses.

The features described above—clothing styles and choices of label to refer to different styles of gender relations—had acquired the sort of social symbolism that sociolinguists have identified for speech variants. As is documented in many cases, speech variants signal social affiliations, social distance, and social identities. Labov (1972), for example, studied the development of speech patterns on Martha's Vineyard during periods of great tourist influx. He discovered that permanent residents began to emphasize speech variants peculiar to Martha's Vineyard so that their discourse became even more distinguishable from that of the incoming tourists. The residents formed an emerging, albeit unorganized, group that set itself off against the tourists. Hill and Hill (1980; see also Hill 1985) have analyzed changes in grammatical forms in Nahuatl and have traced the association of those changes with changes in the valuation of ethnic solidarity. These grammatical markers became a means by which the people in interaction conveyed their stances toward solidarity and thus their affiliation or disaffiliation with one another.

Emergent or incipient groups of this sort are at first unorganized and may remain so. As in the sociolinguistic studies just referred to, the social symbolism and signaling may remain more or less out of participants' awareness. In most speech situations, conversants are not explicitly aware of the sociolinguistic and other sorts of social markers that pervade their interactions. They focus their attention on the topic of the conversation and not on the social symbolism of the speech, gestures, dress, and other markers that are in evidence in the interaction. Thus, while people approach one another and bond together according to similar views and orientations cued by markers, they may have difficulty articulating those views and precisely identifying the cues that signal the views. They may be vague about exactly what causes them to affiliate and disaffiliate with others. Many of the women at SU, for example, described sorority women as snobbish (elitist) and used negative labels to refer to sorority women as a type.[3] Shared evaluations of sorority types seemed important in the formation of friendships, and markers existed for communicating one's stance toward sororities. Still, the women did not necessarily express an antisorority stance directly, nor did they explicitly identify their friendship groups by opposition to the exclusive, elite, possibly upper-class styles of femininity and masculinity that they specifically associated with the most popular Greek social organizations.

From time to time these sorts of emergent groups and the internal divisions that they reflect are expressed overtly. One candidate for student government at SU, for example, set up his campaign in opposition to candidates he identified as "preppie." And, although emergent groups rarely make statements explicitly, as do organized groups, they sometimes express themselves through rituals and dramatizations. These rituals and dramatizations can portray or represent differences of style and stance in symbolic form. Spike Lee's recent film *School Daze* and the high-school initiation described by Schwartz and Merten (1968) both provide examples of how dramas and rituals throw divisions within peer cultures into high relief.[4] We heard of such a representation in our study; one of the women described a humorous skit she had devised for performance in her dorm that caricatured fraternity types and jocks.

For the most part our interviews and observations were not designed to explore the group processes that form and elaborate internal divisions.[5] Our picture of the divisions in the student community came indirectly, through the vocabulary of gender types and through the ways in which peer-group struggles were internalized by the individual women.[6] The internalized conflicts were important in some of the women's lives.

At SU, Susan was embroiled during most of the period of the study in an internalized debate between two standards of feminine attractiveness and styles of gender relations. She fairly clearly contrasted a socialite and a hippie style and tried to choose between them. Cylene, at Bradford, in a less articulated struggle, worried during several of the interviews about the use of sexual attractiveness to manipulate men for the purpose of getting better grades or preference in a job situation. She had observed this behavior by several of her fellow students, and although she condemned such practices, they also intrigued her and thus provoked an inner conflict. In a more overt manner, Aleisha, also at Bradford, became active in trying to oppose a style of feminine attractiveness she thought was ill-considered. She wrote a letter to the editor of the school paper decrying the skimpy outfits and sexually suggestive movements of the school cheerleaders. Aleisha thought the cheerleaders gave a bad impression of the school. Sandy, who clearly felt denigrated by her fellow students for not conforming to a certain feminine style, complained that the others made her feel like "a sloppy little girl," even though she recognized that the notions of feminine attractiveness in vogue at SU conflicted with those in her hometown in another state. In this context we might also recall Kandace's participation in Christian organizations. She had originally become involved in a religious group in high school, partly in response to what to her was a "confusion" about gender relations in her high-school peer culture.

Although these women, except for Kandace, were not part of groups within the student community that were organized to contest issues of sexual attraction and attractiveness, they were drawing upon disputes within the peer group and, most explicitly in Susan's case, searching for friends who shared their views. Even though informal groups of friends at Bradford and SU did not aggressively emphasize their social solidarity, as Willis's Hammertown lads did, the women nevertheless felt the internal divisions within the peer group. They were obviously participating—albeit indirectly—in a form of gender politics within the peer culture (and its subdivisions), as well as in the interpersonal politics of gender relations (see also Holland 1988b).

Peer Groups and the Cultural Production of Femininities and Masculinities

It is important to note that these struggles over styles of romance and attractiveness took shape and were played out within a peer community that included both men and women, rather than within same-sex peer groups of the type described by Willis and McRobbie. The women did sometimes portray men as a class or category of being with certain common characteristics that women had to deal with, but they more often emphasized types of men and types of women. Masculinities and femininities often were paired (e.g., sorority women/fraternity men; Southern women/Southern men). The pairs fit together as the female and male parts of a particular style of acting out romantic gender relations.[7] Women (and men, to the extent that we can judge from our limited data) at Bradford and SU liked or disliked particular styles of gender relations and their associated masculinities *and* femininities.

Another important feature of the struggle over which masculinities and femininities were to be valued was that the struggle took place *within* the peer group. The struggle was not between the peer group and school officials. The university administration was not conceived as particularly important as a source of canons of attractiveness or as an arbitrator of gender relations. As Horowitz (1987) chronicles, since the 1960s universities have generally ceased overt monitoring of student's social and sexual behavior. In any case universities have never maintained the sort of control over the construction of attractiveness that they have over the definition of intelligence and educational achievement. Universities control the distribution of educational credentials, but do not control any comparable credentials of attractiveness. Groups within the student community construct their versions of gender relations more in opposition to other groups within the student community than in direct opposition to the school.[8]

In neither the arena of interpersonal sexual politics nor the arena of intragroup politics was one group attributed supreme authority. The student community did share a vague sense that there was a dominant or prevailing or hegemonic perspective on beauty and on male/female relationships. But the standards of the system were contested and the standings of individuals relatively unclear. The actual arbitrators of attractiveness were difficult to locate and thus to target for attack. Instead the arbitrators became the fellows who came to the mixer, the cute guy sitting in the next row in math class, and the women in the dorm.

Summary

In this chapter we have discussed two levels of the politics of attractiveness and the phenomenology of participating in those levels. At one level, attractiveness is experienced interpersonally, through experiences of forming and conducting romantic relationships and also through experiences of being compared to a normative attractiveness and often found wanting by one's peers. As we have argued, the women in our study, perhaps because they were newcomers to the college scene, spent a good deal of their time and energy embroiled in the interpersonal politics of romance. The women were also involved in another level of sexual politics: contentions within the peer group over the relative superiority of different versions of gender relations and associated images of attractiveness. Although none of the women in our study participated in demonstrations or other overt political activities concerning gender relations and attractiveness, they, like all the other students, were drawn into the low-level, low-profile conflicts that went on constantly over the value of various versions of attractiveness and different sexual preferences. These low-level struggles created groups that were pro- and anti-Greek, pro- and anti-gay, and pro- and anti-preppie. Among the women we studied, the groups were groups of friends with fairly vague identities as groups and relatively unarticulated stances toward styles of enacting gender relations. Notwithstanding the amorphous nature of these groups, it is important to note that they existed and that they were part of the collective creation of femininities and masculinities at Bradford and SU.

Some of the women were also engaged, mostly internally, as individuals by issues drawn from peer-group politics. These issues were cast in terms of personal dilemmas. Susan worried about whether to be a socialite or a hippie. Sandy worried about styles of dressing and whether her behavior was really childish and "without class." Cylene debated about whether it was naive to reject the manipulative advantages of sexual attractiveness.

Finally, we have pointed out that the cultural productions occurring at the level of the peer group appear to have been shaped largely by oppositions within the peer group rather than between the peer group and the university. At Bradford and SU, ranking by attractiveness, in both interpersonal and intergroup politics, was quite different from Willis's lads' experience of ranking by the school according to educational capital. In interpersonal politics, the ranking system was created between individuals who had to convince one another of their relative attractiveness or lack of it. At the intergroup level, no single individual or group had clear authority to rank forms and styles of attractiveness. And although there was a sense that everyone could be ranked on a scale of attractiveness, no such formal ranking ever occurred. There was no credential system for attractiveness and no clear source of an imposed system that could be attacked.[9]

Part 5 *Academics*

12 *Schoolwork for What?*

Ostensibly, women and men go to college to further their educations and to acquire the credentials necessary for future careers.[1] But there is more to college life than classes, studying, and examinations. When the women in our study got to college, they found themselves in a world of peers in which, whether at Bradford or SU, school-work was relatively unimportant. As far as the peer culture was concerned, the women could excel or not in schoolwork, and have or not have serious career plans. These areas were viewed as matters of individual capability, effort, and preference. In this chapter, we address the place of academics in the peer culture and the women's attitudes toward their schoolwork. In the next chapter, we describe how these attitudes, in combination with the women's other experiences during college, affected their entry into the workforce after graduation.

THE PLACE OF ACADEMICS IN THE PEER CULTURE

Amid all their talk about romantic relationships, our informants offered relatively little about the content of courses, the value of different majors, or the viability of various careers. When they did talk with their peers about schoolwork, they tended to complain: classes required too much work, professors were "unfair," or there was not enough time to study properly for a test. They seemed not to know or care very much about the coursework or future career plans of their friends. For example, in our life-history interviews each woman was asked to describe how her high-school friends would have responded if she had experienced trouble with her schoolwork. Almost without exception, the women said that their friends would have done very little, because either they would not have known about the trouble or they would have pretended not to know about it. Most felt that this response

was appropriate. Paula said, "I felt like it was none of their business."

When Paula was asked directly whether she and her friends from
high school ever talked about why they chose their majors, she said,
"No. . . . It's just that we all picked things that we did well in in school."
When Della was asked whether she and her high-school friends ever
got together and talked about schoolwork, she said, "No, no; schoolwork didn't play with our minds."

In general, schoolwork and career decisions seemed to be conceived
by the peer culture as matters of individual choice, not for group
discussion or debate. The women made repeated references to "making my own decision" and "making up my own mind" about what field
to pursue or what major to choose. Aleisha, who spent hours talking
with her girlfriends about her many romantic interests, said when
asked what her girlfriends were majoring in, "I don't know; I never
asked them."

The evidence for women's inclination to think about academic matters in individual terms was corroborated by our survey. When asked
to rate thirteen academic or career-related activities and relationships
that had been identified by members of the ethnographic sample, the
surveyed women rated individual academic achievements as more
important than peer relationships oriented to academic or career interests (see Table 7). Overall, it appeared that the women, although
immersed in a world of peers, tended to deal with academic matters
on their own.

Correspondingly, status in the peer system was not determined by
academic success—in fact, somewhat the contrary. Occasional references were made to "brains" and "intellectuals," but the women were
quick to disassociate themselves from these labels, indicating that they
were not interested in having such terms applied to them and that
they would not gain any status from them. One woman said: "People
thought that I studied a lot more than I did and that was always
looked on negatively: the brain syndrome." Another said something
similar: "Some of my friends . . . and my father call me 'the brain,' but
they're just kidding. I'm glad they don't take it too far." And Paula
spoke disparagingly about a "guy with a 4.0 [a perfect grade-point
average] who wanted to go to Harvard Medical School" but couldn't
get in because "all he did was study."

People in math and science courses, especially, were sometimes
considered "weird," at least in part because they were so serious about
schoolwork. Paula presented the following picture of science students
when she was looking for someone to talk to about getting into medical school:

I need to talk to somebody who knows what's going on . . .
all the people I know are business majors . . . except, I
guess, the people in chemistry class. And I don't want to
get into a detailed conversation [with them] . . . half the
people in chemistry are weird. . . . They could be mad
scientists, . . . hunchbacks, running around with their lab
coats on.

STRUGGLES TO MANAGE SCHOOLWORK AND PEERS

Although schoolwork was deemphasized in the peer
group system, doing schoolwork could not be relegated to a secondary place as easily as some other aspects of life, such as female/
female relationships. No system existed to propel women into close
female/female relationships, but the academic system did exert pressure, because it was necessary to pay some attention to schoolwork
in order to stay in school. The dynamic between the peer and academic systems produced a tension on the two campuses of which most
of the women spoke. During the course of our ethnographic study,
all of our informants struggled—some more, some less—with what
they perceived to be the conflicting demands of schoolwork and
peers.

For most, schoolwork and peer activities were viewed as competing
domains: time spent studying was time spent away from peers, and
time with peers accomplished little schoolwork. One SU woman described the situation as a choice: one could be a "bookworm" or a
person who liked to "have fun." Della, at Bradford, described the
same dichotomy in another way: "The ones that did all the book
studying, they had no social life; the ones that didn't do no book work,
they had a lot [of social life]."

None of the women wished to be viewed as one or the other of these
extreme types. When they arrived at college, they all wanted and
expected to be successful in both schoolwork and the peer system.
Almost from the beginning though, they talked about needing to
study more and "party" less. Most were surprised to find that schoolwork took more time than they had given it in high school, and they
struggled to complete it and do other things as well. One woman at
SU had this to say:

I always liked school, ever since I was very young . . . but
here I haven't done anything for enjoyment in so long. . . .
All I do is work. . . . It always came so easy for me in high
school, and now I've got to compete with somebody just to
get a spot [in medical school], so I almost never have time
to do anything with my friends . . . I'm going crazy.

The struggle with the demands of schoolwork was evident in our survey responses too. One of the survey questions asked about people and activities that had taken more time than expected over the semester and hence had caused the respondent to cut back on other things she normally did. Schoolwork was felt to be extraordinarily demanding by the largest percentage: more than 80 percent of the women surveyed on both campuses felt that schoolwork took an unexpectedly large amount of their time. Jobs and peer relationships were much less likely to be seen as taking up an undue amount of time.

The women in our ethnographic study seemed to agree that peers complained when they devoted too much time to schoolwork. One Bradford woman put it this way:

> Guys will tell you, "Come on, let's go out." And if you tell him you have to study, he'd probably be upset. . . . Some of my friends tell me I'm a partypooper . . . 'cause I usually have to study. A lot of times when [my two closest friends] have somewhere to go, they won't ask me. . . . This sort of bothered me 'cause they were having a good time and I wasn't.

Jobs, in contrast to schoolwork and peers, could be ignored. One woman described her typical day as follows:

> Go to class, go to work, go out to dinner with some friends, . . . relax and watch TV [with friends] . . . study.

When she got a couple of Cs on tests, she decided:

> Work's [the job's] the bother; there's no time left for studying. . . . I think I'm going to have to quit work. You think I'm gonna let that work bother me? Nah!

Occasionally, the women spoke admiringly of other women who could keep peer activities from getting out of control. For example, Della described an older student on her hall as follows:

> She's a girl that sets a good example as a very studious person. . . . I see her studying all the time. . . . She lets you know that studying is very important . . . that you can't just all the time have a bunch of friends over or go out all the time. There's a time for everything; she lets you know.

And Della knew that failure to manage both could have long-term implications:

> My sister . . . has messed up her life along the way, and
> she's still messing up . . . having so many men until she
> don't even have [time] to work.

The women's comments about the need to study more often included irritation at the thought of devoting even more time to schoolwork. Perhaps not surprisingly, the women frequently let themselves
be drawn into impromptu peer activities. One student explained what
happened as she and her suitemates were preparing to leave her
room for a night of studying for the next day's exams:

> We had a spontaneous party . . . everyone was here . . . till
> two in the morning. We made all kinds of daiquiris. . . . My
> parents called [during the party] and I never knew it. They
> couldn't believe we partied the night before exams. *I* can't
> believe we did. I've never done anything like that in my
> life.

Another said:

> I've been doing a lot of things with guys. I know my grades
> are going to suffer. . . . I guess I'll have to buckle down one
> of these days.

And a third had this to say:

> If I do homework every night and on the weekends, I can
> probably do a good job in my courses . . . [but] during the
> week I'm pretty lazy. . . . I try to study but I just go to sleep
> . . . or, you know, somebody'll come along and want to do
> something.

The survey indicated that peer-related factors affected attention to
academics, particularly at SU. One variable, "extraordinary demands
from peers," was negatively correlated for students at both Bradford
and SU with "energy available for schoolwork." That is, the relationship was inverse: women who said that demands from peers were
high also said that energy available for schoolwork was low (and vice
versa), but only at SU was the correlation statistically significant (Holland and Eisenhart 1981:96).

It appears that although the women at Bradford and SU wanted
and expected to do well both in schoolwork and with their peers,
schoolwork seemed to interfere with peer activities by demanding a
lot of time. Peer-related activities, on the other hand, were viewed as
more fun and potentially more rewarding. Thus, they threatened to
overwhelm schoolwork.

THE WOMEN'S ANSWERS TO "SCHOOLWORK FOR WHAT?"

Weiler (1988:34) states that schooling is contradictory for women in a patriarchal society. Although she does not explain exactly what she is referring to, we assume she means that schools, especially universities, are generally regarded as a pathway to upward social mobility, that is, to more elite and better-paying jobs. Yet women have traditionally faced job ceilings and the likelihood of working in jobs that are lower-paying than those of men. Given that the peer system pays virtually no attention to schoolwork, given the job ceilings, and given the likelihood of low-paying jobs, why do women do schoolwork? Do they want an education simply for the pleasure of having one? Do they want to build their own lives by having at least some career—which, as Gaskell (1985) reminds us, has been the traditional view of what women can do with their schooling? Are they seeking husbands who are likely to be of a more advantaged class than the boyfriends they left behind in their hometown high schools?

Among the women in our study, we found three major cultural interpretations of schoolwork.[2] These "developing understandings" of the academic work of college life (see Holland and Eisenhart 1988b) were alternative views of the purpose of schoolwork and also of the women as students. Although we believe that these cultural interpretations were learned before college, they were susceptible to challenges and revision during college, primarily because college schoolwork was more demanding than high-school work had been and because the competing demands of the college peer system were more intense. The combination of forces derailed some of the women but not others, and some sooner than others, depending on which interpretation the individual woman had of schoolwork.

The three interpretations were organized around motives for doing schoolwork: (1) work in exchange for "getting over," that is, finishing college and thereby obtaining college credentials;[3] (2) work in exchange for "doing well," that is, receiving good grades and other academic accolades; and (3) work in exchange for "learning from experts." These orientations to schoolwork affected the women's interpretations of grades, evaluations of teachers, decisions about studying, choices of courses and majors, and feelings about their own performance. During the three-semester period of our main study, each woman seemed to hold one interpretation as a dominant one. Some, however, were aware of the alternative interpretations and sometimes entertained them, if only partially or fragmentarily.

WORK FOR "GETTING OVER"

Ten of the women in our ethnographic study (nine at Bradford and one at SU) viewed the work they did at college as a means of finishing up their schooling—what Rosalind referred to as "getting over." From this perspective, "going to college" and "getting through" the work there was what mattered. Going to college and getting through were important because they led to a degree that could be used to get a good job later. Another way to say this is that attending and completing college and receiving a degree was a means of moving up in life. Cynthia, for example, said,

> I felt like going to college would bring me a good job . . . and I wanted to become something . . . I didn't want to just get out of high school and just set up and just wait for somebody to bring me some money.

Later, Cynthia made it clearer that she viewed simply getting through college as a step toward achieving her goals.

> If I can just pass, I'll feel all right . . . I have to pass to get out of here. It's going to have to be done in order to get myself somewhere in life. It's just a step higher.

Associated with this interpretation was the idea that the work and requirements of college were somewhat arbitrary and simply tasks that somehow had to be completed. The work had no particular significance in and of itself to the students, except as a collection of activities that had to be done or procedures that had to be followed in order to finish. This view was reflected in the women's statements about the kinds of things that instructors required. For example, Rosalind, in talking about what her algebra instructor was like, said,

> She's teaching a whole different way from the way I learned it. I'm used to taking shortcuts and in her class you cannot take a shortcut. You have to go from one step to the next. If you miss a step, the problem is wrong even if you come up with the right answer.

Later she made a similar remark about a history exam.

> You have to write everything in order. You couldn't put one part here, at the top, and another part at the bottom.

And, finally, about a health exam, she complained,

It was a smoking exam. Half the things we covered in class weren't even on the exam. You really had to know something about health to pass that exam!

When the tasks associated with getting the work done became especially bothersome, doing them might simply not be worth the trouble. Because tasks were perceived as arbitrary, with little future return, there was no point in enduring a great deal of hardship to accomplish them. Rosalind likewise expressed this position:

I studied two weeks for that exam . . . I forgot three things which I didn't care to remember because it was just too hard to keep writing.

These obstacles to getting finished were described for most courses and professors. The strategy adopted was simply to persist in order to get the degree. Rosalind, who was asked by her interviewer on numerous occasions whether she might consider changing her major or not completing college, always answered with a resounding "No!"

I wasn't gonna change . . . I want my degree in biology, then I want my master's in physical therapy . . . I wouldn't be satisfied with a bachelor's [or less].

Cynthia, who experienced considerable difficulty in the math courses required for her degree in business, was also determined to continue:

I see myself as a person that knows that if I want this fulfilled in my major, then it's [the math's] going to have to be done. . . . I'm gonna have to get used to seeing it. I'm just hoping I can cope.

For Cylene, buying the books she needed for classes became too much of a burden. She explained that purchasing books took a large share of the meager financial resources she had for college, was difficult to transact because she had problems in getting a ride to the bookstore, and was not likely to do her much good anyway because people in the dorm "borrowed" her books right before the tests. Furthermore, buying books allowed "the white man" at the bookstore to get her hard-earned money. After one semester of buying books, she had seen little return on her investment and decided not to buy them again; she proceeded without the books.

Cylene's feelings about buying books reflected another aspect of the "getting over" interpretation: that the costs of getting an education had to be weighed against the potential return. For the women at Bradford, going to college required financial sacrifice, especially for their parents or the other adults who helped with their expenses. When the costs became too high relative to the anticipated return, some of the women decided to drop out of school. A number of the Bradford women did make the decision to drop out, at least for a semester or two (see Table 3 and chapter 13; cf. Weis 1985).

The women at Bradford who adopted the "getting over" interpretation all recognized that going to class, buying books, studying, taking tests, and writing papers—however the requirements were defined by the school or by individual instructors—had to be done. But one could "get over," or get through, without completing all the tasks individually or fully. For example, some students "traded up on notes," meaning that one student took notes for another who for whatever reason decided not to attend a class. Some students regularly took turns trading up on notes with each other. Some students shared books, and some bought papers that they turned in as their own work.

These women saw themselves as "getting" grades, not "making" grades. Primarily, grades were viewed as tokens that had to be accumulated to get through courses and, eventually, college. They were important because they were necessary for finishing college and obtaining a degree. From this view, "passing" grades, as Cynthia indicated earlier, were what was needed. A grade of C was described as "fine," and a C+ average as "doing real good." Only an F was a problem, because it meant that the course had to be repeated, which meant falling behind and delaying progress toward completion of the degree.

The women were not unaware that grades could be indications of the quality of one's performance. Cylene worried about her mother's disappointment if her grades did not measure up to her cousin's. Rosalind talked about wanting to bring up her 2.8 average. However, getting high grades seemed to be of only secondary importance to the women in this group. As Cynthia suggested, in talking about getting passing grades in order to get out of college and get a good job, grades were only tokens of how well one had adhered to an arbitrary set of requirements; they did not indicate anything about one's future performance in a field of work.

Grades were "given" by teachers in exchange for work completed. Teachers were evaluated in terms of how well they made clear their requirements for grades. Rosalind's dismay about a health teacher's test that did not cover the material discussed in class contrasts with her assessment of two other teachers:

> She told us each and every thing that was going to be on that exam. . . . She gave us an eleven-page outline. . . . She gave us a chance to pass. . . .
>
> My English teacher is pretty nice. . . . He repeats the material two or three times to make sure everyone understands, and at the end of the class, he'll say, "If there's anyone who does not understand, you're welcome to come to my desk." So, I like him.

Teachers were also evaluated on the fairness of their grading, which was determined according to the principle that effort expended should be recognized with an appropriate grade. For Cylene, an appropriate grade was one that reflected the amount of work that one had put in; equal amounts of work should receive equal rewards. Cylene criticized one teacher for giving higher grades to students who had previously taken a course from her, despite the quality of their work relative to Cylene's, and another teacher for giving Cylene and others the same grade, despite the fact that Cylene had turned in more work. For Rosalind, an appropriate grade was one that reflected the time one had put in and not necessarily the skill one had acquired. She made her view clear in responding to the interviewer's surprise that she had made an A in swimming without learning to swim: "He grades you on your time in the pool, coming to class, and how hard you are trying. He grades pretty fairly."

All the women who held this interpretation of schoolwork seemed to be quite certain about their majors. They had come to college with majors chosen in high school or earlier, said they fully intended to pursue those majors, and kept them as long as they remained in college (see Table 3). These women did not believe that they needed to make outstanding grades or otherwise demonstrate special mastery in academic areas. They were simply trying to make grades good enough to finish school and get the credentials they believed necessary to be eligible for the future jobs they envisioned. They did not find the content of schoolwork compelling. Della's comment was typical: "I just did enough [schoolwork] to get over; hey, that's all."

WORK FOR "DOING WELL"

Seven of the women—six at SU and one at Bradford—viewed the work they did in college as a way of gaining recognition for their natural abilities and skills. All seven talked about wanting to do well in school for their parents, but they also all had the goal of doing well as their own. One of them, Linda, put it this way:

> I always wanted to achieve the best, to be the best that I could academically. I always wanted to make As . . . if I made a B, I felt I was a failure within; that if I had pushed a little harder, I could have made an A.

This idea of doing well was related to the idea of being good at, or having a natural ability for, schoolwork in general and at least one subject area in particular. Linda said,

> I'm just not a business mind, [so] econ. is hard for me. My suitemate, she's a business mind, and she whizzed right through econ. I'm just more like science, natural science. It's easier for me. The whole concept seems real easy. It just comes naturally to me.

The ideas about schoolwork held by the women with this interpretation also seemed to have been formed before coming to college. In high school or earlier, they had come to believe in their own academic ability, and they had learned that they did not have to work very hard to do well in school. Kelly said about her high school experience: "I really didn't have to work much to get a good grade." And Susan was able to make very good grades in high school with what she considered to be a minimum of work: "It wasn't the amount of effort you put into it, [what was important was] the grade that comes out of the little bit of effort you [do] put into it."

According to this interpretation, doing well in college should be easy for those who are naturally good at the kinds of tasks or the subject matter of school. That is, good grades should be attainable, and without a lot of hard work. All the women in this group talked about "making" grades in college. For them, good grades were made by combining ability with some, but not too much, work.

Very good grades, preferably A's and certainly no more than a few B's, were the paramount indicators of success. High grades validated that one was "good at schoolwork"; on the other hand, lower grades undermined the valued identity. High grades in a subject area also signified to a woman that she was "suited" for that field as a career. It was assumed that if a woman was naturally good at something in school, then she would also be naturally good at it later in a job or career.

The women selected courses with an eye to demonstrating their ability to do well. Whenever possible, they avoided courses in areas where they were not naturally adept or courses that were known to be hard. When difficult courses had to be taken, the women tried to stagger them across semesters and "balance them out" with easier courses, in order to maintain high grade-point averages.

Teachers were sometimes evaluated in terms of how easy or hard they were, and this information was used by the women to balance their course selections. Teachers were also described as good or bad lecturers; some were funny, and others were hard to get along with because they wanted the work done in quirky ways. However, success in a class was determined primarily by natural ability in the subject area and by willingness to work to make a good grade.

When the women with this interpretation of schoolwork went to college, they expected to be able to make high grades, especially in the subject area chosen for a major. Except for Natalie, they found that making high grades was not as easy as they had expected. It meant working harder in classes and taking a lot more time for studying than had been necessary in high school. The increased difficulty of making good grades led the women to question their natural ability for schoolwork or for their majors. Having to work hard to make high grades suggested that they were not suited for academic work after all, or at least not for the course of study they had initially chosen to pursue. They began to look around for new courses in which they could do better. They considered switching their majors to fields in which they thought they could make the high grades they valued. Five of the seven did change their majors to something they considered easier. Velma, the Bradford woman in this group, gave up on schoolwork and dropped out of school. Only Natalie was able to maintain the valued identity as a good student that she had brought from high school.

Consistent with their "doing well" interpretation, the five women saw changing their majors as a process of "finding themselves," that is, of identifying their natural talents. Since they chose majors they considered easier, they felt they had to forfeit their claims to being good students. They began to search for alternative ways to prove themselves in college and, as a consequence, became even more vulnerable than they had been to pressures to succeed in the peer system.

WORK FOR "LEARNING FROM EXPERTS"

The world of college was very different from the perspective of work in exchange for learning from experts. The five women—two at Bradford and three at SU—who had this interpretation of schoolwork saw college as an environment in which skills could be acquired from experts.[4] They were quite explicit in their expectation that college should provide experts to help students learn. Valecia, an English major who hoped to become a broadcaster some day, organized her view of work in college around the idea that she needed to learn "good English" from her instructors.

> I love speech and English. I like writing and I like talking about what I write, but it's the proper way of [doing it] that I have trouble comprehending. I want to major in [English] and I want to get it down solid. . . . In high school, I was neglected of an English background, so English, it's a lot to learn. But since I got to college . . . the instructor now . . . he's an expert and I'm an amateur. . . . He's published five or six books and he knows every corner of a good paper. . . . I always wanted an instructor that was real strict on the way I write and he is. . . . He's been critiquing me hard. That's why if I get a good grade, I'll feel like I've accomplished something.

Correspondingly, as a self-diagnosed "amateur," Valecia expected the development of good skills to be difficult and to take some time.

> I like English, but I'm having so much trouble. . . . Well, who said it would be easy? Everybody have their problems the first year. . . . I like English. Isn't that part of a major? Something you enjoy doing? . . . Freshmen start out just like a baby . . . having to learn a whole lot of new things. I just can't get downcouraged now because I'm a freshman. I have three more years to go.

Although Valecia was aware that other students had ways of completing their work more quickly, she sounded determined to take the time to learn the material really well:

> When I rush through, I do a bum job. Kids told me ways I can get it out easier, but I don't want to. I want to get the best grade and I want to put forth my best effort.

Karla, who began college tentatively saying she would major in journalism but soon began to contemplate a major in art or physics, was seeking a "broad-based education." (Valecia also mentioned "wanting to have some knowledge" in other subjects, but this aspect of college was overshadowed by her ambition to become good in English.) Karla was primarily interested in exploring different majors as possible careers:

I'm here to gain a really broad-based education and learn
as much as I can. . . . I would like to look at [lots of]
different fields and job opportunities. . . . I would like it if
you could just take courses without having to worry about
degree requirements.

Karla expected to find knowledgeable professors who could evaluate
her talents in a particular field—"When it comes to college, one ex-
pects a professor to be a demigod"—but she was sometimes disappointed. Some teachers' level of mastery of their subject was too low
for them to be of much help to her. This was a special problem in art.

I never had an art teacher I felt was really talented or good
enough where their opinion would mean much as far as
whether I should be an artist.

Peers likewise were not adequate sources of information or help
because their skill level was no higher than Karla's. Also a problem
were teachers who knew the subject matter but whose testing or grading procedures did not provide Karla with accurate feedback about
her growing mastery of a subject. She complained about a French
teacher who did not seem to comprehend the mathematics necessary
to give partial credit and thus obscured the extent of her progress in
French. She also complained about a zoology professor whose tests in
a survey course covered "picky things" rather than the "basic" or
fundamental knowledge that Karla had learned and believed was
most important to have learned. She also believed that some professors, particularly in science, had to be convinced that the women in
their classes should be taken seriously before they would make an
effort to teach them what they knew.

Valecia described professors whose classes were a waste of her time
because she did not learn anything new and professors whose grading
and testing procedures obscured how much she had learned. The
second was a problem even with the respected "strict" English teacher,
who once informed the class members that if he felt a student had
improved, he would give the grade deserved, but if he felt a student
had not improved, he would give an F. When Valecia got an F, after
working very hard in the class and believing that she was "improving,"
she did not want to accept the grade as an indicator of her progress
and complained to the dean about the grading procedure. Her response to what seemed an unfair grade echoed Cylene's, described
earlier, but with one important difference: the issue here was not

simply the hard work and time spent, but the student's perception that she had really improved her grasp of the subject.

Grades were important to Valecia and Karla because they were signs of learning and developing skills. Valecia hoped desperately to get a good grade from her English professor because it would signal progress toward getting English "down solid." Valecia decided to take a course that she had placed out of, but with a low score, in order to learn the material better. Later, when she discovered she was making a C− in a course, she decided to drop it and take it again for a better grade, even though doing so meant she would fall behind her classmates. For Karla, grades in each of the fields she was considering as a potential major were particularly important as indicating her level of mastery and thus something about her chances for a successful career in that field. Grades in these fields were also important because of how they would look on her transcript when she applied to graduate school for further, more advanced study.

Kandace, Aleisha, and Stephanie searched for a somewhat different type of expert at college. These women each had a "cause" that directed their search for experts, most of whom they found outside the university classroom. Kandace came to SU with memories of a drug-dependent relative who had poisoned her family life while she was growing up. She wanted college to be a place of experts who could help her make sense of her experiences and learn from them. Kandace found what she was looking for in some of the extracurricular and religious activities at the university. For her, classwork had some pertinence in providing a theoretical perspective on her situation, but the "real experts" she found at college were other people who had suffered from the same problems. Aleisha was active in causes to advance the position of blacks in U.S. society. She expected to find more accomplished political activists in the university community, as well as in the larger community of which Bradford was a part. Stephanie came to college primarily interested in learning how to create a self-sufficient lifestyle; thus she searched for people, usually older, who had some real-life experience with self-sufficiency.

Four of the five women with the "learning from experts" interpretation changed or added to their majors during college.[5] They did so not so much to "find themselves" as to pursue interests they had and wanted to extend. Aleisha increased the number of requirements she had to meet by choosing a double major, and Karla decided on marine science because it was "more of a challenge" to her. Kandace seemed to find all the challenge she needed in her original major and in her experiences meeting and learning from others she encountered outside the classroom.

SUMMARY

The three distinctive interpretations of schoolwork that we found among our informants can be summarized as work in exchange for "getting over," for "doing well," and for "learning from experts." These interpretations had different implications for the facets of college work, affecting the meaning of grades, evaluations of teachers, allocations of time, decisions about majors, and even decisions about buying or not buying books.

The women with the "getting over" interpretation thought of their school careers in instrumental terms. The work was something that had to be done in order to finish college, even though it apparently had little intrinsic relevance to future work and later life. Their personal identities were not expressed in academic work. The women with the "doing well" interpretation began college with very different expectations. They saw academic work as an opportunity to demonstrate their identities as talented students.

The women with either of these two interpretations tended to end up with what Valli (1983:232) has called a "marginalization" of the worker identity. By the time the study ended, they had little of themselves invested in an identity as a full-time or serious worker, or learner, in school. Although we do not know when in their student careers the "getting over" interpretation first developed, the women having that interpretation appeared to have brought it with them to college. Their life-history interviews made it clear that they had held a "getting over" interpretation of high-school work too. They may have had to work harder in college, but their college experiences apparently did not challenge them to revise their view of what schoolwork was all about.

In contrast, we watched the women with the "doing well" interpretation become discouraged by their experiences in college and reconsider their commitment to identities as workers in school. Their developing understandings led them to a position similar to that of the women with the "getting over" interpretation: little investment in a strong worker identity.

We do not mean to imply that the two groups of women became entirely alike because of their marginalized worker identities with respect to schoolwork. They had taken different routes to arrive at a deemphasis of schoolwork as an important part of themselves. Among other differences, the women with the "doing well" interpretation had experienced a loss of self-esteem while those with a "getting over" interpretation had not. However, despite their different orientations to college, by the end of their sophomore year, all except two (Maureen and Natalie) had deemphasized academic pursuits as a crucial part of their personal identity. Performance in school had remained or had become instrumental, a means to an end, and not especially expressive of themselves as individuals.

Some have suggested to us that the "getting over" interpretation of college could be categorized in cultural Marxist terms as an accurate insight about the nature of the system, a "penetration" of how society works (see the discussion in Willis 1977:119–44). If the work required in college truly is irrelevant and arbitrary, if anything beyond a passing performance in college has little to do with later life, then one could say that a view that discredits the importance of schoolwork beyond its pragmatic, instrumental value constitutes an important insight. At the least the women with the "getting over" interpretation avoided the loss of self-esteem experienced by those with a "doing well" interpretation. But the value of the insight in helping the women to achieve their career goals is open to question.

The analysis of "getting over" as a penetration of the system is reminiscent of Ogbu's (1974, 1987) argument that black Americans accurately perceive that success in school will not, at least alone, permit them to surmount the obstacles blocking their access to societal rewards. In response, they develop "often in collective struggle, . . . a variety of 'survival strategies' . . . to compensate for apparent lack of equal opportunity for equal and fair competition in mainstream economic and other institutions" (1987:325). Perhaps the "getting over" interpretation is a survival strategy that the Bradford women had learned with their black compatriots in high school or even earlier.

Unfortunately for the women at Bradford who hoped for careers in the legitimate sector of the economic system, such survival strategies may turn out to be of limited value. Ogbu argues that when blacks and other "involuntary minorities" discredit the importance of school success for career success, they tend not to recognize that school work habits and attitudes are associated not only with school success but also with occupational success. The analogous limitations of the "getting over" view of work are revealed when it leads students to drop out of school or to take jobs that rank far below their original aspirations. As will be seen in the next chapter, the women with the "getting over" interpretation often inadvertently derailed their own stated ambitions to obtain "good jobs" or to pursue "careers."

A few of the women, those with the "learning from experts" interpretation, arrived at college ready to engage with their work in a way different from that of the others. They saw the work as relevant to acquiring knowledge and skills they wished to have, and they saw mastery of this knowledge as directly important to their self-definition and to their future success. These women were the most likely to seriously pursue careers beyond college.

13   *Pathways to Marginal Careers*

We conducted follow-up interviews with most of the women in the ethnographic study in 1983 and in 1987. Though brief, the interviews gave us some idea of what had happened to them during their last two years of college and their first four years after college. We found that the outcomes differed depending upon their interpretation of schoolwork ("getting over," "doing well," "learning from experts") and involvement in the world of romance and attractiveness. Two of the interpretations of schoolwork, combined with other experiences during college, led to an increasing marginalization of the women's identification with the world of work (see also Eisenhart and Holland n.d.).

Paula was one of the women who began college with the "doing well" interpretation. After experiencing difficulty in making good grades and maintaining interest in her coursework, she revised her view of herself as naturally good at schoolwork and scaled down her career aspirations. By 1987 she had married and had subordinated any career ambitions remaining from college to those of her husband.

The outcome of Paula's college career illustrates what happened to fourteen of the seventeen women who held a "getting over" or "doing well" interpretation of schoolwork. The other women also had come to college with strong academic records. They said they wanted to have careers but did not have much of a notion of themselves in a career. By the time they had been out of college for four years, only three—Maureen, Linda, and Natalie— were pursuing careers, in the sense of being engaged in a job sequence that requires a high degree of commitment and promises continuous professional development (see Rapoport and Rapoport 1976:9).[1] For the most part, we found that the other fourteen women had made career "decisions" that had led them into "traditional" roles for women in work settings and in families.[2]

In this chapter we first describe what happened to the women who held each interpretation of schoolwork as they progressed through college, entered the workplace, and started their own families. The educational, occupational, and social outcomes described are those that had been realized by nineteen (83 percent) of the women in 1983 and seventeen (74 percent) in 1987. We found that as the women progressed through the first two years of college, the majority seemed to have had unrewarding or disappointing experiences with school-work and to have turned increasingly to the peer culture for reward-ing experiences. That is, for most the world of schoolwork remained or became of limited importance, and the world of social activity, romance, and attractiveness became more central. There were some important differences between the black and white women that obliged us to refine the concept of "marginalized worker identity" into two parts: marginalized identification with career and marginal-ized identification of self as a significant breadwinner. Much about marginalized career identities should become clear as we review our findings within the framework of the three interpretations of school-work and peers.

"Getting Over" and Enjoying Peers

We have already observed that the women with the "getting over" interpretation of schoolwork brought with them to college marginalized identities as workers in school, or in other words, as learners. As we followed these women through their first two years of college and afterwards, we found that they did not become any more interested in or identified with schoolwork. On the other hand, their views of themselves as romantic partners to men were, in con-sonance with the peer culture, important for all but one (Sandy, at SU). All of the Bradford women in this group had steady boyfriends or a series of romantic relationships with men during their freshmen and sophomore years. They all devoted considerable time to manag-ing and maintaining these relationships. Sandy also seemed to be affected, but in a different way; she felt rejected by the peer culture and had rejected it. She became involved in a close and time-consuming relationship with a woman friend.

With two exceptions, the women with the "getting over" inter-pretation had no serious trouble doing "well enough" in their school-work and having time enough for friends. For them, only minor adjustments were necessary to participate in both worlds. One woman in this group put it this way: "I like Biology; it wasn't hard at all. I came out with a B. . . . I didn't ever go to class. . . . I was doing a lot of things with my friends. . . . I didn't learn anything, but I passed all my tests." Another said, "I never did bad to where I needed to change my ways." When Della started to have some trouble in her classes, she decided to quit her part-time job, with no regrets, in order to have more time to study and to preserve her "free time" with her friends and boyfriends.

Others decided to spend more time at the library or in their rooms in order to get their studying done, but without seriously disrupting their peer relationships. Usually, extra studying was done in the company of friends or boyfriends or was timed to coincide with the schedules of others the women wanted to be with. Della, who had always studied at home alone during high school, excitedly told the researcher one day during the middle of her freshman year: "I found a new way to study—with my friends."

In fact, the women in this group found schoolwork so boring and unrewarding in and of itself that they had to rely on their friends to keep them at it. Some reported that they stayed in school only because of pressure or encouragement from others. At one point Della said, "I was thinking of quitting school and [my boyfriend] told me, 'If you quit,' he was gonna whip my butt. . . . So, I can't quit." In another case a Bradford woman reported that she had avoided flunking out only because her friends insisted she study more so that she would not have to go home and be separated from them.

In the cases of Deidre and Sandy, friends pulled the women in other directions, and the women's interpretations of schoolwork were not motivating enough to keep them in school. These women dropped out of school before the end of the ethnographic study. Deidre came to believe that her goal of "getting a good job" could be better achieved elsewhere. "It's boring here . . . studying for four years. And most of the two-year colleges will find you a job. It's like guaranteed employment, and here it's not." Being at Bradford also interfered with Deidre's relationships with her hometown boyfriend and some close girlfriends from high school who attended the community college in her hometown. Before the end of her second semester in college, she had stopped going to class or studying. She stayed until the end of the semester only because another "home girl" was struggling to complete her courses and wanted Deidre's company. As a friend, Deidre thought it was her "obligation" to attend the other woman's classes with her and to help her with homework.

Sandy dropped out of school apparently because she wanted to devote as much time as possible to her developing relationship with her woman friend. About this she said, "[T]here's probably not gonna be another time in my life when I can just sit down and just be friends."

Immersed in a peer-dominated system that paid little attention to academic work or career preparation, and holding a cultural interpretation of schoolwork that focused on getting credentials in order to get a job, some women found insufficient incentives for staying in school. Even those who did remain in school often wondered if the distant goal of finishing a degree was worth even the limited effort they expended on schoolwork. At one point Della said, "I'm here for an education . . . [but it isn't very important to me] because if I can get a job in my field, where I want to be, . . . school would have no value." These women found no support in university life for developing or further elaborating their views of themselves in future careers, regardless of their majors, grades, or announced aspirations for future jobs.

It is not surprising, then, that of the ten, four left school without graduating, and that of those we contacted who were working in 1983, all but one held clerical or low-level technical jobs. When we talked to Rosalind in 1983, after she had dropped out of school, she said she had not been able to keep going to school in the face of what to her were arbitrary courses. She had not returned to Bradford for the 1982–83 school year because she was tired of "going to the same classes over and over." She was thinking of enrolling in a technical school. When asked what was the most satisfying aspect of her college experience, Rosalind said, "Nothing."

In 1987, when we talked to others who had held the "getting over" interpretation, we found that most had held a series of short-term and sometimes part-time jobs. They had not found these jobs very rewarding, but they needed money. Phyllis's case is illustrative. In college she had majored in business administration. The job she got afterwards was as a keypuncher.

> The first job I had was [at] a keypunch company, and the only thing I did was enter data. . . . [I took the job] because I was anxious. I wanted to get started and make some money as soon as possible. I worked there for six months and then I got hired [as] a computer . . . equipment operator. Then I was promoted to . . . a regular computer operator. . . . I would like for my career to be more prosperous . . . right now I'm in a position where I feel like I'm kinda standing at one point. I wish I really liked what I did.

There was one thing that Phyllis was pleased about. Unlike most of the others with the "getting over" interpretation, who were already or almost married when they graduated, she had not married until recently. About this, she said, "Right now, I'm just happy with the idea of having a husband."

Cynthia, who married before she graduated, had held clerical positions in four companies. Her first job was part-time. She moved when full-time work became available elsewhere, and she moved again for more money. She also had a baby.

Sybil, who had majored in social work, wanted a full-time job in her major but could not find one, so she first took a part-time, short-term job in social work and at the same time worked as a sales clerk "so I could pay off my debt for college." She enjoyed the social work, but when her job was completed, no additional work was available. She found work as a receptionist; she said simply, "I needed a job; that's why I took that one."

Charlotte married right after college graduation and soon had a baby. Like the others, she needed income, and she accepted a job as a sales clerk. "I had the baby and we needed the money," she said, "and the job came open. [So when it came open,] I just took it."

Maureen proved to be an exception among the women with the "getting over" interpretation of schoolwork. Although she had entertained the idea of dropping out of college ("because it's so boring"), she had decided against it. Her decision seemed to be motivated by a desire to avoid having to get a job ("I've never had one") and by the fact that she found college coursework "easy." She also felt pressure from her parents, both of whom had college degrees, who had agreed to support her fully as long as she stayed in school. They had also convinced her that a Ph.D. was the credential necessary for a "good job" in psychology, her field of special interest. Maureen did graduate (although three years late and from a different school) with a degree in psychology and at the time of the last follow-up interview had applied for a doctoral program in psychology.

Our ethnographic material about the "getting over" interpretation of schoolwork tended to be confirmed by our survey data from Bradford, although the survey was not designed to determine cultural interpretations of college work. In fact, we had trouble interpreting the survey results from Bradford until we realized that the women there tended to view the university as arbitrary. According to the survey results, the Bradford women tended to stick with their original majors and to be certain about the careers they wished to pursue. What ambivalence they had was, like that of their fellow Bradford

students in the ethnographic study, focused on the worth of the credential relative to its costs. Costs included time, energy, anxiety,
money, and the sacrifice of other interests (such as competing peer
relationships and activities). Survey respondents who felt that the
costs were unfair or not relevant indicated less commitment to pursuing training in their majors (see Table 1; Holland and Eisenhart
1981:89).

"Doing Well" and Succumbing to Peers

The seven women who held the "doing well" interpretation of schoolwork were the most vulnerable to reducing career commitment as they tried to handle the demands of both peer and academic systems. Their experiences with schoolwork at college were
more than boring and unrewarding: they were disappointing and
discouraging.

From the vantage point of this interpretation, doing well in college
should be easy for those who are naturally good at the tasks or the
subject matter of school. Good grades should be attainable without a
lot of hard work; it should be possible to make high grades and have
time left over to be with friends and do other enjoyable things.

All of the women in this group, like most of the others, faced the
situation of having to work harder in college to make the same grades
they made in high school. In general, those with the "getting over"
interpretation chose not to work harder and so made lower grades.
But those whose major interpretation was "doing well" had a more
worrisome problem. Not being able to do well was a challenge to their
identity of being good at schoolwork. Not doing well in the chosen
major was a blow to the idea of why one was in college—to study a
subject at which one was naturally good.

Five of the seven women with the "doing well" interpretation responded to the demands of college work by reconsidering what courses
to take and what to major in. Their difficulties led them to question
what coursework and, by extension, what types of occupation, they
were best suited for. One woman, who was having a great deal of
trouble deciding on a major, put it this way: "I really don't know what
I'm going to get into. I guess I should start talking to somebody. It
makes me nervous so I always keep pushing it back in my mind."

Eventually, all five of these women scaled down their ambitions and
notions of self. They came to see themselves as "average" rather than
"good" at schoolwork and before the end of their sophomore year
switched to what they believed were less demanding courses and ma-

jors (see Table 3). Kelly, like Paula, was faced with reconciling herself to a lower rank after only a few weeks of college. She dropped her goal of becoming a doctor, dropped her premed major, and switched to international studies before the end of her first semester. Kelly said, "I came from a background of good grades, tops in the class, never really worrying about it, [but in college] I'm just a face in the crowd . . . just average here. . . . It's a lot harder than I thought. . . . I wish I could have done a lot better." Linda, another SU woman who scaled down her commitment to schoolwork and switched her major from physical therapy to nursing, which she perceived as less demanding, also talked about the problem of "being average" at college: "I don't want to be average. . . . But, right now, I guess that's just what I'll have to content myself with because I don't know if I can do any better."

By the end of her freshman year, Kelly seemed to have resigned herself to a diminished commitment to doing well academically, at least at SU. She stated that the next year she planned to get more involved in extracurricular activities "because I wouldn't use this time any better." That is, she did not believe that more time spent studying was likely to help her make better grades: "It's just like [the time] would be wasted." Consistent with this statement, Kelly began her sophomore year by accepting a job as manager of the men's hockey team. She had no particular interest in hockey and knew nothing about the game or the players; she simply responded to an ad for the position because she wanted to use her time "more productively" to make some money. The job required her to work every afternoon and to take numerous out-of-town trips during the hockey season, for which she missed classes. When we attempted to contact Kelly in the spring of 1983, we were not able to talk directly to her, but we found out that she had dropped out of school.

Kelly's difficulties with schoolwork seemed to bring her to question whether she really was good at academic work. Her statements and eventual decision to allocate less time to her studies suggested that she had relinquished her identity as a good student—an identity that had been important to her in high school. Concomitantly, her investment of herself in her career as a student, as a school worker, had been attenuated. In this sense Kelly's experiences led her to a marginalization of her worker identity. Like the female clerical workers in Valli's (1983, 1986) study, Kelly did not seem very much attached to an identity as a full-time, serious worker. By 1987 she had returned to SU and graduated. She had gotten married almost immediately after graduation and had started working in a series of part-time clerical positions. She explained that "there's not a whole lot else to do around here" (where her husband's job was). She also had two children.

Linda had a similar experience and response. Like Kelly, Linda realized that she would have to work harder in college to make the good grades she had come to expect in high school. Linda rethought her ideas of herself in light of her orientation toward doing well. She decided that she did not have what it took; she talked about herself as lacking mental and physical stamina, as being lazy, and as not having the intellect to do the work. Although the process was painful, she too adjusted her ideas of herself and "accepted" a view of herself as being average.

> I'm just very disappointed with myself. I wanted to do so much better than this. You can't be average and get into the medical field. And I don't want to be average. . . . But, right now, I guess that's just what I'll have to content myself with because I don't know if I can do any better.

One part of Linda's scaling down was to switch her major from physical therapy to nursing, because nursing required a lower grade-point average. Both Donny, Linda's boyfriend since high school, and his mother, also a nurse, encouraged Linda to enter nursing. Although Linda scaled down her aspirations and her view of herself, she worked to obtain her nursing degree and she took a nursing job immediately after graduating. She was working at the same job in 1987. By that time she had been married and divorced from Donny and was about to marry a doctor. On the basis of what she told us about her plans, we wondered whether her statement of many years earlier, that she would leave her job for a family or her husband's career "with no qualms" (see Chapter 1), was about to come true.

Compared to Kelly and Linda, Susan came up with a more novel solution. She modified and eventually switched her view of school-work. In high school Susan had made good grades with little effort. She had been considered good at math and science. It soon became clear to her that at SU more work was necessary to make good grades, and she encountered a chemistry course that required more studying than she felt motivated to do. She received a D in the course and became convinced that she did not want to take another chemistry course ever again, although up until the end of her first semester she had spoken of chemistry as a possible major. Susan portrayed her poor performance as stemming from lack of interest. She described herself as being "slack" and "lazy," and the work as boring and un-

interesting. She resorted to doing only the bare minimum because she
did not know what she "wanted to do." The work had no meaning for
her, and doing well had lost significance for her. By the end of her
third semester, she was saying, "Right now I'm at this point in my life
where I don't talk about schoolwork a lot cause I don't know what I
want to do, but . . . I always have got so much work to do . . . for
nothing." She daydreamed about taking a semester off.

Meanwhile Susan was spending a great deal of time with friends she
described as "mellow"—who got together a lot to drink, do drugs, and
listen to music. They were less like her socialite friends from high
school, who worried about their social reputations and pursued ex-
pensive leisure activities, and more like her friends from a male prep
school, who were not so reputation-conscious and were more caring
toward others. Her search for and her talk about friends seemed to
reflect an effort to sort out the kind of person she wanted to be.

As Susan proceeded through school, she rejected a concern with
social reputation and getting rich. She moved toward a definition of
herself as a "hippie . . . a peaceful deadhead." But she still did not
know what she wanted to do in life. Without knowing exactly what she
wanted to achieve, without having a worthwhile goal for future work,
the work of college did not seem compelling. She preferred to spend
time with her friends, and she would have liked to quit school and "go
skiing out west."

Susan still had trouble giving up her image of herself as being good
at schoolwork. Her sister was also in college and doing well:

> [She's] real smart. Well, she's not real smart, she's as smart
> as me, but she's more responsible and she studies more. . . .
> She just got her license to operate the [special equipment
> associated with her major]. . . . Mom and Dad, like if she
> got that, it's like . . . "Yes, Susan, [and] what are you going
> to do?" [I think] "Oh, shut up! I don't want to hear about
> that right now."

In the spring of her freshman year, Susan went to see a counselor:

> I was really getting bummed out about school, because I—I
> still kind of worry about not doing anything, you know. . . .
> I do what I have to do . . . the bare minimum . . . my grades
> aren't bad, they're about . . . a B or C average, . . . I'm just
> used to, well Mom and Dad are used to me having As and
> Bs, and so I was, you know, just kind of bummed out
> about it.

Susan did not scale down her ambitions or even her view of herself as smart. Instead she questioned the goal of working for grades: one must know what one wants to do or achieve, or the work is a waste of time. She did believe that a college degree would lead her to a better-paying job than she might get otherwise. In fact she often talked about the "paths" that one must take to get to various jobs. By the end of her sophomore year, she had settled for working for a degree in exchange for a job that would "pay more than being a waitress," but she was still searching for a more important goal.

By the end of her senior year, Susan had quit school for a semester. She still had not found a goal, but had come back to SU to work for a math degree, because it was the easiest to finish in the fewest semesters. She had reoriented to a "getting over" perspective. In our follow-up interview a few weeks before her graduation in 1983, she said: "Yeah, [I did] well enough. It doesn't take that high grades to get out of here. You just got to stick with it for a while."

Susan still had not found something she considered worth doing in a larger sense, although one of her courses in her last semester, an introductory course in education, had provoked her interest. The teacher happened to be upset about the mistreatment of the lower classes in the American educational system. Susan was impressed by his concern and thought perhaps she could make a difference. She considered going into math education.

Instead, Susan worked as a waitress and seasonal employee at various resorts, traveling along with the tourist business. The outcome of her struggles with schoolwork, at least by 1987, seemed to be a marginalization of her worker identity. She had come to view work instrumentally, primarily as a means of making money. Even had she become a teacher and invested herself in an education career, she still would have been a case of what Deem refers to as "leakage": the loss of a woman from the pool of those with abilities in math and science—specifically, the loss of a woman who majored in one of those subjects in college but failed to continue to graduate school or to obtain a high-paying, high-status "nontraditional" job (Deem 1978:100).

Although Susan did not have much invested in herself as a worker in 1987, she was excited about one thing: she finally had a boyfriend. She had taken longer than the others who had held the "doing well" or "getting over" interpretations to find a romantic relationship, but she finally seemed to have managed it and sounded very happy about it.

As they reduced their commitment to schoolwork, most of the SU women with the "doing well" interpretation began to devote more time and energy to romantic and other peer relationships. They all spent more and more time during their freshmen and sophomore years worrying about finding the right man with whom to share a romantic relationship. All of them had relationships with high-school boyfriends when they first came to college, but for one reason or another all but Linda decided they were not satisfied with these relationships and looked, ever more urgently as time went on, for better prospects. Linda, who "broke up" with her high-school boyfriend during her freshman year, began dating others; after she and her boyfriend got back together, she spent more and more time away from SU with him at his school.

In sum, it appears that as these women divested themselves of strong student or schoolwork-related identities, they invested more of themselves in romantic identities. In contradistinction to the popular idea that women who cannot find husbands have careers, these women, who could not do as well as they wanted to at schoolwork, had boyfriends.

Lisa's interpretation of schoolwork at SU was difficult to categorize. She may have originally held a "doing well" interpretation, but we were not able confidently to place her in this group because her views about schoolwork were so affected by her boyfriend. Lisa's interest in maintaining her romantic relationship seemed completely to overwhelm her own ideas about her career and future. Although she was exceptional in our study, her orientation toward schoolwork and a future career, like some of her other experiences at college, seemed to presage what some of the other women, especially in the "doing well" group, would face as they become more heavily involved in and committed to their romantic relationships.

Lisa had an older steady boyfriend who had entered SU before she did. When asked why she selected SU, she said: "I always wanted to go here because [my boyfriend] was here." In most things that Lisa did at college, including her academic work, she followed her boyfriend's lead.

> He has a lot to do with the way I am. . . . He is the main person who . . . I imitate—not imitate, I wouldn't say, but base my behavior. That's it: base my behavior. . . . He's like a big brother who really cares a lot. . . . You know, the big brother is all the time [saying], "Well, I don't think you should do this," or "That guy's just taking advantage of you," or something like that . . . just pointing out situations I wasn't aware of at the time . . . because they were, you know, new to me or something.

One specific decision that Lisa based on her boyfriend's advice was her reconsideration and eventual choice of a college major. She had begun college planning to major in art but soon came to feel, after some questioning by her boyfriend, that she would need to find something else—a field in which she could hope to get a job. At first she thought about art therapy, but her interest was really captured by a course she was taking in her boyfriend's major. Her boyfriend convinced her that she was not suited for that field. He also pointed out to her that if she majored in it they would have to find two jobs in that field later. Lisa abandoned that idea and settled on a major in speech pathology, with her boyfriend's approval, saying: "He probably knows best. . . . He knows me so well." Lisa also noted that she did not expect to be well-paid as a speech pathologist, but at least she would be able to find work: "There are a lot of jobs in that, even around here."

Thus it appears that Lisa was letting her boyfriend take the lead in determining how she would think about her coursework and her job prospects. As she envisioned her future with him, she allowed him to set the parameters of her occupational life.

Velma, at Bradford, at first seemed to escape the difficulties associated with the "doing well" interpretation. In contrast to the women described above, she seemed to be able to make the grades she wanted and to resist, though just barely, the temptation to join in more peer activities:

> I know one night I had a biology exam the next day, and I came so close to that campus dance, but something was saying, "No, you stay and study for your biology exam." And I did well on that exam and I was so glad I stayed. . . . I think I still could have went to the party and took my exam too, but I probably wouldn't have made as high.

At the same time, she claimed to have a boyfriend at home and to be very shy around men on campus.

> I have a hard time to look in a [man's] face. I play with my nails, anything. It happened this past weekend. This guy said, "All I could see was your ear." I'm going to try to do better. . . . I think I'm nervous if I look in their face. I start trembling, heart beating fast. If I'm turned the other way, it's ok. . . . It's just the opposite sex. If it's a female, [I'm] ok.

It became evident by her sophomore year that Velma was not going to be able to maintain her momentum. She became more and more popular with men and dropped out of college before 1983.

Of the women in this group, only one, Natalie at SU, was able to continue to do as well in college as she had in high school. She did not change her major, and she did not feel that she had to sacrifice time spent with friends in order to accomplish her academic goals. She also did not become very much involved in romantic relationships. She never had a boyfriend during the time of our ethnographic study, although she participated actively in campus social activities like parties and mixers. Natalie, unlike the others with the "doing well" interpretation, seemed to have a special kind of support from her family. She had ongoing help and assistance in learning about her specific career choice—to become an insurance specialist—from her father, who introduced her to the insurance specialists he knew and arranged for her to visit several firms. She also got advice about courses and professors from her older brother, who had attended SU and had also majored in math.

Everyone in this group except Velma graduated from college. In 1987 Linda had become a nurse, Lisa (whom we will discuss with this group) had taken a job in education, and Natalie had become an insurance specialist. The others were working in clerical or other low-paying jobs, like waitressing or cleaning. Two of the ones with better jobs, including Lisa, described themselves as "following" their husbands or husbands-to-be, that is, choosing their jobs or residences according to their husbands' careers. Linda seemed poised to follow suit. Only Natalie, who still had no serious romantic relationships, was pursuing her own career.

The women in our survey at SU were, as a group, similar to those in the ethnographic sample who held the "doing well" interpretation of schoolwork. Many were not certain whether their declared majors were the best ones for them.[3] Many were still in the process of winnowing their best subject from among their perceived abilities. They were sensitive to experiences and indications that could be taken as either confirming or disconfirming their talents for a particular major. For them, "comparative evaluation of major"—the balance of rewards, perceived ability to succeed, and costs associated with the major—was the main predictor of "commitment to pursue training in the chosen major" (see Table 1 and Holland and Eisenhart 1981:89). They did not seem to question the legitimacy of the costs of college training, as did the women at Bradford who saw much of the coursework as arbitrary. Not surprisingly, their assessment of the legitimacy of the costs was not associated with their commitment to pursue training, as it was for the women at Bradford. Concerning career path, the SU women appeared in the survey to be uncertain as to which aspects of themselves they should develop; the Bradford women were more likely to be uncertain whether the costs of college were worth the benefits of following the chosen paths. Although the SU women also expressed pragmatic concerns, they were less likely than the Bradford women to view college primarily as a place where one goes to obtain the credentials needed to pursue a career.

The survey data also suggested that for SU women peer activities and relationships affected commitment to pursue majors, through the intervening variable of "energy available for studies." "Extraordinary demands from peers" was inversely related and "indirect help/happiness from others" was positively correlated with "energy available for studies." At Bradford, none of the peer-related variables was strongly associated with "energy available for studies" (Holland and Eisenhart 1981:94).

"Learning from Experts" and Managing Peers

The women with the "learning from experts" interpretation believed that the purpose of doing academic work at college was to master an area of expertise for use in the future. Although concerned about good grades and obtaining their degrees, these women were more interested in finding "experts" in the university setting, especially in subjects they wished to pursue. For them, low grades were setbacks, but they were taken as indicating lack of mastery, not lack of ability. Professors were sought out not because they were easy or entertaining but because they could teach a subject of interest. Some viewed college as a place to get to know, and to talk at length with, a variety of more experienced people—professors, older students, townspeople—who could help them develop the special expertise they desired to have.

These women also participated in campus peer activities and romantic relationships, but they had a sense of wanting to contain these activities so they could pursue their other interests. One of the women in this group, Karla, chose a boyfriend who already had extraordinary demands on his own time. Because he could only go out occasionally and she was not very much interested in the activities of her other peers, she managed to be free, in comparison to women in the other groups, to pursue her career interests at college. Similarly, Stephanie's boyfriend lived in another city and was busy with his own interests there; they saw each other only infrequently, and she was free to do other things.

Karla and Stephanie were the only women with the "learning from experts" interpretation who had boyfriends while at college. The two Bradford women in this group refused to let their relationships with men become "too close." When a relationship started to become intense, they "cooled off" the relationship and did not jeopardize the time they devoted to academic interests. One said, "I don't believe in getting serious with guys; I think I'm too young. They have a lot on their hands . . . to get an education. And so do I."

Thus, with an interpretation that made schoolwork important to them and the ability or luck to keep their romantic and other peer relationships from taking too much time away from school-related interests, these women were able to maintain a commitment to themselves as career-oriented. All of them graduated from college, and all but Stephanie pursued their final college majors into graduate work or jobs in their fields of study. (Stephanie pursued her interests, but not her major, after college.)

To sum up: only a few (18 percent) of the women in our ethnographic study with a "getting over" or "doing well" interpretation of schoolwork pursued their college career interests after graduation; a much larger proportion (80 percent) of the women with a "learning from experts" interpretation pursued theirs.

ROUTES TO MARGINALIZATION OF CAREER

Overall, these outcomes suggest that the majority of women in our ethnographic study did not finish college with a clear or strong sense of themselves as future or potential career women. By default, most seemed to be falling into a reliance on men and marriage for economic support.

The women who held the "getting over" and "doing well" interpretations of schoolwork differed in some of their specific views, in their particular struggles with schoolwork, and in their insights about their own experiences. They also differed in the degree to which cross-gender attachments became more important in self-definition than work activities. But by and large, sixteen of the eighteen women in these two groups (seventeen plus Lisa) either saw or grew to see romantic relationships as closer to the core of their interests than careers. Significantly, as the women's career identities became marginalized their romantic relationships became more central.[4] For the remaining two, and for the five women with the "learning from experts" interpretation of schoolwork, the two areas were more equal in importance. By balancing romantic relationships more conservatively against schoolwork, these women left themselves freer to pursue strong career interests in college—and usually managed the transition to a career in the world of work.

Routes to Identification of
Self as Future Breadwinner

Adrienne Rich (1980:643) has written that long-term relationships with men, marriage in particular, are unequal contractual
arrangements in which the woman's position is considered low-status
and without a means of gaining power. We found that many of the
women in our study ended up, by 1987, married and with jobs that
were relatively low-paying, low-status, that they did not particularly
value, and that they saw as secondary or supplemental to their husbands' careers. We have already suggested that these outcomes occurred at least in part because of their unrewarding and disappointing experiences with their schoolwork and their subsequent increased
participation in the peer culture. These outcomes were also linked, we
believe, to the women's ways of thinking about their economic futures, that is, to their ways of thinking about being breadwinners.

To a degree, the thinking of the black women at Bradford and the
white women at SU about their futures as breadwinners differed in
ways consistent with black and white patterns in the U.S. population
as a whole. Although existing research, including the present study, is
not sufficient to account for the similarities and differences we found
at Bradford and SU, the women were undoubtedly heirs to the
themes heard in their families and communities of subcultural traditions reflecting different, though related, experiences. No one can
adequately distinguish the contribution of the shared structural position of gender from the contributions of cultural tradition, social
class, and race, until additional cases studies become available, particularly case studies of historical depth. However, we can tentatively
address the differences here.

The women at Bradford tended to be from lower-middle-class
families living in communities in the South where family farms and
manufacturing have declined, especially in the recent past (see, for
example, Heath 1983; Wood 1986). Black men in particular have
experienced difficulty in securing other sources of economic stability.
Nationwide and in the South, perhaps as a result of economic pressure, there has been a marked increase in the number of families—
both black and white, but more so for black—headed by women
(Farley 1984; Rodgers–Rose 1980:39). Black women from communities with increasing economic instability for black men, including
our informants from Bradford, may grow up with the realization that
they will have to provide financially for themselves and their children.
They probably do not expect that they will ever be fully supported by

a man. A look around them would suggest that a man may not be able to provide enough for the family, but that a man and a woman who both work can provide a higher family standard of living.

Southern white women, especially those of the middle and upper classes (whose mothers and grandmothers might have attended the women's college associated with SU before it became coeducational), are more likely to have anticipated considerable support from men which would relieve them from the necessity of working outside the home. Because of societal favoritism, white men could bring home significantly more money than women. Through marriage, white women traditionally have had access to more resources than through the job market.

The different orientations of the Bradford and the SU women should be interpreted in light of these historical and contemporary inequalities in access to economic resources. In 1979–81, when we conducted the main portion of the ethnographic study, our informants at SU did not mention the possibility that marriage might not be a lifelong means of support (cf. Weis 1988, on high school students). The business of being attractive to men and maintaining a relationship with a man was salient to them, as it probably had been for their mothers and grandmothers. They seemed to take for granted that their husbands would or could be the primary breadwinners. The Bradford women valued boyfriends and potential husbands, too, but they often stated explicitly that although men might be of economic assistance in the future, having to rely upon them for continuous financial support was not wise. This difference existed between the black and white women in our study despite rumors of improvement in the relative earning power of women to men and blacks to whites in the recent past, and despite the overall increased instability of American marriages.

Women's View of the Future at SU

While they were in college, the women at SU implied in numerous ways that they could expect men to support them in the future. When Linda said that she would give up her "job" in favor of her husband's "career" or in order to raise a family, with "no qualms at all," and when Lisa said that she knew her future job as a speech pathologist would not pay well, it was pretty clear that they were counting on men for substantial economic support. Karla, who could not understand why her roommate wanted to work so hard in school when she was planning to marry someone who did not want his wife to work, evidently accepted that in some typical marriages the woman stayed home while the man worked to support her. Susan, as she cast about for a goal for her life, suggested that marriage might be a fallback to work. In describing her plans for supporting herself in the future she said, "Five years is enough time to goof off. I'll be twenty-six by then and that's not that old. I can get married or something."

Two of the women at SU—Natalie and Stephanie—were exceptions to the rule. We have already quoted Natalie (in chapter 10) as she talked about her childhood dream of "marrying rich" and her eventual disillusionment with the dream. Her sister's difficult experience with a husband who could not hold a job made an impression on Natalie. Her desire not to repeat her sister's experience, together with her expectation that someday she would fall in love and want to marry, led Natalie to think about how she could do both. Her solution was to develop her own career as an insurance specialist and to look for a romantic partner who would not "bankrupt" her. Interestingly, she had not found anyone by 1987, when she was progressing through the steps of her apprenticeship as an insurance specialist, but she hoped that she would soon.

Stephanie also questioned the idea that men should provide economic support for their wives. She seemed to believe in a marriage partnership in which both people pursued their own interests and contributed roughly equally to household maintenance. For her, this idea went along with a desire to have both partners acquire the skills necessary for a self-sufficient household. She had come to believe, along with her high-school boyfriend and a group of older women who were his friends and later hers, that self-sufficiency was desirable in a world of environmental poisoning and nuclear weaponry.

It is likely that ideas about men's economic support of their wives had surrounded the SU women all of their lives. Many expressed positive feelings about their mothers who had stayed home while their children were young. Several mentioned that their fathers, in particular, thought that they and other women were going to college primarily to find husbands who would support them. Paula reported her father's response when she called home to tell her parents about her bad grades during her first semester as a sophomore:

> He has decided that when I meet somebody, . . . I'll get married quickly. I said, "You mean I'm up here doing all this for nothing . . . to find a man and stay home and raise a family?" I don't know . . . but that's what my father thinks.

Importantly, Paula was not angry at her father's response; she seemed pleased that he thought she was attractive enough to draw a man quickly.

Most of the SU women, like Paula, seemed to take for granted that a woman married in exchange for support from a man. This source of support was considered reliable, as long as one found the right man, and could be seen as a fallback, as it was for Lisa and Susan, if one's own career or earning power did not turn out well. Even Karla and Natalie, who had some difficulties accepting the pattern, did not really object to it, if it worked.

The View at Bradford

At Bradford the view was somewhat different. Men were seen as potential, and certainly desirable, economic contributors, but so were the women themselves. Men were also seen as possible financial drains. Velma captured the ideal of most of the Bradford women in the study when she listed what she wanted in a husband:

> Well-disciplined, well-educated, stable background, good-paying job, ready to play the father role: see that everyone is comfortable [financially]—the wife, child, and himself. [The mother role] . . . the same things and listen to everyone's problems and take care of the house.

The possibility that a man might totally support a woman had its appeal for some women. One said, "I'll take a man to support me . . . he'll have to pay me half of his money." The interviewer then asked about the woman's desire for emotional ties with a man.

> I have to look out for other ties first. . . . I don't never want to be poor again. . . . I don't really want to work. . . . For financial reasons I [will], but otherwise I don't want to.

And several of the Bradford women reported, with some pride, that their parents and friends noticed how many gifts and other financial benefits they were able to get from romantic partners.

But women at Bradford also voiced fear that men could drain away resources. They believed it was important to protect oneself from such situations. Della expressed this sentiment in describing why she was not ready to marry the man to whom she was about to be engaged.

> He expects us to be engaged [this summer] and married by the first of the year. . . . I don't want to be his wife yet, 'cause I want to have my own money. I . . . don't want him always getting my money. . . . He already asked me to get

a savings account with him cause he knows I got a hunk in
the bank. . . . But I'm not going to do it because he'll spend
$150 on one suit. . . . I ain't gonna do it and then be
broke. . . . He wants me to put enough in so [he can buy a
car]. But then he thinks he gonna take my car . . . but I'm
gonna put it in my name. . . . He can't do nothing about it;
it'll just be in my name. You just got to think of the tricks
for these guys. . . . You just got to watch that you're pre-
pared for them.

This view, which is reminiscent of Natalie's response to her sister's
situation, was prevalent at Bradford: men were nice to have around,
especially if they could provide economic benefits, but a woman had
to protect herself from men who might wreck her own financial position.

It is likely that the women at Bradford had been surrounded all
their lives with these ideas about the economic relationship of men
and women. Although the Bradford women recognized much more
of a need to look out for their own economic position, they, like the
women at SU, did have hopes for romantic partners who would provide them with some economic benefits they did not expect to be able
to obtain by themselves.[5]

SUMMARY

For a majority of the women, their developing interpretations of schoolwork, together with their unrewarding and disappointing academic experiences and the availability—not to mention
the pressure—of the peer culture, led to a marginalization of or a
failure to develop their ideas of themselves as having careers in the
future. They either were content for a career to be marginal or non-
existent in their lives or did not notice what was happening.

Most of the white women did not expect to be primary breadwinners in the future. At least they did not spend much time thinking
about what would happen to their lifestyles or their potential families
if they became the main money-earners. Only one talked about economic independence in the future and planned for it. The rest, except for Stephanie, who envisioned an equal partnership, were either
silent on the subject or voiced some expectation of being part of a
couple in which the man earned most of the money.

The black women were much less sanguine about the likelihood of
being supported by a man. A number of them had originally come to
Bradford in order to improve their earning potential and thereby
their economic futures. For them, Adrienne Rich's predicted future

of economic dependency on a husband was not a likely option, whether they wanted it or not.

Despite the differences between the women at Bradford and SU, many of them ended up at roughly the same place relative to the world of work and careers: with very little solid identification with a career, with lower academic *and* career achievement than they had intended, and with lesser credentials and training than they had expected. As we have seen, over the first two years of their college careers many of the women shifted more and more of their interests and energy away from college work and toward the peer group, with its emphasis on romance. It may not be surprising, then, that the discontents they voiced were generally with men, rather than with the university and what they might have seen, given their original goals, as disappointing educational outcomes.

14   *Women's Discontents with the University*

The women at Bradford and SU did complain about the treatment they received as college women. Some, like Della, expressed dissatisfaction with professors for not taking them seriously as students. But in comparison to how much they complained about the things that happened to them in romantic relationships with men, they expressed little discontent with the overall system of gender relations as promoted by university officials and university policy. The university provided an important setting for learning and enacting gender relations, but it was not a primary target for the women's opposition (as in the cases described in the literature for working-class and racial minority students; see chapter 3).

At Bradford there was some apprehension that the university, despite its history as a black school, discriminated against blacks. White professors particularly, and to some extent black professors, were accused of showing favoritism toward white students or the ethos of white America. Most of the women in our study resigned themselves to this racial discrimination and tried to avoid professors or situations in which they knew discrimination to exist. A few joined or organized groups committed to fighting societal discrimination against blacks. None of the black women showed interest in groups or causes to end discrimination against women, either on campus or in society.

At both Bradford and SU the women tended to respond as individuals to their discontents with gender relations. They tended to develop personal and somewhat idiosyncratic strategies for dealing with their problems. They only relied upon friends and others for help with interpreting and evaluating their experiences.

In the following pages we describe the types of dissatisfactions with school that occupied the women, the ways they interpreted them, and their responses to them (see also Holland and Eisenhart 1988a). Though few in number, these instances suggest how treatment by schools and their representatives—the teachers— was interpreted by the women, and they foreshadowed situations that the women were likely to encounter later as adults and workers. It is pertinent here to wonder if the other women had similar complaints that they simply did not voice. Were they so used to not being taken seriously by those who held powerful positions, like their teachers, that they no longer noticed? We suspect as much.

We also suspect that some of the women did not really believe that gender discrimination affected them personally in any systematic way, and that the remainder who did apprehend gender discrimination felt that they were clever enough as individuals to circumvent it when they encountered it. For instance, when the women with the "doing well" interpretation of schoolwork scaled down their majors and chose less demanding and usually more female-dominated fields of study, they did not even consider the possibility that their decisions might have anything to do with gender discrimination. In their view they were realistically assessing their individual abilities and interests. Those who, like Della, complained about professors who treated women as sexual objects tended to assume that some men were "just like that" and not that the gender hierarchy gives men license to publicly treat women in demeaning ways.

Several of the women complained about classroom incidents in which they were not taken seriously as students. Della's experience (see chapter 9), when a male teacher drew attention to her body by looking her up and down during class, is an example. She took his behavior as a gender insult: she complained about his being taken with her body and clothes and about his emphasizing that aspect of her in class. Her response was to feel uncomfortable and embarrassed by the incident—and to resign herself to his behavior.

Della knew that she was not being taken seriously as a student or a learner in this university classroom. She knew that her professor, at least in this instance, was perceiving her in terms of her gender and was highlighting her contribution to the class in terms of her attractiveness as a woman. In other words, the feedback that Della received about her role as a student was modeled on the pattern of gender relations emphasized in the peer culture. She was treated as being on the sexual auction block. As Gearing et al. (1979) have pointed out, not being taken seriously as a student has dire consequences for learning. As long as "experts" do not believe that a novice desires or deserves the information and knowledge they possess, they are unlikely to create opportunities for her to learn or to demonstrate any learning she might have acquired. Experts spend little time or energy on such a student, and the student is unlikely to learn much.

Karla had some experiences similar to Della's, but she dealt with them differently. Karla took science courses in which there were few women. She complained that at least some of her science professors failed to take their female students seriously (Holland and Eisenhart 1988a). Karla's response to this situation was more active than Della's, but it was still a personal one: she decided to make sure that all her science professors knew her name and that during each class period she asked at least one question. This way, she reasoned, the professors would not be able to ignore her as they did other female students. They would not be able to bury her identity as a student in her identity as a woman (as Gearing might put it), and would thus not be able to deny her access to their expertise.

Sandy had experienced a similar situation, but with a high-school math teacher:

> This one [high-school] teacher, he started out the year by saying they had a new book and anytime they came across a mistake, he'd say, "Oh, that's because a woman wrote it." And Marcie [a friend] was a Sixties person, up with women's lib, and all that good stuff. Whenever Marcie or another girl would go up to put problems on the board, the teacher would go, "It figures you couldn't be right, you're a girl." Well, he had no right to say that. . . . And Marcie got real mad, and she picked up the math book and threw it at him, and she said, "You're so chauvinistic, and you're a real pig." Well, you just don't do that at our school, so he took her to discipline court. And she explained that he was cracking on women . . . and they told the teacher he was wrong.

It is worth noting that Sandy thought the problem was solved when the school administration reprimanded the offending teacher.

Our last example is Karla's complaint about one of her teachers from high school, whose opinion she had valued. Her problem began when the teacher visited and then wrote to her at college. He sent her one of Freud's books to read and proposed that they meet to discuss the book. She read the book and went to meet him excitedly, ready to have an intellectual discussion. Instead, she discovered that he wanted to become her lover. She tactfully tried to put him off, on the grounds that he was married. When she refused his advances, he attacked her verbally. He argued that if she was really the intellectual she claimed to be, she would be open-minded about having lovers regardless of their marital status. When she continued to refuse, he charged that she could not cope with her sexuality. Karla decided she had to do something really dramatic to get rid of him:

> I decided what this man needs is to dislike me . . . [so I got a] big, really mean-looking football player to write a letter to the guy, saying he'd break his face, . . . saying he and his buddies would descend upon him like ugly on egg . . . if he ever [contacted] me again. Now, I don't think that I have to worry about [him] anymore.

But Karla did not stop thinking about the experience. She began to see school as comparable to Rich's "sexualized workplace" (1980). She became wary of male teachers.

> But, you know, this has caused me to do a lot of thinking about the nature of the human male. Here is a man you would never suspect . . . upstanding member of the community, seemingly happily married. What more could he want? And trying to seduce an eighteen-year-old girl . . . and an intellectual seduction, too. It's made me a little leery of older male teachers who act incredibly friendly, because there have been a lot of them, that I always looked upon as just really nice people who were interested in their students. But now this whole other dimension has been added of, "Hey, wait a minute; maybe he's not interested in my intellectual development."

These examples illustrate the nature of the women's complaints about not being taken seriously and their responses to these situations. They suggest that the women did not encounter direct barriers to nontraditional behavior and aspirations but were nevertheless liable to encounter the assumption that they were not serious. When older male teachers treated them as sex objects or as incompetents, they knew that they were not being taken seriously as students.

The examples reveal that the women blamed the individuals, not the schools or society, for their problems. Della accused the particular professor and wondered why he had singled her out. Sandy also blamed the teacher and believed that the school could provide a remedy. Unlike the others, Karla had an understanding that brought the school and gender systems—specifically the link between them—into question. She seemed to learn that the practices of male authority figures in the school might not be in her best interest as a student, but she seemed to conclude that the solution lay in her own vigilance and not in trying to alter the school or gender systems.

That there are few complaints in our data about not being taken seriously in school might be interpreted to mean that schools in general do take their women students seriously and thus provide no target for widespread dissatisfaction or opposition. Our analyses here and elsewhere (Eisenhart and Holland 1983; Holland and Eisenhart 1988a) indicate that a better explanation is that the school and its representatives were not the salient feature of most of these women's lives. Most of the women were absorbed in problems with their peers. Because they were busy adapting to the peer culture with its emphasis on romance, the university itself was relatively less important to them, either as a source of prestige or as a target of opposition and resistance.

Despite our informants' limited discontent with the way they were treated as women at the university, we did find evidence that the pattern of gender relations promoted by the campus peer culture extended into the university classroom. There was every reason to believe that once the women entered the workplace, they would encounter it again. We suspect that the tendency to link women's prestige and work contribution to their physical attractiveness to men—a tendency that a few of the women noticed in their high schools and colleges—might become more obvious to them in the workplace. In her study of women in a high-school office-education program, Valli (1986) found that the women were being taught to make themselves sexually attractive on the job (and to take care not to go overboard). Their work performance in their intern positions was judged, at least in part, by how attractive they looked. Those who were considered attractive found the "best" job placements.[1]

SUMMARY

We found that the women's discontents with the university were minimal compared to their discontents with romantic relationships (see chapters 9 and 10). What a few complained about in the university environment was that they were not taken seriously as students or learners. Their complaints seem to us to indicate an extension of gender relations, as constructed according to the cultural tradition of romance, into the classroom and teacher-student interaction dynamics. They also foreshadow what the women were likely to experience in the workplace.

Only one woman, Karla, saw the pattern as systemic, in that she began to suspect the friendliness of her male professors in general and to adopt a wary attitude toward all of them. She also saw male professors in some areas, notably science, as likely to treat female students as not really serious about schoolwork. Karla saw their behavior as an obstacle to be gotten around. The other women simply blamed particular individuals for problems and tried to avoid those individuals. None saw their problems as part of a systemic, society-wide barrier to be confronted and attacked.

Part 6 *Conclusions*

" 'Cause I'm a Blonde"

Because I'm blonde, I don't have to bake.
I talk like a baby and I never pay for drinks.
Don't have to worry about gettin a man . . .
If I keep this blonde and I keep these tan.
'Cause I'm a blonde. Yeah Yeah Yeah
I see people work and it just makes me giggle.
'Cause I don't have to work I just have to giggle.
'Cause I'm blonde. B-L-O-N-D
'Cause I'm a blonde. Don't you wish you were me?
I never learned to read and I never learned to cook.
Why should I bother when I look like I look?
I know lots of people are smarter than me.
But I have this philosophy. So what?
'Cause I'm a blonde. Yeah Yeah Yeah
I see girls without dates and I feel so sorry for 'em.
'Cause whenever I'm around all the men ignore 'em.
'Cause I'm a blonde. Yeah Yeah Yeah
They say to make it you need talent and ambition.
Well I got a TV show and this was my audition.
um ok what was it? . . . ok Don't tell me.
Oh yeah, o.k. "Duck Magnum duck!"
'Cause I'm a blonde. Yeah Yeah Yeah
I took an IQ test and I flunked it, of course.
I can't even spell VW, but I got a Porsche.
'Cause I'm a blonde. B-L-I-N-D [*sic*]
'Cause I'm a blonde. Don't you wish you were me?
I just want to say being chosen this month's "Miss August" is
like a compliment I'll remember as long as I can. Right now I'm
a freshman in my fourth year at UCLA, but my goal is to become
a veterinarian because I love children.
'Cause I'm a blonde. Yeah Yeah Yeah
Girls think I'm snotty and maybe it's true.
With my hair and body, you would be too.
'Cause I'm a blonde. B-L . . . I don't know.
'Cause I'm a blonde.

From Julie Brown's recording *Goddess in Progress*. Lyrics copyright 1984 by Rhino Records. Reprinted by permission of Julie Brown.

15   *Unfinished Lives*

The women at Bradford and SU would have had no trouble understanding the woman and the world of gender relations caricatured in Julie Brown's song " 'Cause I'm a Blonde," although some would certainly have booed her "philosophy" and her idea of beauty.[1] They would have known what Miss August was talking about, because they knew all about the culturally constructed world of gender relations implicit in the lyrics of the song. If from nowhere else, they were familiar with this world from their experiences at Bradford and SU in the early 1980s. Miss August describes what a woman's sexual attractiveness supposedly can be worth: attention from men, freedom from cooking, freedom from work, easily won fame (on TV, no less), awards, and the accoutrements of wealth. For very little work and very little in the way of accomplishments, the song implies, an attractive woman can get intimacy, fame, and wealth from men.[2] No doubt Miss August would have agreed with Weiler's (1988:34) point that the role of schooling for girls in a system of patriarchy is contradictory. Miss August makes it very clear that education isn't necessary.

" 'Cause I'm a Blonde" resonates with the style of gender relations prevalent at Bradford and SU. The women in our study faced a situation in which their social and emotional life on campus was profoundly affected by their sexual attractiveness to men. Drawing upon a very old tradition, the peer cultures at both universities interpreted gender relations and sexual attraction in terms of romantic love. Even though men and women paired up according to an equivalent level of attractiveness, and even though women and men exchanged tangibles and intangibles of supposedly equal value, their relations turned out to be unequal. They were unequal because women's attractiveness—and in some sense, social

211

worth— was a function of their appeal to men, whereas men's attractiveness and social worth were reckoned according to their appeal to women *and* their success in sports, music, business, and other fields.

THE SEXUAL AUCTION BLOCK

Miss August implies that other women would like to have the same "symbolic capital" that she has—the same stunning physical attractiveness—so that they can also do well in life:

> I see girls without dates and I feel so sorry for 'em.
> 'Cause whenever I'm around all the men ignore 'em. . . .
> 'Cause I'm a blonde. Don't you wish you were me? . . .
> Girls think I'm snotty and maybe it's true.
> With my hair and body, you would be too.

Although many of the women, especially the ones at Bradford, might have disputed Miss August's idea of blondes as extremely attractive, the women at both universities were concerned about their own attractiveness. Those at SU especially talked a lot about working to improve their looks. But it is at this point that the song drifts away from the women's experiences as we heard them. For the women in our study, the more disturbing experiences came not so much from comparing themselves to other women, but rather from irritating, upsetting, and potentially devaluing experiences with men. Although attractiveness was often talked about as a personal essence, in fact it was affected by the prestige of the men a woman attracted and by their treatment of her. Hypothetically, an unattractive woman had to settle for the "nerds," men as unattractive as she. Her other option was to go out with a more attractive man and put up with bad treatment commensurate with the discrepancy in their attractiveness.[3] In either case, being on the sexual auction block was risky for the women because men often did things—from ignoring them to sexually assaulting them—that in the logic of the cultural system indicated that the women were not particularly attractive and were therefore low-status.

As we have repeatedly argued in this book, the women in our study did not have any choice as to whether or not they would be involved in gender relations. As has been characteristic on college campuses since the 1920s, the peer cultures at the two universities we studied were organized largely around gender relations. The women in the study were around their peers all the time. Their actions and the actions of others were constantly interpreted as romantic actions, and the women had to come up with some response to the peer emphasis on gender relations.

The women negotiated the sexual auction-block aspect of campus life in a variety of ways.

Creating a Protected Niche

Most of the women did enter into romantic relationships, though not always wholeheartedly. Though some seemed to enjoy romantic relations for their own sake and a few exploited them, or at least were tempted to exploit them for what could be gotten from the men involved, others seemed uneasy and tried to find a more comfortable or protected niche away from risk to their prestige. At Bradford the protected niche was created by forming a serious relationship with one man, among those one went out with, and by trying to keep quiet the nature of one's feelings and activities. At SU the protected niche was created by finding a "Mr. Right," someone who was attractive and treated one well. The women converted their symbolic capital—their sexual attractiveness—into the benefits to be gained from more or less exclusive heterosexual relationships. Such relationships usually took up a lot of time and exposed the women to a number of demands.

The women's experiences in the world of romantic relationships both affected and were affected by their experiences with schoolwork. In a number of cases we saw women's career identities erode: those with the "doing well" interpretation did less well in classes than they expected to, and those with the "getting over" interpretation became more and more bored with the seeming futility of schoolwork. As their career identities eroded, their focus on romantic relationships increased. Next their efforts at schoolwork decreased, then their rewards from it decreased, and their focus on romantic relationships further increased (see also Henry 1965:179).

Postponement and Limitation

The women who did not get so caught up in romantic relationships did so by postponing or limiting their involvement in various ways. Some claimed absentee boyfriends who seldom if ever showed up. One woman gloried in a boyfriend who had lots of work and so only had limited time to see her; another participated diligently in "man-hunting" activities but in our interviews never showed any interest at all in finding a romantic relationship; still others tried to postpone their wedding dates as long as possible; and one "broke up" with the man she actually intended to marry later. Most of these responses accomplished two things: they limited the energy the women needed to devote to romantic relationships, and at the same time they at least partially removed the woman from the sexual auction block, as far as peers were concerned.

These women, most of whom were successful in school, were managing to control their involvement in heterosexual relationships, but, as some of them found out, they could not remove themselves totally from the sexual auction block. They could not prevent themselves from being evaluated for their sexual attractiveness and treated primarily from the frame of sexualized gender relations. Several especially resented being treated by professors according to their sexual attractiveness. A number seemed to believe that sexual relations would become the frame of interaction between themselves and male professors or bosses at work, if and only if they wanted them to. Others, like Karla, were beginning to realize consciously that they as women were *always* vulnerable to being treated from the perspective of sexualized gender relations.

It was unclear to what degree the women consciously recognized that their vulnerability to bad treatment from men could seriously depreciate their attractiveness, their symbolic capital. It is likely that they did recognize their vulnerability at some level, for those who were uncomfortable with being on the sexual auction block—most of the women in the study—had had some upsetting experiences. Although none told of experiences of "date rape," we heard of incidents when a woman was verbally chastised or ridiculed for refusing intercourse. It is likely that some of the women's efforts to remove themselves from the sexual auction block were designed to decrease their vulnerability to such possibilities. Because the system worked in such a way that a woman's prestige suffered because of bad treatment from males, no matter the circumstances, it is likely that women avoided confiding in others about men who tried to assault them. The logic of the system was that a man's treatment was a sign of the woman's status. Establishing a protected niche gave individual women some security from having their sexual attractiveness, an important source of their social worth, devalued, but in ways that conformed to the system and thereby confirmed it—or at least did not attack it.

Heretics and Dropouts

A few women explicitly opposed various aspects of gender relations as construed by the peer group, and one woman more or less extricated herself from the pressures of peer culture by entering into an intense friendship with another woman. These opposers thought and acted more or less on their own. They sought no group support for maintaining their idiosyncratic views, even though some campus organizations might have offered a forum for exploring alternatives to the peer culture.

ON THE ABSENCE OF WOMEN'S GROUPS TO
OPPOSE MALE PRIVILEGE

A good proportion of the women in our study were involved in romantic relationships as prescribed by the peer culture. With its focus on heterosexual relations and romance, the peer culture did not provide a fertile ground for women's solidarity. Julie Brown's " 'Cause I'm a Blonde" paints crudely the broad outlines of the context of women's relationships with one another. Miss August's relationships with other women are determined by her relationships with men. The important people are men; other women make up the audience. Although a more complicated situation existed among the black women at Bradford, because of their concern for avoiding manipulation by male and female peers alike, the women at both schools tended to have fragile relationships with one another.

Many of the women at both universities actually had doubts, reservations, and criticisms concerning the system of gender relations in which they were enmeshed. But they did not join together to change the situation. Their criticisms were piecemeal and not coordinated: one woman objected to boyfriends being shown off; another was determined to avoid having to depend on a man financially; another was upset at having been treated like a sex object by a professor. The criticisms were socially unorganized; the women voicing them created or joined no women's groups to oppose male privilege in gender relations.

Two points could be made about the absence of participation in oppositional women's groups among the young women in our study. First, there was a very large vocabulary for designating types of men and types of women and a plethora of clothing styles, hairstyles, residence choices, words, and so forth, that the students treated as marking stands for or against groups such as sororities and fraternities, "preppies," and lesbians and gays. These markers signaled what might be called emergent groups or factions within the peer community. Students formed associations and friendships with other students who had similar orientations.[4]

Despite the large variety of social markers, there did not seem to be any for the participants in our study to use to recognize other women or men who shared their particular reservations about gender relations. There was little evidence of discourse appropriated from the women's movement, for example, that could be taken as an indicator of shared sentiments. Instead, the gender-marked terms that existed were associated with the cultural model of romance and attractiveness. Their meaning was based on—and therefore took for granted—the assumptions of the model. Terms did exist that indicated stance toward the women's movement, like "libber" and "feminist," but even those terms tended to be absorbed into the model as indicating types of women who were not very sexy (Holland and Skinner 1987:106).

None of the formal groups that did exist seemed to attract the women's attention. During the study none of our informants took any courses that might have offered, by virtue of their subject matter or the reputation of the teacher (e.g., as a feminist), an opportunity to meet classmates who shared their concerns.[5]

A second and more complex point about the absence of participation in or formation of women's groups among the women in the study concerns the nature of the peer system and gender relations. The sexual auction block was run primarily by peers, not by the university. It was run on a very informal basis—there were no numerical grading systems for attractiveness, no authority to do the evaluation, and no formal credentialing system. Because attractiveness was a function of attraction as well as looks, individual couples negotiated their attractiveness relative to one another. Forming a romantic relationship with one man was usually sufficient to protect a woman from negative evaluations from other men and women. Just as getting a boyfriend was enough to remove one of Lees's London high-school girls from the slag category, getting a boyfriend was enough to satisfy doubts about a Bradford or SU woman's attractiveness. As a result of these features of the system there were no clearly demarcated low-status groups—no publicly, unanimously designated set of unattractive women. This system was very different from that faced by the working-class students described in the literature (see chapters 3 and 4). They were publicly graded by the school as having inferior academic standing and thus were created as a clearly marked low-status group (see also Lacey 1970).

In the absence of any public designation of a disadvantaged group, those who might have felt individually disadvantaged by the system, like Sandy, were perhaps unlikely to recognize others who felt the same. Not only were there no publicly designated groups, there was also no clear, shared target of oppressive ranking. Since there was no clear authority adjudicating attractiveness, who or what could a woman blame for messages that she was unattractive? Sandy blamed individual women—acquaintances—for criticizing her. Others who felt similarly criticized no doubt had in mind other sources for the criticism; or perhaps they just had a general sense of feeling unattractive.

The absence of a clear target of oppressive ranking was, in turn, a likely blockage to the realization that women as a group were disadvantaged by the system in comparison to men. To have recognized that they were disadvantaged as a group, the women would have had to see beyond the differences among themselves, as ranked by attractiveness, and beyond the proof of their own individual attractiveness as validated by boyfriends. They would have had to see their shared basis for opposing the ranking itself. These were great difficulties that the women would have had to overcome in order to form groups to oppose their collective disadvantage in the sexual auction system. The administration of the system by the peer group made the blockages quite profound.

CONTESTED IMAGES OF ATTRACTIVENESS AND DIVISIONS WITHIN THE PEER COMMUNITY

The campus cultures at Bradford and SU held to a homogeneous interpretation of the basics of gender relations. Yet though there was general collective accord about the nature of gender relations and their interpretation according to the cultural model of romance and attractiveness, there was dissent about what was attractive. Factions within the peer community supported different styles of acting out sexual attraction and thus different images of attractiveness. Low-level conflicts—and as we know from our interviews, private struggles of conscience—went on over stances toward different sexual preferences and over the value of "preppie" or other upwardly mobile styles.

The internal divisions within the peer community were important for two reasons. First, the emergent groups were coed: that is, they involved both men and women. Men made denigrating remarks about preppies just as women did, and preppies themselves came in both female and male versions. Gender issues, in other words, were constructed in such a way that groups of women and men joined against other mixed groups; groups of women did not join against groups of men. Second, there is a hint that at SU these internal divisions linked gender to other social divisions such as class. Perhaps if we had been able systematically to research the vocabulary of gender types at Bradford, as we did at SU, we would have found the sorts of differences depicted in Spike Lee's *School Daze* (1988), which portrayed groups on a black campus vying over images of attractive-ness—images that related race and class to gender. In the film the groups were divided over race-related images of attractiveness: the Wannabees represented a light-skinned image that approached the concept of beauty presented in " 'Cause I'm a Blonde"; the Jigaboos, an opposition black, Afro-American image. Thus contestations over class and race were inextricably confounded with gender.

In any event, it is clear that some women in the study were drawn not only to doubt the peer culture's insistence on romance, but also to contest which image of attractiveness would dominate. These were two different sorts of struggles. The first involved the women as individuals, trying to cope with gender relations as culturally con-strued in the peer culture. The second involved the women as poten-tial members of emergent coed factions that were contesting images of attractiveness. The emergent factions took the basic patriarchal ground rules of gender relations for granted and disputed only what styles and forms were to be considered most attractive.

THEORETICAL IMPLICATIONS

The points just summarized have implications for the the-oretical literature on women and schooling viewed from a cultural-production perspective.

Romance: An Imposition on Women, or a Part of Women's Resistance?

The girls and young women in McRobbie's studies (espe-cially 1978b) seemed preoccupied with constructing romantic images of themselves. McRobbie argues that, supplied with material from teen magazines such as *Jackie* (see McRobbie 1978a, 1981), they elab-orated romance as part of their resistance to the harsher social real-ities of school and work. Lees (1986), in contrast, persuasively argues that the girls and young women that she studied in London were oppressed by a system of gender relations couched in terms of ro-mance. Romance was part of the oppressive system they encountered, not some sort of celebratory culture of resistance they developed in response to an oppressive system.

Our research corroborates Lees's analysis. The pieces of the cul-tural tradition featured in her British schools were different from those we found in the American universities, but both systems of gender relations were constructed from the longstanding tradition of romantic love. In these different peer cultures, males held the privi-leged positions in gender relations. In our findings, as in Lees's, the face of patriarchy most directly confronted the women in the world of romance and attractiveness.

In an essay subtitled "Sex Differences in Love," the sociologist of emotions Arlie Hochschild (1983:255) makes the argument that because women are so directly and personally affected by the organization of gender relations, they are more likely to be pragmatic about such relations and less given than men to flights of romantic fantasy:

> Men, having a more romantic notion of love, cast a different map over their experience than do women. . . . The romantic rendering of love [by men] suggests a less managerial, more passive stance toward love. Romantic love is by its nature something that cannot be controlled; it occurs automatically, "at first sight," and is predestined. Love feelings are in a particular way ascribed, not achieved. Indeed, the data suggest that men manage and work on love less. . . . On the other hand, women understand love more as something which can, in its nature, be managed and indeed they seem to perform more feeling work upon it. By de-romanticizing love, women appear to professionalize it more. Why?
>
> The answer, I suggest, is that young men hold hegemony over the courtship process while at the same time women, for economic reasons, need marriage more.

Our point, and Lees's as well, both extend Hochschild's propositions. School and college peer cultures insist that a woman's social worth, her social prestige, is mostly a function of her sexual attractiveness. Hence gender relations are serious business for a women, not only because of the ultimate economic and social importance of marriage, but also because her sexual attractiveness is so immediately emphasized in the peer culture she participates in during her school career.

It is certainly conceivable that the women in our study could have focused exclusively on the parts of the tradition of romantic love that concern flights of rapture, emotional wholeness, and undying union with another person. It is conceivable that they could have built an oppositional culture of romance drawing upon these themes. Some did seem to enjoy pursuing romantic relationships, and some who were in steady relationships did talk about their happiness in those relationships. However, none of the women seemed to be caught up in ideals of love; nor were any of them in love with the idea of love. The cultural tradition of romantic love conceivably could have been drawn upon in fresh ways as a source of material for opposing the version of gender relations that we found at Bradford and SU; but we found no evidence of such an occurrence.

In sum, our findings, in combination with the other literature, suggest that although romance-as-opposition does occur at times, it is likely that it must usually coexist as a form of resistance with a peer-run system of male-privileged gender relations that draws upon the same tradition of romance. Gender relations interpreted in the cultural idiom of romantic love are more aptly described as imposed upon girls and young women, than as constructed by them as a counterculture in opposition to gender discrimination. It is equally significant that though Lees (1986) primarily argued against the romantic entrapment path suggested by McRobbie (1978b) and repeated by Willis (1981b:207), she did report that some of the girls she studied emphasized romance. These were girls who were alienated from school and from learning or training for a career. Her finding parallels our conclusion that decreasing investment in schoolwork coincided with increasing investment in romantic relationships.

Is the Peer Group a Site of Cultural Production or a Site of Cultural Reproduction?

In their efforts to overcome the bias in social-reproduction theory that conceived students as passive pawns of school and society, Willis (1981b) and other researchers at CCCS (Hall and Jefferson 1976) and elsewhere have emphasized the peer group as a source of cultural production. They have successfully demonstrated that students and youth react to the constraints they face in the larger society. In this sense young people become part of the larger picture of social reproduction, but not a site of reproduction in themselves. Ogbu's work has presented a similar picture for black Americans.

For the women we studied, the campus peer society and culture was the major purveyor of male privilege. From this standpoint, the peer culture emerges as one of the major sites of reproduction of the patriarchial gender hierarchy.

Opposition to Patriarchy as Compared to Opposition to Class, Race, and Age Hierarchies

The literature suggests that oppositional youth groups are more likely to develop in response to class, race, and age hierarchies than in response to gender hierarchies. Capitalistic, racist, ageist societies produce dissident youth groups that act out oppositional stances. Patriarchal societies are less likely—or have been less likely—to spawn dissident youth groups protesting male privilege.

Our study indicates that for young women, patriarchy is mediated most virulently by the peer group—not by school officials who are socially distant in age and authority, but by peers who may sleep in the same room and even in the same bed. In our study the system of romance and attractiveness, the system that undergirded male privilege in gender relations, was maintained much as the system of honor is maintained among the male Kabyles (Bourdieu 1977; see chapter 7). It was *not* maintained in the manner Bourdieu contrastingly describes for the system of "educational capital" in France (Bourdieu and Passeron 1977). In Kabylia the system of privilege is sustained through face-to-face relationships. Because a man of honor has greater symbolic capital, he has an advantage, but maintaining that advantage goes on in a hands-on manner on a day-to-day basis. In France, on the other hand, the schools do much of the work of preserving the advantage of the elite classes. They certify the "educational capital" of the elite in a way that means the elite scarcely have to encounter working-class people. Symbolic violence—the degradation of another group's cultural capital—is accomplished with little need for individual, hands-on work.

At Bradford and SU, the sexual auction block was run by peers, not by the university. The university did not constitute an institutionalized source of "sexual attractiveness capital" as the schools in France were a source of "educational capital" (see Bourdieu and Passeron 1977; Bourdieu and Saint-Martin 1970). The system was accomplished by the peer group in face-to-face interactions, without the aid of institutional credentials.[6]

The system of sexual attractiveness among Bradford and SU students and the system of honor among the Kabyles shared other similarities. In both cases the symbolic capital was validated relationally and there was no system of precise measurement that could specify the amount of symbolic capital that someone had. Although there was probably greater agreement among the Kabyles about which families were less honorable than others than there would have been as to who was less attractive at Bradford and SU, in both systems no ratings were handed out by a central authority or collective institution. It is important that among both the Kabyles and the university women we studied, the system for distributing symbolic capital was personal and imprecise and was not clearly associated with an authority that could be singled out for deliberate opposition.

We get no hint from Bourdieu that there were any men in Kabylia who resisted the honor system, but there probably were.[7] They probably opposed the system in ways similar to those that we found for the women in our study and that Fordham and Ogbu (1986) found for individual black high-school students dealing with their peer cultures.[8] The kind of resistance that we found, and that Fordham and Ogbu found—which consisted of various forms of strategic compliance in combination with "dodging the system," along with radical but internal critiques of it—may characterize systems that are maintained in a personal and face-to-face way. In a system in which authority is not personified and no permanently disadvantaged group is clearly and publicly created, opposition may tend to remain internalized and idiosyncratic.

Our argument, in short, is that the form of opposition to patriarchy in the schools is a function of the way in which the system of male privilege in gender relations is carried out. In the United States, race, class, and age hierarchies, as they are reflected in schools, are mediated largely by school authorities. Gender hierarchies, as they are reflected in schools, are mediated largely by peers.

Two nuances of our conclusions about peer cultures should be noted. First, we are not arguing that peer groups are unimportant as mediators of class, age, and race hierarchies. Indeed, as indicated by the research of Schwartz (1972) and Fordham and Ogbu (1986), peers are important in the formation of what might be called, in correspondence with the idea of gender regimes (Kessler et al. 1985:42), race, class, and age regimes. Peers, in other words, definitely contribute to forming the pattern of practices that constructs various kinds of racial or social-class "types" among staff and students and orders them in terms of prestige and power. But for race and social class, we would argue, school authority, as represented by the staff, school policies, and texts, figures more prominently as a target for opposition than it does for gender. For gender, standards of attractiveness and forms of gender relations seem to emanate from peers, not from socially distant school authorities.

The second nuance concerns the sexism of these peer cultures. The cultural-production literature, as described in chapters 3 and 4, ties the creation of youth cultures to structural features of the larger society. Exactly how and why the peer cultures of the school-age population come to be sexist is disputed, but the sexism of the schools and larger society is always implicated, no matter what the particular explanation. The point of our conclusions about peer groups is not that the sexism of the university and society at large is irrelevant, but rather that the most effective mediation or communication of male privilege to girls and young women is through the peer group. The form of mediation is important, we argue, because it significantly affects the ways in which girls and young women respond to the gender hierarchy and thus participate in the day-to-day constitution of the hierarchy.

The Intersection of Race and Gender

According to production theory, the black women in our study should have responded differently from the white women, because they had to confront race *and* gender hierarchies. Black women face a double or perhaps a triple oppression in American society.[9] Those in our study who were of working-class background faced class and race constraints in addition to the gender constraints also experienced by the white women. Our findings revealed differences that seemed attributable to the additional barriers faced by the black women. The prevalence of the "getting over" interpretation of schooling at Bradford and the corresponding near-absence of the "doing well" interpretation there are understandable given the social and economic climate in which the black women had grown up. Ogbu's work (1974, 1985, 1987) has shown that black students often view schooling as having questionable significance for their futures, given the job ceilings that black Americans face. The creation of a "getting over" interpretation makes sense in such an environment.

The black women in our study seemed less focused on finding a man than the white women were and less expectant of future economic support from men. This response makes sense in light of the economic discrimination against black men in U.S. society. To the extent that the gender relations black women enter into are with black men, the women are less likely to be able to expect significant financial support as a concomitant.

These two differences between black and white women, as it turned out, did not overshadow the importance of the gender barriers that all the women shared. Both the black and the white women faced a system of gender relations organized in such a way that men were afforded a privileged position. Both groups found themselves on the sexual auction block, and both spent a great deal of time and energy on romantic relationships. The majority of women—black and white—faced a system that left them on their own to develop, or not, in careers and to prepare themselves well, or not, as future breadwinners. In two-thirds of the cases, the women's notions of themselves in careers tended to diminish. Although the "getting over" interpretation of schoolwork at Bradford was quite different from the "doing well" interpretation at SU, neither attitude proved sufficient to get the women through their classroom experiences without erosion of their original commitment to careers.[10]

Attractiveness and the Intersection of Gender, Class, Race, and Age Privileges

There was an additional way—implied though not explored in any depth in our study—in which gender and race intersected.[11] Attractiveness, found to be a major feature of gender relations, clearly had the potential to articulate symbolically not only gender but also the other major dimensions that affected the women's *structural* position. Prestigious forms of beauty were not race-, class-, or age-neutral.

Through the "black is beautiful" movement of the past decades and through individual efforts, the hegemony of white forms of attractiveness has been strongly contested. Sara Lawrence Lightfoot (1988: 310) provides as example of this struggle when she speaks of the efforts of her mother: "She was determined that her daughters would 'know that they were beautiful.' She knew, of course, that the whole world might not value our beauty, that as Negro girls we would suffer society's preoccupation with white skin, blond hair, and blue eyes. But she wanted us to be assured of our beauty within the family." To what extent this struggle is finished, at least within the black community, is not clear. Spike Lee's *School Daze* suggests that it is not. But whether finished or not, its importance for black women is clear. To the extent that white forms of attractiveness are promoted in the media, in beauty contests, and in other public places, and are valued more than black forms, black women begin life—in the terms of the larger society—with less sexual capital than white women (see also Lakoff and Scherr 1984:245–76; Schofield 1982:127–52).

A similar point can be made with respect to class and age. We suggest, though from our impressions and not from systematic research, that during the time of the study, styles of personal appearance requiring a degree of wealth to create, maintain, and modify were favored over styles not requiring wealth (see also Fussell 1983: 51–75); personal features unworn by poverty and age were favored over features that were so worn. These impressions are worth mention because they point to a possible significance of gender relations and the intertwined emphasis on attractiveness that deserves further attention. The prospect of being ranked by attractiveness to men unites all women in terms of the sexual auction block they face. But to the extent that a race-marked, class-marked, age-marked form of beauty is maintained as the hegemonic form of attractiveness in the society at large, this common vulnerability to ranking by attractiveness divides white women from black, wealthy from poor, and young from old (see also Lakoff and Scherr 1984:280).

FURTHER QUESTIONS

As it happened, none of the women we followed were active in the women's movement. In fact, they were not especially engaged, either pro or con, by other women concerned with women's issues or issues of sexual preference. Although one of the women was excited by a lecture given by a prominent visiting speaker identified with the women's movement, we heard relatively little talk identifying female friends, acquaintances, or even campus figures either by their sexual preferences or their involvement in the women's movement. This was true even though organized women's and gay groups existed, at least at SU, and advertised their meetings and activities in the student paper, and even though women's issues were discussed in articles and letters in the papers on both campuses. From all the indications we have, our sample group's lack of involvement in the women's movement was typical for the two campuses at the time. It was not especially surprising, in that, first, most of the women were from small towns and cities in the state and, second, feminist activity on campus, although present, was the work of a small minority of faculty and students. The latter point was especially true for Bradford, where racial barriers were a more salient concern than gender barriers.

Regardless of whether women students actively involved in the women's movement continue to be in the numerical minority on campuses, the body of case studies on women's responses to schooling remains deficient without a study of the cultural productions and social practices of a women's-issues organization. The same is true of groups characterized by opposite political stances, such as antiabortion positions. Despite their possible minority status in student populations as a whole, the active and vocal members of such groups would provide a different and, for that reason informative, view both of the particular system of gender relations that we found and of more general processes of cultural production and internal student politics characterizing women's response to schooling.[12]

Also needed is a study of young women students just now entering college. These women presumably have had more exposure than the women in our group had to a range of discourses—both from the women's movement and from its recently revived opposition. How have these discourses been appropriated? Is the system of gender relations that we found still being recreated in the student peer groups?

We strongly suspect that the system of gender relations we have described is neither ephemeral nor easily dismantled; it reflects male privilege in the society at large, privilege that is still in place and that possibly has become even more firmly entrenched, with the rightward turn of American politics and institutions evident in Supreme Court rulings on affirmative action and abortion in the late 1980s. It is remarkable, and perhaps indicative of robustness, that the system of gender relations among the youth described by Lees (1986) and Griffin (1985) in England and the system found in our study in the southern United States are simply variants of a common model. However, the system of gender relations we have described is not graven in stone. Historical events—like the waning and waxing of the women's movement or high-court decisions and reactions to them—surely affect the ways in which young women respond to gender relations with their peers. Studies of young women in other regions and of different historical periods can only add to our understanding of what is a very complex process operating within a long-term historical struggle over women's rights.

There are also questions to be answered about the participation of young *men* in the system of gender relations. Although funding constraints obliged us to exclude men from our main study, we did learn about aspects of men's view of the system, at least at SU, from our supplementary studies of gender terms in the peer culture. What we learned underscored the need to know more about men's vantage points. Men's terms for women ("bitch," "scag," "honey," etc.; see Holland and Skinner 1987:84) encoded three major dimensions of comparison: (1) relative prestige as a sexual possession/companion, (2) relative tendency to be overdemanding and engulfing, and (3) sexiness. The first distinction in particular indicates that we need to know much more about how women figure in the ranking of men relative to one another within the peer group. Some studies of gender relations among other groups and in other societies argue that women and actions toward women may be used to form and cement alliances between and among men (e.g., Levi-Strauss 1969; Whitehead 1976). Perhaps the systems at Bradford and SU had similar features. In any event we need to know more about young men's participation in and orientation to the peer culture and its emphasis on romance and attractiveness.

From a cultural-production perspective, a question of even more significance is how localized systems of gender relations like those at

Bradford and SU link to larger systems (such as the standards of attractiveness promoted by the fashion and cosmetics industry) and to other major societal structures of patriarchy. This question concerns the formation of campus peer cultures, which are overwhelmingly sites of social reproduction, not just cultural production. The issue of continuity in gender hierarchies or "regimes," as Connell (1987) and Kessler et al. (1985) refer to them, is thus pushed back to the question of how such peer cultures come about.

We know from Horowitz that similar campus cultures have been around in the United States since the 1920s and that at least some of their features date to the late 1700s. Horowitz argues that campus cultures formed in opposition to faculty efforts to control (male) students and make them perform academically. Her account bears some similarity to the explanations given by Willis, Ogbu, Hebdige, and Brake, among others, for the formation of oppositionary, antischool subcultures among working-class and racial minority students.

What has not yet been explained is why gender relations are constituted as they are in these peer subcultures. In his review of studies of British peer subcultures Brake (1980:137–54) makes the interesting observation that despite profound differences among the many youth subcultures and between the youth groups and the dominant cultures, these subcultures leave traditional gender relations virtually unchallenged. Only homosexual groups and avowedly feminist groups have sought to rearrange gender relations. All the others— the mods, the rockers, the hippies, the lads, the college men of Horowitz's account—although promoting different styles of sexuality and attractiveness, have maintained a similar form of gender relations, in which males are in the privileged position.[13] Why should this be so?

Willis answered the question of why the lads of Hammertown were sexist by explaining that in fashioning their response to the British class structure they drew cultural elements from their own working-class backgrounds. They celebrated themselves in opposition to the way the school desired them to be by developing themes of superiority taken in part from working-class culture. One of the themes they happened to choose was a working-class masculinity built in part in opposition to femininity; so the lads acted out a virulent sexism.

In a review of the available research on youth cultures (primarily male), Brake (1980) also argued that youth cultures and work cultures are a response to class position. He, more than Willis, relates these cultures to social-psychological aspects of validating self-worth and acquiring valued identity in the face of the working conditions presented by the society. Thus he sees the sexism of these youth cultures not as an epiphenomenon, as Willis implies, but as directly connected to the fact that British society is not only capitalistic but also patriarchal. He quotes Stoltenberg (1975:35):

> Under patriarchy, the cultural norm of human identity is by definition—masculinity. And under patriarchy the cultural norm of male identity consists in power, prestige, privilege and prerogative as over and against the gender class women. . . . Male bonding is institutionalized learned behaviour whereby men recognize and reinforce one another's *bona fide* membership in the male gender class . . . male bonding is how men learn from each other that they are entitled under patriarchy to power in the culture. Male bonding is how men get that power and male bonding is how it is kept.

In effect Brake argues that men, including male youth, operate in relation to other men and to women so as to maintain male privilege, *especially* when they are disadvantaged by class, race, or age, or when they are members of the privileged classes but not faring well in competition with other members of their class.[14] Youth subcultures, then, to the extent that they are constructed by males, tend to reflect patriarchal structures.[15]

A third explanation for the sexism of peer groups concerns the opposition of youth groups to the age hierarchy that is so heavily emphasized in the schools. As we have briefly argued here (chapter 6) and in more detail elsewhere (Eisenhart and Holland 1983), youth groups produce school-oppositional cultures that appropriate forbidden signs of adult status (see also Coletta 1976; Willis 1981b). This appropriation, which emphasizes activities that are hard for school officials to control, such as displays of sexuality and the acting out of more mature styles of masculinity and femininity, begins at an early age. We observed it among fifth- and sixth-graders in the mid-1970s, and more recent research would no doubt reveal examples among even younger children. To the extent that ageism affronts youth groups, one could expect to find aspects of adult gender relations elaborated and exaggerated in the peer groups (see also Schwartz 1972).

While there is no general consensus about how most youth groups come to be sexist, there is agreement that they do not produce this sexism in a vacuum. All the proffered explanations link the sexism of the youth groups to the patriarchal nature of the larger society; the links need, however, to be better theorized.

The final major question raised by our study, but left only partially answered, concerns divisions *within* the peer group and the actions of both men and women with regard to these divisions. As pointed out by Connell (1987:248), heterosexual gender relations crosscut the dichotomized worlds of sexual ideology (see also chapter 3). Masculinities are frequently culturally defined in tandem with corresponding femininities. In the present study, for example, the masculinity associated with fraternities was paired in the students' minds with the femininity associated with sororities. Tensions within the peer group were more between coed groups who favored different styles of attractiveness (each with its masculine and feminine versions) than between men and women per se. Men and women, in other words, teamed up to promote valued styles of attractiveness.[16] As argued by proponents such as Connell, struggles of this kind are important because they are a way not recognized by production theory in which fundamental change can come about in the system. Further, the present study suggests that these contestations may be an important means by which women think about and try to decide upon their futures. Several of the women in our study—exemplified by Cylene, Susan, and Sandy—personally internalized these struggles. They debated them as a way of making decisions about their future lives (see Chapter 11; see also Holland 1988b).

Again, further work is necessary to link the struggles over styles of attractiveness to structural aspects of society. Although at Bradford and SU attractiveness was negotiated between particular men and particular women in face-to-face interactions, also in play were hegemonic forms of attractiveness that advantaged some and disadvantaged others. What was the significance of these hegemonic forms for the struggles within the peer groups over forms of attractiveness? And to what extent do gender relations in peer groups and in the United States at large not only organize relations between men and women but also provide a powerful symbolic idiom—the idiom of attractiveness— that figures in struggles over the social position of the working class, racial minorities, and the elderly? To what extent do contested forms of masculinity and femininity within the peer group relate to, and at the same time possibly produce, new groups that would redefine the major societal divisions?

ON GROWING OLDER

The women in our study left college—some happily, some apprehensively—poised to begin their adult lives in a society in which their social and economic lot in life will continue to be profoundly affected by their sexual attractiveness to men. While in college, they had tended not to focus directly on the ultimate consequences of acquiescing to a system that pegs a woman's fate to her sexual attractiveness. Instead they had searched for and tried to create niches of safety from the sexual auction block. Few seemed to recognize that their vulnerability to evaluation by the criteria of the auction block could follow them—regardless of their willingness for it to do so—into their adult lives and into the workplace.

Despite their surface acquiescence, it could not be concluded that these young women passively acquiesced to male privilege and remained uninvolved in gender issues. In fact they were very active in trying to bypass the parts of the peer system of romance that they disliked and in trying to do the best they could for themselves within the perceived limits of their romantic relationships. They voiced various complaints, some quite radical, about the gender status quo. And they actively engaged, although indirectly, in the struggle between factions within the peer community over forms of feminine and masculine attractiveness. These struggles affected their choices and paths through college and their ultimate orientations toward their postcollegiate lives. The striking feature of the women's opposition is that most of their criticisms were made privately, not publicly; they opposed the system as individuals, not as members of a group. We witnessed a great deal of personal, socially unorganized, individual struggle and a great deal of creative work in order to produce individualized meaning systems to render the situation livable—for the time being.

What will happen in the future? One advantage of the kind of study we have done, and of the longitudinal view that we have taken, is that the likelihood of future change is obvious. When we saw the women regularly during the months of our research, they were constantly undergoing experiences that challenged their various understandings of their situation and made them reconsider their strategies. They were clearly going to encounter changing circumstances as time went on. We studied the women at an age when the appearance of most was probably the closest it would ever come to the hegemonic forms of attractiveness. The women's symbolic capital, their attractiveness, is likely to decline with age. What will happen as the years go by and they become less attractive? What will happen if they discover problems with depending on men for economic support? Linda evidently had no trouble in finding a new husband after her divorce from Donny, but what will happen if she and her second husband divorce when she is older and less attractive? What will happen to Paula and her children if her husband, whose career she is putting ahead of her own, dies or leaves her? And what of gender relations at the workplace? What will happen as the women discover that the sexual auction block extends into the workplace?

For now, a good portion of the women in our study seem to have acquiesced to the social structures of male privilege in the United States. Their future courses, however, are not predetermined. The women are channeled by their pasts, but their pasts have provided them with resources and understandings formed in the experiences that they have lived through. They will surely have their understandings challenged in the future, and they may well take actions different from the ones we have seen. Their stories are far from finished.

Appendix
Research Design and Methods

A three-semester period, from near the beginning of the informants' freshman year to the middle of their sophomore year, was chosen for intensive study of the twenty-three women in the ethnographic sample. During this time we expected the women to be getting accustomed to college coursework, to be choosing majors, and to be living virtually twenty-four hours a day with their peers. From the ethnographic study we hoped to find out which aspects of campus life were salient to them, which were problematic, and how the women on the two campuses differed.

The Ethnographic Interviews

Informants were formally interviewed nine times over the course of the three semesters. The interviews were designed with a "talking-diary" format that encouraged each woman to recount and discuss her experiences and concerns in her own terms. Similar open-ended questions were asked each time. First the woman was asked a general question about what had been going on in her life since the last interview. Then she was asked questions which focused her responses only by naming broad topical areas of interest in the study: college coursework, majors, activities, family, friends, and boyfriends. Questions took the form: "Tell me what's been happening in your thinking about your college coursework [activities, boyfriend, etc.] since the last time we talked." The interviewer pursued, probed, and asked for clarification of the informant's responses. Once the set of topics or areas had been covered, the interviewer asked about other subjects known to be of interest or relevant to a particular informant.

A second type of interview, the "life-history" interview, was conducted near the end of the study, in the middle of the women's sophomore year. As in the talking-diary interviews, the questions addressed broad topics and were open-ended. The first part of this interview asked the informant to recall everything she had ever thought about becoming as an adult, to describe any ways in which she had tried to learn more about her interests and any individuals who had helped her think about them, and to tell what had happened to her various ideas over time. The second part of the interview asked the informant to talk about her high-school friends and to make comparisons between her high-school friends and her friends at college. All of the talking-diary and life-history interviews were tape-recorded and transcribed.

The Ethnographic Observations

During the three-semester period, the researchers participated with the informants each month in a range of campus activities involving peers. The researchers wrote up their observations of these activities. Activities to participate in and observe were selected from the list of usual activities reported by each informant. Researchers were instructed to pay particular attention to behaviors and conversations that might reveal the women's attitudes toward school, their majors, their future plans, their friends, and their boyfriends.

Analysis

Analysis of the ethnographic cases involved reading and rereading the approximately two-hundred typed pages of fieldnotes and interview transcripts accumulated for each informant. We attempted to maintain an inductive appreciation of our data. On the basis of our initial readings of the data we categorized the women's college experiences into four types: schoolwork, romantic relationships, friendships, and family relationships. We then reread and coded the data into these specific categories and into several subcategories. Following the general procedures outlined by Spradley (1979, 1980) we searched for patterns within and across the categories.

THE SURVEY

The survey was developed from a preliminary analysis of the ethnographic data. In particular it was designed to test a multivariate model, a "continuation model," of women's likelihood of pursuing majors chosen by the middle of the sophomore year, with special attention to the influence of peers. The model (graphically presented in Holland and Eisenhart 1981:90) was derived from the ethnographic data and then translated into questions— 357 in all. The survey instrument included questions about the respondents' involvement in the kinds of campus activities described by the ethnographic sample, about peer groups, about social relationships, and about majors and coursework.

We drew a random sample from each university but excluded women who were participants in our ethnographic study. The final sample included 362 women (179 at Bradford and 183 at SU). The hypothesized factors yielded multiple correlation coefficients of .591 for Bradford and .676 for SU, both significant at the .0001 level (Holland and Eisenhart 1981). In this book we rely primarily on the ethnographic material, supplemented by the survey and by other materials where appropriate. For a fuller account of the survey data see Holland and Eisenhart (1981).

THE LANGUAGE (ETHNOSEMANTIC) AND CULTURAL STUDIES

The first of these studies, Study A, was designed as a means of discovering the shared implicit knowledge that female and male undergraduates at SU had about cross-gender relationships. The study, and additional ones along the same lines, were conducted by Holland between 1978 and 1983 and were not originally designed as part of the study that is the focus of this book. However, as the results were analyzed, it quickly became clear that the findings were convergent. Both studies were yielding comparable information about cultural interpretations of gender relations. We decided to subject both sets of interviews to the same sort of analysis as the interviews in Study B described below. For a more detailed discussion of the methods and the findings of the ethnosemantic work see Holland and Skinner (1987).

In Study A, after an initial elicitation of gender-marked terms from twenty-six female and sixteen male informants, comparable numbers of women and men (most of whom were attending SU) were asked to sort selected lists of the types of males and females. Women sorted the male types; men, female types. Then they were asked to describe the different types they had grouped together and to compare and contrast terms. Multidimensional scaling procedures were used to obtain a visual representation of the patterns of comparison and contrast in the terms and descriptions.

In Study B, five women from SU, three older women, and two older men, were each individually interviewed five times. Each was asked to tell about first and subsequent memories of one person, usually someone with whom the informant had had a relatively long relationship. After the informant gave an account in his or her own terms, the interviewer asked in-depth questions about the informant's impressions of and reasoning about the person, often requiring the informant to express explicitly information or beliefs about males and females that the informant might otherwise have taken for granted.

We found (as fully described in Holland and Skinner 1987) that the ethnosemantic analysis of gender-marked terms afforded by Study A was incomplete. When we joined the results of Study A with the in-depth interviews from Study B and the ethnographic interviews from the present study, we found that the meaning of the terms rests upon the cultural model of romantic relationships. The methods used for inferring cultural models from interview material are described in general in Quinn and Holland (1987) and for the cultural model of romantic relationships in particular in Holland and Skinner (1987).

THE FOLLOW-UP INTERVIEWS

In 1983, when members of the ethnographic sample should have been graduating from college, an attempt was made to recontact them by telephone to learn about their coursework, choices of major, friends, and career plans since 1981. In these interviews we probed particularly into their plans for work or continued study after college and for information about romantic relationships and their expected implications for the women's futures. In 1983 we were able to contact nineteen of the original twenty-three informants.

In 1987 we tried again to contact the original twenty-three women by phone. This time we wanted to learn what they had done after leaving college and what plans they had for the future. We were able to reach seventeen of the twenty-three (all of whom were among the nineteen contacted in 1983). Information on the graduation status of all the women was obtained from the universities in 1987.

The follow-up telephone interviews were collected by researchers who had not participated in the original study, although they were familiar with the

data from it. These researchers taped their conversations with the informants, and the tapes were transcribed. We ourselves were in the midst of
analyzing the ethnographic data and did not consult the follow-up data until
after the ethnographic analyses were complete. Thus we were not aware of
the close associations among the women's orientations to schoolwork, their
romantic experiences, and their occupational choices until long after the full
data were compiled. Although our ignorance of the follow-up data may have
limited useful feedback during the research process, it conversely had the
virtue of having served as an informal curb to bias toward the conclusions
presented here.

Notes

Chapter One

1. There is an enormous anthropological literature on schools and many school ethnographies. See the long list of case studies in the education and culture volumes edited by George and Louise Spindler. Edited anthologies include Roberts and Akinsanya (1976a, 1976b). The relevance of this literature to issues of social reproduction is described in chapters 2 and 3.

2. At the same time, John Ogbu, an anthropologist working in schools in the United States, was forcefully revealing the same dynamic interaction between the schools and black students (Ogbu 1974).

Chapter Two

1. For important contributions to the growing literature on critical, self-reflexive ethnography see, for example, Clifford and Marcus (1986), Clifford (1988), Marcus and Fischer (1986), and Crapanzano (1980).

2. Theories of cultural production and practice are the current reformulations of early social-reproduction theory. We describe them and their significant departures from social-reproduction theory in chapter 3.

3. Most of Holland's pre-1982 publications are listed under Clement.

4. Due to budget constraints, NIE would not fund us to follow a male sample. Recently Bradley Levinson—under Holland's direction—conducted a small study of male students at SU using a research design similar to the one reported here. If his sample is indicative, men may discuss their classes and majors more than women do, at least in school contexts (Levinson, personal communication, 1988). Some other research of Holland's (1988a) at SU also suggests some marked differences between male and female students' orientations to the university.

5. As used in local newspapers and in university publications, "historically black" indicates that the school was begun under segregation as a college for black students. A further implication is that the school is still predominantly or mostly attended by black students. "Historically white" is the corresponding term for colleges and universities for white students.

6. Readers who have neither spent years earning doctoral degrees nor spent hours each week preparing classes may find

our original view of students' interests naive, and our statement that the nature of student interests "still is hard to grasp," perplexing. For us in our roles as teachers, our findings raise troubling questions about the ways in which college education is organized in the United States, and needling doubts about the worth of our own work in providing college educations. It is tempting to go on as though our original assumptions were still intact and so avoid facing up to our questions and doubts.

7. In order to highlight the importance of the peer group—an importance that we think is inadequately recognized in the literature—we paint school authorities in simple strokes. We write as though school officials are always powerful mediators—agents and functionaries—of class and race structures and are unanimous in an oppressive stance toward working-class and racial minorities. Although school officials do in some sense always serve as functionaries of the system, the people who fill those jobs are usually neither powerful as individuals nor of a single mind in their treatment of the under-privileged. The literature is very clear on these points; Weiler's (1988) and Giroux's (1988) are but two recent books addressed to teachers' efforts to change the schools and thereby the society. Our portrayal also glosses over the fact that students differentiate between and among teachers. In our earlier study in the desegregated elementary school, we were daily aware that individual teachers had reputations among the students—both black and white—for being more or less prejudiced, and that student reactions to them varied according to how discriminatory they were perceived to be. Students, in other words, do not perceive or relate to school authorities as some undifferentiated, monolithic mass (see also Connell et al. 1982). In the present book we have left aside these more complex views of the role of school authorities in order to focus on the peer group. For the women in our study, the message of male privilege was more momentously delivered by peers, in the dorms, at parties, and on the streets, than it was by faculty and other administrators in the classroom and in advising sessions. The book is devoted to analyzing women's experiences of gender hierarchy in the peer group and to analyzing the shape of their responses to male privilege, as a function of that experience.

CHAPTER THREE

1. "Patriarchy" is used here to refer to a social system that privileges males over females. It does not refer to a characteristic of each and every individual male and female. As Connell (1983:44) puts it: "Though not all men oppress all women, it is still true that there is a general oppression of women by men. This is precisely the defining point of patriarchy. All women live and act in conditions shaped by the structural fact of men's supremacy, even those women, the Thatchers and Gandhis, who are very powerful indeed."

2. There are a number of excellent accounts of reproduction theory. Critical reviews include Willis (1981a, 1981b), Giroux (1983a), Connell (1983), Lakomski (1984), and Apple (1982), among others. Insightful summaries appear in MacLeod (1987), Valli (1986), and Weiler (1988).

3. Bourdieu has concerned himself with the reproduction of privilege in societies and not with capitalism per se.

4. In contrast to Bowles and Gintis, the radical education theorists just cited rejected economic reductionism and analyzed the schools as more or less autonomous sites of the reproduction of class divisions.

5. We are discussing limitations of such studies in explaining social reproduction. The studies contribute important information about aspects of social reproduction, but are not comprehensive. They are of considerable value for what they do reveal, including in some cases the in-the-classroom view missed by social-reproduction theorists. As Erickson (1987:341–51) argues, the approaches are complementary, not exclusionary. The continuing importance of work such as Heath's (1983) and Rist's (1973) cannot be denied.

6. For a more detailed yet concise overview of the streams within liberal formulations of education and the conservative formulations they oppose, see McCarthy and Apple (1988:11–16).

7. See Connell (1983: chapter 10) for a trenchant critique of role theory in general, and Kessler et al. (1985:34–35, 42–47) on sex-role theory in particular. Valli's (1986) critical remarks on socialization theory are similar.

8. See Giroux (1983a:266–74) for a detailed critique of Bourdieu. Giroux's telling criticisms of "habitus" are especially important given the enthusiasm with which that concept has been received in anthropology and other fields. See also MacDonald (1979–80:149–50) who, while appreciating many of Bourdieu's concepts, notes the difficulty of reconciling "habitus" and "resistance." Bourdieu (1977b:82–83) himself points out that revolutionary action depends upon "possession of a discourse capable of securing symbolic mastery of the practically mastered principles of the class habitus." Since "habitus" was developed by Bourdieu to counter what he considered a serious overemphasis on linguistic mediation, it deemphasizes discourse and thus the link to "revolutionary action." We do find some indications that Bourdieu (1977a) noted resistance among working-class boys against bourgeois school culture, for example, but his theoretical apparatus diverts attention from such opposition.

9. Certain American sociologists of education should be cited here as well. Good examples are Apple and Weis (1983), plus the full-length monographs of Weis (1985) and Valli (1986).

10. Ogbu was far from the first anthropologist to carry out ethnographic research in the schools or to notice student resistance. However, he was one of the first to explicitly relate what he was finding to the structural features of the society. A lively debate continues in the anthropological literature over the importance of structural features versus cultural differences in explaining poor school outcomes for minorities (see Clement 1978, Erickson 1987, Trueba 1988).

11. The reader should be advised that "production" theory is only one of the avenues of refinement and improvement that has been attempted regarding reproduction theory. Another avenue, for example, examines the contradictions within and between sectors of society, such as the school and the economic sectors. In Althusser's analyses the various sectors were assumed to be interrelated, but not interdetermining; hence contradictions between sectors would probably arise such that reproduction would not be smooth and mechanistic. Wolpe's later work pursued this possibility. As Weiler (1988:340) describes, Wolpe introduced complications into the picture of the reproduction of women's economic subordination by emphasizing the relative autonomy of the schools, which meant that contradictions would be apt to occur between the schools and the workplace—and result in tensions at the workplace. A similar idea constitutes the backbone of a recent study of the reproduction of the mostly female clerical labor force in the

United States (Valli 1986), which also emphasizes disparities between school and workplace. Presumably worker resistance stems in part from these contradictions.

Giroux (1983a) presents this emphasis on contradictions among sectors and two other streams of reproduction theory, the cultural-reproductive model and the hegemonic-state–reproductive model. He critiques all three as they were developed up to the early 1980s and finds them all in need of more attention to resistance. What he in the end calls "resistance theory" is closely akin to what we are describing here as "production theory."

12. Biological theories, which account for gender inequalities by recourse to inbuilt psychobiological differences between the sexes, are not considered social theories and hence are not addressed here.

13. Unfortunately for the newcomer to the literature, these theories are also referred to as "social-reproduction" theories. Whereas they relate more directly to biological reproduction, the social-reproduction theory discussed in the first part of the chapter, it will be recalled, refers to the recreation of class, gender, and race hierarchies and to the role of schools in that recreation (Arnot 1982:70).

14. Theories of schooling that consider class, gender, and race to be three irreducible dynamics are referred to as taking a "parallelist" position (McCarthy and Apple 1988:23).

15. In her talk Yanagisako suggested further that our tendency to define gender in relation to "sexual" activities may be culturally bound. Other ways of defining gender may exist that are not so closely tied to sexual intercourse. Discussants argued that the definition of "sexual" activities should certainly be expanded to permit the possibility that in other societies, especially ones where women bear many children, parturition, lactation, and other activities related to childbearing could well be the central activities constituting gender. Practices related to the treatment of bodily fluids such as semen are another possibility as well.

16. According to Wexler's (1987) critique of the "new sociology of education" in the United States, this shift in focus occurred before the theorists grasped the nature of postindustrial, postmodern societies. In such societies the important contest for control is in the arena of semiotic production, *not* economic production. As yet unenlightened by the poststructuralists, these education theorists, according to Wexler, have failed to recognize that the television-viewing room, the movie theater, and other places of encounter with mass discourse may be more important than classrooms when it comes to shaping the subjectivities of the next generation.

Wexler is right to insist on the importance of the mass-media texts that assault all of us, young and old, every day. However, his proposals for renovating critical educational theory may be unnecessarily drastic. For example, the British cultural studies associated with the CCCS, which Wexler virtually ignores, have included a focus on these texts all along. There is no need to reject all the theoretical work on cultural production to date, as Wexler would seem to have us do, in order to accommodate media-transmitted texts. As Johnson (1986, 1987), writing from the tradition of CCCS work, cogently argues, the insights derived from text-based studies and their emphasis on signifying practice are powerful indeed, but these texts are only one moment in a much more complex process of cultural production.

CHAPTER FOUR

1. For an insightful discussion of the feminist presence at CCCS and of the adoption of British cultural studies by U.S. feminist scholars, see Long (n.d.).

2. The reader should recall that we are discussing school-age populations and that the amount of research focused on girls' and young women's involvement in youth cultures is limited. Although the women's movement was under way outside these schools and among older women, no such campus group has as yet been ethnographically described.

3. As was described in chapter 3, not all, in fact, not even a majority, of working-class boys respond to society and to schooling according to this ideal type. We moved from production to practice theory precisely because production theory ignored internal differences between and among the groups of students in school. As will be seen, production theory is flawed for the same reason when it is applied to gender hierarchies and to women's response to schooling. In order to account for internal divisions in the study described here, as well as in other studies of gender and social reproduction, it has been necessary to go beyond production theory.

4. Sharpe's (1976) study, conducted around the same period with working-class London girls of roughly the same age, revealed patterns similar to those found by McRobbie. Her study was a survey and was not placed in the context of what we are calling production theory (see also McRobbie 1980).

5. This study, which is cited extensively below, drew girls from three schools. One of the schools was attended by a large number of ethnically different students; another was attended by white working-class students; the third was a girls-only school attended by white middle-class girls. The researchers interviewed and carried out group discussions with approximately one hundred girls.

6. There is some ambiguity in the description that Lees (1986:68–69) gives of the girls' friends who were boys. In the last sentence of the section it is left unclear whether none of the entire set of girls mentioned a boy by name when asked who their friends were, or whether "none" refers only to the set of girls who "had little or no contact with boys."

7. In our two-year ethnographic study of fifth- and sixth-graders in a desegregated elementary school in the city of Bradford (the site of one of the universities described in the present study) we described the students as participating in a peer culture constituted by both boys and girls, even though the friendship patterns were heavily skewed to same-sex friendships. The peer culture was described as involving both boys and girls because the cross-gender contacts as well as themes of male/female interaction (e.g., romantic engagements, sexual activities) were very important in the culture. We also analyzed the peer groups as responding to the age hierarchy—created by the school's rigid age segregation—they encountered in the school (Eisenhart and Holland 1983).

8. This chapter addresses women's *response* to schooling. References to work on school ideology and gender—ideas about gender-specific abilities, eligibilities, and futures put forth in the formal agenda and practices of the school—are given in chapter 3, especially in the section titled "Social-Reproduction Theories of Gender."

9. It is unclear, however, that this behavior constitutes resistance to gender hierarchies or is rather part of a larger peer-group defiance of school-

mediated age hierarchies. Sexual behaviors were important in the peer cultures we studied in the fifth and sixth grades; we argued that peer cultures form in part in response to the age hierarchy that the students face (see Eisenhart and Holland 1983). The school defines students as children (nonadults) and denies them markers of adult status, yet constantly communicates that older students have more prestige and privilege. Aping adult sexuality is one way to act out opposition to the school's position. Willis (1981b:15–18) makes a similar argument regarding the lads' emphasis on their sexuality and sexual prowess vis-a-vis the Hammertown teachers. School social relations are based on asymmetrical relationships partially related to age differences. Acting out sexuality—defined as the privilege of adults—defies that asymmetry.

10. Lambart (1979:158–59), in her study of a grammar school for girls, also found antischool behavior among the members of "Sisterhood," a group of girls in their third year. The girls broke school rules, used parts of their school uniforms for playful purposes, and sometimes acted disrespectfully to teachers. Lambart does not associate this behavior with resistance to gender oppression, but rather attributes it to competition over academic standing fostered by the school: "In conclusion, it should be stressed that, despite its deviance, the Sisterhood existed as a focus for girls with more than average ability. This feature can be added to its members' characteristic mischief and inherent disrespect for teachers. These may, indeed, have been a function of what some members of the Sisterhood probably considered relative failure."

11. Although the point was not fully developed theoretically by Fuller (1983), the Afro-Caribbean women frequently contrasted their styles in school with those of their male compatriots. Arnot (1982:78) has suggested the possibility that young women, at least those of the working class, celebrate their femininity through a "rejection of male culture which stresses the value of hierarchies . . . , objective over subjective knowledge, and individual competition over cooperation." While Fuller's young women did not endorse these particular values, they did reject male values and styles of knowing and succeeding. This suggestion of Arnot's about young women's response to schooling should be followed up to a greater extent than it has been. Although we did not find such an emphasis, Luttrell (1989, n.d.) did. Her study focused on older women returning to school.

12. This idea seems closely related to the popular idea that women try to escape work by getting married. In our studies we heard female as well as male students say that many female students come to college to find husbands.

13. Wilson (1978) describes a similar system of gender relations in the peer culture of a group of 13- to 15-year-old girls. In their world—they participated in a "delinquent" subculture—the label of opprobrium was "lay," not "slag." Most of them described themselves as "one-man girls." They interpreted their sexual relations with their boyfriends within the ideology of romance and the intention of marriage. Unlike the girls Lees describes, they had a term, "easy boys," for boys who went with many girls and thus could spoil a girl's reputation.

14. Weis (1988), in a 1985–86 study in a U.S. high school, also found critical attitudes toward marriage among female students. However, she attributes their views to shifts in the economy that have rendered working-class males less employable.

15. Here we begin to see the power of production theory over reproduction

theory. Deem (1978), who described the structure of the schools as helping to reproduce the gender status quo, depicted the schools not as actively restricting women to the courses they were taking, but as providing training that reproduced women's position, fostering a climate that promoted the traditional sexual division of labor and benignly looking on while women made decisions that would confine them to traditional women's work both at home and in the labor force. Deem was limited in where she could turn to explain these "choices." Willis's point about the sexism of the lads presages the more extensive argument to this effect by Lees. The present study tells a similar story, although the sexism of the university peer groups is much less overtly virulent than that of the groups described by Willis and Lees.

16. In contrast, the working-class high-school girls in McRobbie's (1978b: 100) and Lee's (1986:131–33) studies were doing twelve to sixteen hours of domestic labor at home per week.

CHAPTER FIVE

1. All proper names used in reference to the study are pseudonyms. We have further attempted to conceal the identity of the participants in the study by changing some of the details of their activities. Our aim is that the individual women should not be recognizable even to friends who knew them during the period of the study.

2. Given NIE's focus, the ethnographic study was originally designed to focus particularly on women who were interested in careers involving math or science.

3. Our ability to discover what was distinctive about women's experiences at college would have been enhanced by the inclusion of male comparison groups. Unfortunately, NIE was unwilling to fund the male component of our college study. Recently (1987–88) Bradley Levinson has undertaken a roughly parallel study of a small number of freshmen men at SU.

4. In reviewing choice of major among the students who volunteered for the study, we discovered differences in the distribution of math and science majors on the two campuses. A significant number of the SU volunteers named "pure" math or science majors, whereas none of the Bradford volunteers did. In contrast, many more Bradford than SU volunteers named business and therapeutic fields (which might be categorized as "applied" math or science). This situation led us to distinguish "pure" from "applied" math or science fields and to select women with somewhat different majors as representative of the math and science group on each campus. The SU sample included several pure math or science majors, whereas the Bradford sample included only applied math or science majors. (Table 3 includes a list of the entering majors of the women in the ethnographic sample.)

CHAPTER SIX

1. By "gender relations" we refer to relationships and interactions between males and females that have to do with sexualities and sexual activities, including intercourse. Although "sexual relations" has been used as the appropriate label in some of the literature, we will refrain for now from using that term because it is popularly used in the United States to refer to only a very limited aspect of gender relations, sexual intercourse.

2. SU was one of the schools Horowitz studied. Unfortunately, she did not

include any historically black colleges in her sample. Thus, while her work was especially helpful for SU, it was of more limited relevance to Bradford.

3. Moffatt (1989:50–53) makes a cogent critique of Horowitz's account of recent changes in campus culture. He argues that campus forms are now less distinctive than they were in earlier periods, that campus culture now has much in common with a widespread youth culture. The form of gender relations we saw at Bradford and SU, while exhibiting a continuity with past college cultures, may thus be characteristic for youth groups outside of college as well.

4. American colleges and universities began to designate courses as women's studies courses beginning in 1970. By the mid-1970s, when SU established its program, women's studies had emerged as a distinctive and integrated field with its own journals (Hunter College Women's Studies Collective 1983:5–6).

CHAPTER SEVEN

1. Some of the material in this section was originally published in an article by Dorothy Holland and Debra Skinner, "Prestige and Intimacy: The Cultural Models behind Americans' Talk about Gender Types," in *Cultural Models in Language and Thought,* edited by Dorothy C. Holland and Naomi Quinn (Cambridge: Cambridge University Press, 1987). The segments are reprinted with the permission of the publisher.

2. "Attractiveness" is polysemous, and its meanings are interrelated. For a clear exposition of another such term and its relationship to a cultural model, see Quinn's (1982) analysis of "commitment" in Americans' cultural model of marriage.

3. Although some of the past literature has suggested that men have derogatory terms for women, but not the reverse, our research found that women have just as many negative names for men as men have for women (see Holland and Skinner 1987).

4. In order to convey more of the women's *vulnerability* to men's assessment of their value in this sexual market, we prefer the metaphor of a "sexual auction."

5. The women appeared not to agree on the the amount and kind of sexual intimacy appropriate for different stages of a romantic relationship. Our impression of a lack of consensus among the women derived mainly from their allusions in the interviews to their own sexual experiences and activities and from differences among them in the interviews and observations in their criticisms of men and of other women. Given the original purposes and design of the study, we did not directly query the participants as to their sexual activities or their judgments as to what activities were appropriate when. Nor did the women spontaneously discuss their sexual activities to any great extent in the observations. The more important point is that sexual activities—whatever they are in particular—are given meaning by the system of gender relations. (See Moffatt 1989, for an ethnographic study in which students were queried, mostly through anonymous essays, about their sexual activities and attitudes. The method got around the students' discreetness about sex in public discussions and produced a great deal of research material. Unfortunately for our purposes, Moffatt is less explicit than we would like about the system of gender relations.)

6. Bradford women also concerned themselves with finding and attracting men, but they seemed to have less trouble. Their talk about searching for men did not have the same urgency as some of the SU women's talk.

7. According to Rothman's (1984) account of the history of "courtship" in America, the transition to "going steady" is no longer as clearly marked as it was in the past.

8. According to Rothman (1984), cohabitation has been added as an optional step preceding marriage. During the period of our ethnographic study, none of the women we interviewed considered full-time cohabitation.

9. Zetterberg's (1968) essay on the "secret ranking" suggests a somewhat similar ranking system for American society in general. Several of his examples come from work or office contexts.

10. Schur (1983:145–63) summarizes other research that comes to the same conclusion.

11. And, in fact, since these industries, in part, define beauty, they *can* make both women and men more attractive—if one has enough money. A hegemonic—socially ascendant—feminine attractiveness is presented through the media and, although Americans tend to talk as though attractiveness is inborn, in fact it is a lot easier to look like the the media's examples of beauty if one has money. While money certainly does not ensure that one will be perceived as attractive, it can help. Money can buy the appurtenances associated with being attractive, like well-made, stylish clothes, grooming aids, and even items like diamonds and furs that are thought of as gifts given by men to attractive women. Further, wealth enables one to avoid skin- and hair-damaging jobs, provides time to manicure one's nails, and permits the hiring of others to undergo the frazzling tasks of taking care of oneself and one's possessions. More extensive changes, such as cosmetic surgery, are available to the wealthy but not the poor (see also Haug 1986).

12. Given the focus of our study, we can only make suggestions as to the possible relationship between ideals of attractiveness found at Bradford and SU and ideals of attractiveness ascendant in the society at large. Although addressing a broader topic than attractiveness, Connell's (1987:183–90) discussion of forms of masculinity and femininity that are hegemonic (or, in the case of femininities, "emphasized") at the level of the society as a whole is very useful. He reviews literature on the topic, gives a brief but helpful explanation of Gramsci's use of the term "hegemony," and lists common misunderstandings of the concept, including the mistaken idea that hegemony implies "total cultural dominance, the obliteration of alternatives" (p. 184; see also Scott's 1985 reformulation of the concept). We do not wish to be understood as claiming that there is a single form of feminine attractiveness that totally dominates in the United States, with no contest from minority groups and no alternative cultural forms.

13. Consistent with the argument we are making here, Lees (1986) found that the only way a London girl could redeem herself from the category of "slag" was to get a steady boyfriend.

14. Social-psychological research finds similar patterns of gender-differentiated forms of attractiveness around the country (Patzer 1985). Berscheid, Dion, Walster, and Walster (1971), for example, monitored the dating activities of a sample of men and women of college age over a year's time. They found that for women physical attractiveness was a much better predictor of

dating experience than for men. For women the coefficient of correlation between physical attractiveness and dating was .61; for men, only .25.

Patzer (1985) summarizes a great deal of the social-psychological research carried out in the United States on physical attractiveness. Most of the research has been limited by the presumption that attractiveness is an essential characteristic of an individual (and not a function of how one is treated by others) and by a disinterest in the broader cultural meaning systems in which attractiveness is important. Despite these serious limitations, many of the studies, such as the one by Berscheid et al., can be readily linked to the cultural model of romance and the other aspects of gender relations we found at Bradford and SU.

15. Weyr's novel *Pretty Girls* (1988) conveys a sense of the lives of college women that is in accord with our findings. The novel, which is set in a predominantly white Southern university, dramatizes the importance of attractiveness and the role of men as its arbitrators.

16. In women's eyes, these are the "jerks," "nerds," and "assholes." Not only are they unattractive, they are too insensitive to tell when women do not like them. They are hard to get rid of.

17. Lees (1986) blames the different demands on female sexuality for women's "misinterpretation" of sexual desire as romantic love. She argues that the notion of "slag" is internalized, so that women cannot admit simple sexual attraction—that is, without love—even to themselves. Thus they "fall in love" many times.

18. Our cross-gender comparison in the present study is based on limited information, including Levinson's research (see note 4 to chapter 2) and our own research with men in the ethnosemantic studies.

CHAPTER EIGHT

1. Segments of this chapter were originally published in an article by Dorothy Holland and Margaret Eisenhart, "On the Absence of Women's Gangs in Two Southern Universities," in *Women in the South: Proceedings of the Southern Anthropological Society,* edited by Holly Mathews (Athens: University of Georgia Press, 1989). The segments are reprinted with the permission of the publisher.

2. In the setting studied by Schwartz and Merten, the valuing of this type was disputed by another group of girls who were mostly from working-class backgrounds and who were referred to as "hoods" by the sorority girls. They valued loyalty and sincerity more than the sorority girls did.

3. In these respects, relationships among women at Bradford were similar to those described by Lees (1986:72–73) among her informants in London.

4. Our informants were freshmen and then sophomores during the year-and-a-half period of the study. School policy at Bradford tended to discourage the Bradford women from joining sororities until their sophomore year. Although some of the women were interested in sororities, none joined during the study at Bradford or at SU. As a result we did not study sororities directly.

Sororities are organizations that could conceivably strengthen ties among and between women and serve to promote group opposition to patterns of male dominance. However, we received no indication that sororities fostered different sorts of alliances than those we found among nonsorority women. Sororities' reputations among the students were phrased in terms of the themes that were important on the respective campuses. At both universities there was an element of prestige attached to belonging to a sorority. Some of our Bradford informants thought of acceptance by a sorority as being "honorable"—as showing that one had respect. At SU, sororities were associated with elitism. Those who disliked sororities at SU referred to sorority girls as "snobby." SU sororities were talked about as bases for activities related to finding and maintaining romantic relationships, as were female friendships in general. Nonetheless, because our data are limited on the subject of sororities at Bradford and SU we cannot rule out the possibility that one or more of the campus sororities fostered more female solidarity for its own sake than we found among the women in our study.

CHAPTER NINE

1. Presumably Della would have been less upset if the man who admired her legs had been her age or a professor she considered a possible romantic partner. It is just this continuity with culturally acceptable gender relations that made the professor's behavior, a behavior that would be proscribed in many legal codes as "sexual harrassment," so upsetting to Della. He disregarded her feelings and so belittled her. He also laid bare her vulnerability to evaluation on the sexual auction block, no matter whether she cared to be so assessed or not.

2. The women in fact varied in terms of their practical knowledge and expertise in the conduct of romantic relationships. They varied in the degree to which they identified with the world of romance and the extent to which they had formed an identity of themselves as a romantic type. For a more theoretical discussion of the formation of romantic identity and motivation, see Holland (n.d.) and Holland, Cain, Prillaman, and Skinner (n.d.). Both make explicit an underlying neo-Vygotskian approach.

3. See also Holland and Eisenhart (1988a) for an analysis of the women's discontents with and solutions to problems with romantic relationships.

CHAPTER TEN

1. Sandy was from the Northeast. The discrepancies she described between valued styles of femininity in her hometown and at SU are a reminder of regional differences in peer cultures in the United States.

2. There is some comparative material on involvement in the women's movement from a different region of the country. Mirra Komarovsky (1985) conducted a study at an elite women's college in the Northeast during the same period as our study. The official policy of the school was feminist. While our group tended to come from towns and small cities in the South, hers tended to be from northeastern urban and cosmopolitan backgrounds. Nonetheless, the proportion of college women Komarovsky reports as being involved in the movement—even in the more likely population of her study— was relatively low. Only 13 percent of the entering freshman class and 26 percent of the senior class said they felt a need to engage in collective action to improve the status of women (p. 122). Although difficult to compare with our study because of the use of different methods and different forms of analyses, these findings and others from Komarovsky's study indicate that more, but not a great deal more, of her respondents than ours were inclined to interpret relationships with men in a way that would challenge patriarchy. Evidently regional differences, or at least differences attributable to feminist

school policy or urban background, did exist at the time of the studies, but they were perhaps not as large as might have been expected.

Another source for comparison is Moffatt (1989). Although not focused on women's perspectives, Moffatt, in his participant-observation study of college life at Rutgers University in the mid 1980s, found little involvement with the women's movement. The undergraduate women, he reports, sometimes implied that feminist and other political critiques of gender inequality sounded dated to them: "In my two years in the dorms, I never heard an undergraduate woman spontaneously complain that she had been subjected to sexism by her professors or by other college authorities—and most women when I ask them about it directly, said such things had never happened to them. In the opinion of most female undergraduates in the dorms, apparently, the political battles for the equality of the sexes had largely been won" (p. 49). Moffatt also points out (pp. 223–29) that in their comments on sexuality women undergradates showed little feminist influence.

CHAPTER ELEVEN

1. See Holland and Skinner (1987) for further descriptions and analysis of this armamentarium of insults.

2. Although an exact picture is difficult to outline from her interview material as presented, Lees (1986:133) alludes to a class distinction that intersected with the "slag" and "drag" ways of being a girl. A "scrubber," for example, was a slag who was dirty and presumably lower class. A "tart" had a higher class standing. Lees (1986:136) quotes Christine Keeler—the call girl involved in the Profumo scandal—as being upset with her biographer for referring to her as a "scrubber" rather than as a "tart." Keeler felt that she had always had some class and that Jack Profumo would not have gone out with a scrubber.

3. Antisorority feeling was less marked at Bradford, or at least there was less negative talk there about sorority women. Bradford's school policies, unlike SU's, tended to make it difficult if not impossible for freshmen women to join sororities.

4. In *School Daze* (Columbia Pictures, 1988) a student struggle at a black college over gender relations and attractiveness is explicitly presented. The "Wannabees" (girlfriends of the campus fraternity men, who dress, act, and style their hair as "white" as possible) actually confront the "Jigaboos" (girlfriends of the political activists, who dress, act, and style their hair in black, Afro-American modes)—in a beauty shop (Wallace 1988). The film adroitly satirizes gender relations within the two groups, making it clear that different canons of attractiveness accompany different notions of proper gender relations. The film's plot revolves around a campus struggle over which style has greater value.

5. For an example of methods better suited to the study of group processes involved in internal divisions among college students, see Moffatt (1989), especially chapter 3. Eckert (1989) provides a comprehensive account of the emergence of two major divisions—the "jocks" and the "burnouts"—within a Detroit high school.

6. Weyr's novel *Pretty Girls* (1988) includes an interesting use of one of these terms. The three women friends in the book refer to themselves as the

"Amazon Club." They are critical of their male friends who don't date "Amazons."

7. Homosexual styles were an exception to this pattern of pairing masculinities and femininities as companion parts.

8. The universities did, in fact, cooperate with (and for some activities, allocated funds and personnel to) the Greek fraternity and sorority system, athletic programs, Homecoming, and to other activities that supported and favorably publicized some forms of masculinities and femininities (see also Coleman 1961, Eder and Parker 1987, Kessler et al. 1985). Further issues of sexual orientation no doubt came up in some of the women's classes; professors in their role as authorities can relay particular interpretations of homosexuals, for example. Nonetheless, in the eyes of the women in our study, the proponents of styles of attractiveness were students.

9. The media is a potential target of opposition, in that it definitely promotes forms of feminine attractiveness that are biased toward some groups—e.g., whites—and not others. As pointed out in note 12 to chapter 7, our study design did not address such questions. The few indications that we do have suggest that opposition is played out among emergent groups with their various appropriations and modifications of media forms, rather than aimed directly at the media itself.

CHAPTER TWELVE

1. Segments of this chapter were originally published in an article by Dorothy Holland and Margaret Eisenhart, "Women's Ways of Going to School: Cultural Reproduction of Women's Identities as Workers," in *Class, Race, and Gender in U.S. Education,* edited by Lois Weis (Buffalo: State University of New York Press, 1988). The segments are reprinted with the permission of the publisher.

2. In the terminology of cognitive anthropology these cultural interpretations are much like the "cultural models" described in Holland and Quinn (1987; see also Holy and Stuchlik 1981). The three interpretations were understandings of school and schoolwork that the women had learned from others, much as they had learned the cultural model of romance from others. The three interpretations were identified using the same methods of discourse analysis described in Quinn and Holland (1987) for the uncovering of cultural models. We refrain here from calling them "cultural models" because they seem to be portions of more encompassing models that subsume schoolwork, such as models of success or perhaps of survival. Additional analysis would be necessary to identify the larger models.

3. We use the term "getting over" to mean the process of completing something that consists of a challenging set of hurdles or obstacles. The term itself was used by the Bradford women in our study, and the contexts of its use suggested this meaning to us.

4. The observant reader will notice that our discussion of the women's orientations to schoolwork has accounted for 22 of the 23 women in our ethnographic study. The orientation of the last woman was considered an exception—a very telling one. Her situation will be described in chapter 13.

5. Table 3, which shows changes in college majors, implies only three changes in the "learning from experts" group. Stephanie, the fourth change counted in the text, changed her major within the category listed in the table.

CHAPTER 13

1. All three of these women were pursuing careers, but only two—Maureen and Natalie—had maintained a strong worker identity. Lisa, although categorized as an exception in her interpretation of schoolwork and so not part of the seventeen discussed in this section, showed a pattern similar to Linda's.

2. We use the term "traditional" to refer loosely to the general pattern of female preference for and choice of certain college majors, occupations, and other adult activities. Correspondingly, "nontraditional" is applied to majors, occupations, and other activities conventionally associated with men and usually considered to be higher-status, more lucrative, and more career-oriented than those associated with women.

3. The reader should recall that we surveyed random samples of *sophomore* women.

4. As summarized earlier, the ethnographic and survey samples both revealed a preponderance of the "doing well" orientation at SU and of the "getting over" orientation at Bradford. If the processes revealed by the ethnographic data can be generalized—and the survey results give some assurance that they can—this marginalization is the predominant pattern.

5. Perhaps some at Bradford were beginning to give up on these hopes. A number of the Bradford women with the "getting over" interpretation mentioned when we talked in 1987 their interest in returning to school as a means of improving their earning potential, but none had yet done so.

CHAPTER FOURTEEN

1. Valli's findings become more understandable when viewed as an extension into the workplace of the cultural model of romantic relationships and its implications for gender relations. Women who are judged attractive, and act accordingly, can expect good treatment from men; those who are judged to be unattractive, or who act in unattractive ways, should not expect very good treatment. The message of the office-education program and the workplace situation is that occupational rewards come to women for being physically attractive and not primarily from other contributions they might make.

CHAPTER FIFTEEN

1. " 'Cause I'm a Blonde" is from Brown's album *Goddess in Progress*. Other songs on the album, especially "I Like 'em Big and Stupid" and "The Homecoming Queen's Got a Gun," also draw delightfully on the way in which gender relations are construed in the United States.

2. This perspective is not dissimilar from an analysis given by Brake (1980: 139). He identifies sexual attractiveness as women's main social source of power in most male-dominated workplaces, although he is careful to point out that the power is "illusory" in a material sense.

3. The latter option may often be the one taken. Hochschild (1983:256) gives a succinct summary of research findings on U.S. marriage patterns: "Men tend to marry down, i.e., marry women with less education and lower occupational status, while women marry men they can 'look up to'—and through whom they are structurally mobile."

4. Emergent groups have the potential for coalescing into more formal groups. On occasion in the past—for example, in the 1960s—they have done so on the two campuses. During the course of our study, however, no such event occurred.

5. Now, ten years later, Bradford and SU students have probably incorporated ideas from the women's movement and possibly from groups opposing the women's movement. It would be instructive indeed to know how the discourse has been appropriated and the extent to which it has fostered the sharing of criticisms and concerns about the treatment of women on campus and in the larger society. (For some comparative material on involvement of university women in the women's movement on other campuses during the period of the study, see chapter 10.)

6. The system of attractiveness did have some elements more comparable to the French educational system than the system of honor in Kabylia. Although there was no credentialing system for attractiveness comparable to educational credentialing in France, in both cases the valued styles of comportment were promoted by powerful institutions: educational capital by the French schools, standards of attractiveness by the American public media. No agency existed to certify how attractive a young woman was, but the cosmetic and fashion industries daily worked hard to remind the students at Bradford and SU (as well as other Americans) of accepted standards of beauty and how they might be achieved. See Haug (1986: esp. 72–78) for an analysis of how such "commodity aesthetics" operate.

7. Perhaps Bourdieu was sensitive to indications of dissent when he was doing his field work, but found none to report. We doubt, however, that he would have focused on dissent. His theoretical work in the 1970s, at least before *Distinction,* seemed to assume mostly inert recipients of the dominant order, and his concept of "habitus" leaves little room for individual dissent (see also Bloch 1985:32).

8. Fordham and Ogbu (1986) traced out the relationship of individual students to the dominant peer culture in a Washington, D. C., high school. All the students had to cope with "the burden of acting white," a problem generated by the definition and derogation of "acting white" in the peer culture. In response to white privilege in the society, the peer culture had elaborated an oppositional stance, but it was no more totally successful than the school in defining the individual black students. The peer culture maintained the system that favored acting black instead of white in a face-to-face, personal manner. See also Fuller's (1983) account of a related pattern in British schools.

9. See McCarthy and Apple (1988:24) for a critique of this metaphor of "linear additions."

10. As we have argued elsewhere (Holland and Eisenhart 1988b), although the differences in two of the cultural interpretations ("getting over" and "doing well") did not result in a difference in the maintenance of a worker identity for the women, it would be a mistake to forget them. These interpretations, if maintained, might be important in later life. Women with the "doing well" interpretation, for example, are likely to have different concerns when it comes to the education of their children than women with the "getting over" interpretation.

11. There were no struggles over race-related forms of attractiveness that we noted. The campuses in our study were relatively homogeneous racially; SU had a small percentage of black students, and Bradford a small percentage of white students. The study took place long after the active period of the black movement at SU during the 1960s and early 1970s and preceded the wave of racial incidents that began to be reported in the later 1980s from

the University of Michigan, Dartmouth, the University of Massachusetts at Amherst, and elsewhere. No issues of attractiveness between black and white students engaged the attention of the women in our study at the time.

12. There have been many rich studies of women's groups in contexts other than schools (see Bookman and Morgen 1988; Ginsburg 1989).

13. See Hebdige (1979:61–62, 88–89) for a discussion of a possible exception, the Bowie-ites. Their style of dress and demeanor at a symbolic level disrupted the taken-for-grantedness of gender identities. See also Brake (1980:149).

14. At one point in his analysis Brake (1980:152) summarizes what middle-class men do when they become disappointed with their lives in the competitive structures of education and career. When their identity and status desires are not fulfilled by their careers, they turn to the identity provided by their families. This pattern is reminiscent of the pattern we found for SU women with the "doing well" interpretation: when they encountered difficulty in the education structure, they invested more of themselves in gender relations.

15. Brake goes on to suggest that young women and girls have difficulties in organizing to challenge male privilege in the youth groups in which they participate because they have few nonsexist cultural resources to draw upon, from their families or communities or popular, mass-media culture. In his estimation, "changes in girls' attitudes will [have to] come from the influence of an older age group, and through the medium of feminism" (1980:154).

16. A related issue concerns the degree to which the budgets and policies of schools support—although indirectly—some forms of masculinity/femininity in the peer culture, but not others. In his study of adolescent societies in high schools Coleman (1961) pointed out the effects of school-supported athletic teams and contests, for example, in shaping peer cultures (see also Kessler et al. 1985). Moffatt (1989:37–40) discusses a more general point. He argues that college support for, and therefore increased control over, extracurricular activities has reduced the areas in which students can practice a collective autonomy.

References

Acker, S.
    1981 No Woman's Land: British Sociology of Education, 1960–1979. *Sociological Review* 29(1):77–104.

Althusser, L.
    1971 Ideology and Ideological State Apparatuses. In *Lenin and Philosophy and Other Essays,* 127–86. London: New Left Books.

Anyon, J.
    1981 Social Class and School Knowledge. *Curriculum Inquiry* 11(1): 3–41.
    1983 Intersections of Gender and Class: Accommodation and Resistance in Gender and Gender Development. In *Gender, Class, and Education,* ed. S. Walker and L. Barton, 19–37. Barcombe, Lewes: Falmer Press.

Apple, Michael W.
    1978 The New Sociology of Education: Analyzing Cultural and Economic Reproduction. *Harvard Educational Review* 48, no. 4 (November):495–503.
    1979 *Ideology and Curriculum.* London: Routledge and Kegan Paul.

Apple, Michael W., ed.
    1982 *Cultural and Economic Reproduction in Education: Essays on Class, Ideology, and the State.* London: Routledge and Kegan Paul.

Apple, Michael W., and Lois Weis, eds.
    1983 *Ideology and Practice in Schooling.* Philadelphia: Temple University Press.

Arnot, M.
    1982 Male Hegemony, Social Class and Women's Education. *Journal of Education* 164(1):64–89.
    1984 A Feminist Perspective on the Relationship between Family Life and School Life. *Journal of Education* 166(1):5–24.

Barrett, Michele
    1980 *Women's Oppression Today: Problems in Marxist Feminist Analysis.* London: Virago Press.

Bartky, Sandra Lee
    1982 Narcissism, Femininity and Alienation. *Social Theory and Practice* 8(2):127–43.

Beauvoir, Simone de
    1961 *The Second Sex.* New York: Bantam Books.

Becker, Howard S., Blanche Geer, and Everett C. Hughes
    1968 *Making the Grade: The Academic Side of College Life.* New York: John Wiley and Sons.

254   References

Bernstein, B.
    1971   *Class, Codes, and Control.* Vol. 3. 2d ed. London: Routledge and
            Kegan Paul.
    1980   Codes, Modalities and the Process of Cultural Reproduction: A
            Model. *Pedagogical Bulletin* no. 7. Lund, Sweden: Department of
            Education, University of Lund.
Berscheid, E., K. K. Dion, E. Walster, and G. W. Walster
    1971   Physical Attractiveness and Dating Choice: A Test of the Match-
            ing Hypothesis. *Journal of Experimental Social Psychology* 7:173–
            89.
Bloch, Maurice
    1985   From Cognition to Ideology. In *Power and Knowledge: Anthropo-
            logical and Social Approaches,* ed. Richard Fardon, 21–48. Edin-
            burgh: Scottish Academic Press.
Bookman, Ann, and Sandra Morgen, eds.
    1988   *Women and the Politics of Empowerment.* Philadelphia: Temple
            University Press.
Bourdieu, P.
    1977a The Economics of Linguistic Exchanges. *Social Science Informa-
            tion* 16(6):645–68.
    1977b *Outline of a Theory of Practice.* Trans. Richard Nice. Cambridge:
            Cambridge University Press.
    1984   *Distinction: A Social Critique of the Judgement of Taste.* Trans. Rich-
            ard Nice. Cambridge: Harvard University Press.
Bourdieu, P., and J. C. Passeron
    1977   *Reproduction in Education, Society and Culture.* Trans. Richard
            Nice. London: Sage.
Bourdieu, P., and M. de Saint-Martin
    1970   L'excellence scolaire et les valeurs du système d'enseignement
            français. *Annales* 1 (January-February): 147–75.
Bowles, S., and H. Gintis
    1976   *Schooling in Capitalist America: Educational Reform and the Contra-
            dictions of Economic Life.* New York: Basic Books.
Brake, Mike
    1980   *The Sociology of Youth Culture and Youth Subcultures: Sex and Drugs
            and Rock 'n' Roll?* London: Routledge and Kegan Paul.
Campbell, A.
    1984   *The Girls in the Gang: A Report from New York City.* Oxford: Basil
            Blackwell.
Capellanus, Andreas
    [c. 1180] *The Art of Courtly Love (Tractatus de Amore).* Trans. John Jay
            Parry, 1941. New York: Columbia University Press.
Clark, Burton R.
    1960   The "Cooling-out" Function in Higher Education. *American
            Journal of Sociology* 65(May):569–76.
Clark, Burton R., and Martin Trow
    1966   The Organizational Context. In *College Peer Groups: Problems and
            Prospects for Research,* ed. Theodore M. Newcomb and Everett K.
            Wilson, 17–70. Chicago: Aldine.

Clement, D. H.
    1978 Ethnographic Perspectives on Desegregated Schools. *Anthropology and Education Quarterly* 9(4):245–47.
Clement, D. H., M. Eisenhart, J. Harding, and J. M. Livesay
    1978 *Moving Closer: An Ethnography of a Southern Desegregated School.* Final report for the National Institute of Education. ERIC ED 161 969. Washington, D.C.
Clifford, James
    1988 *The Predicament of Culture: Twentieth-Century Ethnography, Literature and Art.* Cambridge: Harvard University Press.
Clifford, James, and George E. Marcus, eds.
    1986 *Writing Culture: The Poetics and the Politics of Ethnography.* Berkeley and Los Angeles: University of California Press.
Coleman, J.
    1961 *The Adolescent Society: The Social Life of the Teenager and Its Impact on Education.* New York: Free Press.
Coletta, Nat J.
    1976 Cross-Cultural Transactions in Ponapean Elementary Classrooms. *Journal of Research and Development in Education* 9(4):113–23.
Connell, R. W.
    1983 *Which Way is Up? Essays on Sex, Class and Culture.* Sydney: George Allen and Unwin.
    1987 *Gender and Power: Society, the Person and Sexual Politics.* Stanford: Stanford University Press.
Connell, R. W., D. J. Ashenden, S. Kessler, and G. W. Dowsett
    1982 *Making the Difference: Schools, Familes and Social Division.* Sydney: George Allen and Unwin.
Cowie, C., and S. Lees
    1981 Slags or Drags. *Feminist Review* 9:17–31.
Crapanzano, Vincent
    1980 *Tuhami: Portrait of a Moroccan.* Chicago: University of Chicago Press.
Daly, M.
    1978 *Gyn/Ecology: The Metaethics of Radical Feminism.* Boston: Beacon Press.
Davies, Lynn
    1979 Deadlier than the Male? Girls' Conformity and Deviance in School. In *Schools, Pupils and Deviance,* ed. L. Barton and R. Meighan. London: Nafferton Books.
    1983 Gender, Resistance and Power. In *Gender, Class and Education,* ed. Stephen Walker and Len Barton, 39–52. Barcombe, Lewes: Falmer Press.
Deem, Rosemary
    1978 *Women and Schooling.* London: Routledge and Kegan Paul.
Deem, Rosemary, ed.
    1980 *Schooling for Women's Work.* London: Routledge and Kegan Paul.
Delamont, Sara
    1980 *Sex Roles and the School.* London: Methuen.

Delphy, C.
    1977   *The Main Enemy: A Materialist Analysis of Women's Oppression.* London: Women's Research and Resources Centre.
Eckert, Penelope
    1989   *Jocks and Burnouts: Social Categories and Identity in the High School.* New York: Teachers College Press.
Eder, Donna, and Stephen Parker
    1987   The Cultural Production and Reproduction of Gender: The Effect of Extracurricular Activities on Peer-Group Culture. *Sociology of Education* 60(3):200–13.
Eisenhart, M. A., and D. C. Holland
    1983   Learning Gender from Peers: The Role of Peer Groups in the Cultural Transmission of Gender. *Human Organization* 42(4): 321–32.
    n.d.   Gender Constructs and Career Commitment: The Influence of Peer Culture on Women in College. In *The Cultural Construction of Gender,* ed. Tony Whitehead and Barbara Reid. Champaign: University of Illinois Press. In press.
Eisenstein, Z. R., ed.
    1979   *Capitalist Patriarchy and the Case for Socialist Feminism.* New York: Monthly Review Press.
Erickson, F.
    1987   Transformation and School Success: The Politics and Culture of Educational Achievement. *Anthropology and Education Quarterly* 18(4):335–56.
Farley, R.
    1984   *Blacks and Whites: Narrowing the Gap?* Cambridge: Harvard University Press.
Folb, E.
    1980   *Runnin' Down Some Lines: The Language and Culture of Black Teenagers.* Cambridge: Harvard University Press.
Fordham, Signithia, and John Ogbu
    1986   Black Students' School Success: Coping with the Burden of "Acting White." *The Urban Review* 18(3):176–206.
Fuller, M.
    1980   Black Girls in a London Comprehensive School. In *Schooling for Women's Work,* ed. Rosemary Deem, 52–65. London: Routledge and Kegan Paul.
    1983   Qualified Criticism, Critical Qualifications. In *Achievement and Inequality in Education,* ed. Jane Purvis and Margaret Hales, 124–41. London: Routledge and Kegan Paul.
Fussell, Paul
    1983   *Class: A Guide through the American Status System.* New York: Summit Books.
Gallimore, R., J. W. Boggs, and C. Jordan
    1974   *Culture, Behavior and Education: A Study of Hawaiian-Americans.* Sage Library of Social Research, no. 11. Beverly Hills: Sage.
Gaskell, Jane
    1985   Course Enrollment in the High School: The Perspective of Working-Class Females. *Sociology of Education* 58(1):48–59.

Gearing, F., T. Carroll, L. Richter, P. Grogan-Hurlick, A. Smith,
W. Hughes, B. A. Tindall, W. Precourt, and S. Topfer
    1979 Working Paper 6. In *Toward a Cultural Theory of Education and Schooling*, ed. F. Gearing and L. Sangree, 9–38. The Hague: Mouton.

Ginsburg, Faye D.
    1989 *Contested Lives: The Abortion Debate in an American Community.* Berkeley: University of California Press.

Giroux, H. A.
    1981 *Ideology, Culture and the Process of Schooling.* Philadelphia: Temple University Press.
    1983a Theories of Reproduction and Resistance in the New Sociology of Education: A Critical Analysis. *Harvard Educational Review* 53(3):257–93.
    1983b *Theory and Resistance in Education: A Pedagogy for the Opposition.* South Hadley, Mass.: Bergin and Garvey.
    1988 *Teachers as Intellectuals: Toward a Critical Pedagogy of Learning.* Granby, Mass.: Bergin and Garvey.

Gramsci, Antonio
    1971 *Selections from the Prison Notebooks of Antonio Gramsci.* Ed. and trans. Quintin Hoare and Geoffrey Nowell Smith. New York: International Publishers.

Griffin, C.
    1985 *Typical Girls? Young Women from Schools to the Job Market.* London: Routledge and Kegan Paul.

Hall, S., and T. Jefferson, eds.
    1976 *Resistance through Rituals: Youth Subcultures in Post-War Britain.* London: Hutchinson Press.

Hartmann, H. L.
    1979 The Unhappy Marriage of Marxism and Feminism: Towards a More Progressive Union. *Capital and Class* 8:1–33.

Haug, Wolfgang Fritz
    1986 *Critique of Commodity Aesthetics: Appearance, Sexuality and Advertising in Capitalist Society.* Trans. Robert Bock. Minneapolis: University of Minnesota Press.

Hawthorn, Geoffrey
    1987 *Enlightenment and Despair: A History of Social Theory.* 2d ed. Cambridge: Cambridge University Press.

Heath, S. B.
    1983 *Ways with Words: Language, Life, and Work in Communities and Classrooms.* Cambridge: Cambridge University Press.

Hebdige, D.
    1979 *Subcultures: The Meaning of Style.* London: Methuen.

Heer, Friedrich
    1962 *The Medieval World: Europe, 1100–1350.* Trans. Janet Sondheimer. New York: The New American Library.

Henriques, J., W. Holloway, C. Urwin, C. Venn, and V. Walkerdine
    1984 *Changing the Subject: Psychology, Social Regulation and Subjectivity.* London: Methuen.

Henry, Jules
    1963 *Culture against Man.* New York: Random House.
Hill, Jane H.
    1985 The Grammar of Consciousness and the Consciousness of
           Grammar. *American Ethnologist* 12(4):725–37.
Hill, Jane H., and Kenneth C. Hill
    1980 Mixed Grammar, Purist Grammar, and Language Attitudes in
           Modern Nahuatl. *Language in Society* 9(3):321–48.
Hochschild, Arlie Russell
    1983 Attending to, Codifying, and Managing Feelings: Sex Differ-
           ences in Love. In *Feminist Frontiers: Rethinking Sex, Gender and
           Society,* ed. Laurel Richardson and Vesta Taylor, 250–62. Read-
           ing, Mass.: Addison-Wesley.
Holland, D. C.
    1988a Culture Sharing across Gender Lines: An Interactionist Correc-
           tive to the Status-Centered Model of Culture Sharing. *American
           Behavioral Scientist* 31(2):219–34.
    1988b In the Voice of, in the Image of: Socially Situated Presentations
           of Attractiveness. *IPrA Papers in Pragmatics* 2:106–35.
    n.d.   How Cultural Systems Become Desire: A Case Study of Amer-
           ican Romance. In *Cultural Models and Motivation,* ed. Roy D'An-
           drade and Claudia Strauss. Cambridge: Cambridge University
           Press. Forthcoming.
Holland, D. C., C. Cain, R. Prillaman, and D. Skinner
    n.d.   Symbols and the Formation of Social Selves. In preparation.
Holland, D. C., and M. A. Eisenhart
    1981 *Women's Peer Groups and Choice of Career.* Final report for the
           National Institute of Education. ERIC ED 199 328. Washington,
           D.C.
    1988a Moments of Discontent: University Women and the Gender
           Status Quo. *Anthropology and Education Quarterly* 19(2):115–
           38.
    1988b Women's Ways of Going to School: Cultural Reproduction of
           Women's Identities as Workers. In *Class, Race, and Gender in
           American Education,* ed. Lois Weis, 266–301. Albany: State Uni-
           versity of New York Press.
    1989 On the Absence of Women's Gangs in Two Southern Univer-
           sities. In *Women in the South: An Anthropological Perspective,*
           ed. Holly Mathews, 27–46. Athens: University of Georgia
           Press.
Holland, D. C., and N. Quinn, eds.
    1987 *Cultural Models in Language and Thought.* Cambridge: Cambridge
           University Press.
Holland, D. C., and D. Skinner
    1983 Themes in American Cultural Models of Gender. *Social Science
           Newsletter* 68(3):49–60.
    1987 Prestige and Intimacy: The Cultural Models behind Americans'
           Talk about Gender Types. In *Cultural Models in Language and
           Thought,* ed. D. C. Holland and N. Quinn, 78–111. Cambridge:
           Cambridge University Press.

Holy, L., and M. Stuchlik, eds.
    1981 The Structure of Folk Models. In *The Structure of Folk Models,*
          ASA Monograph 20, 1–35. London: Academic Press.
Horowitz, H.
    1987 *Campus Life: Undergraduate Cultures from the End of the Eighteenth
          Century to the Present.* New York: A. A. Knopf.
Hunter College Women's Studies Collective
    1983 *Women's Realities, Women's Choices: An Introduction to Women's
          Studies.* New York: Oxford University Press.
Jenkins, R.
    1983 *Lads, Citizens, and Ordinary Kids: Working-Class Lifestyles in Belfast.*
          London: Routledge and Kegan Paul.
Johnson, Richard
    1986–87 What is Cultural Studies Anyway? *Social Text: Theory, Culture,
          Ideology* 16(Winter):38–80.
Kelly, Amy
    1937 Eleanor of Aquitaine and Her Courts of Love. *Speculum* 12:
          3–19.
Kelly, G. P., and A. Nihlen
    1982 Schooling and the Reproduction of Patriarchy: Unequal Work-
          loads, Unequal Rewards. In *Cultural and Economic Reproduc-
          tion in American Education: Essays in Class, Ideology and the
          State,* ed. M. Apple, 162–80. Boston: Routledge and Kegan
          Paul.
Kessler, S., D. J. Ashenden, R. W. Connell, and G. W. Dowsett
    1985 Gender Relations in Secondary Schooling. *Sociology of Education*
          58(1):34–48.
Komarovsky, M.
    1985 *Women in College: Shaping New Feminine Identities.* New York:
          Basic Books.
Labov, William
    1972 On the Mechanism of Linguistic Change. In *Directions in Socio-
          linguistics: The Ethnography of Communication,* ed. John J. Gum-
          perz and Dell Hymes, 512–38. New York: Holt, Rinehart and
          Winston.
Lacey, Colin
    1970 *Hightown Grammar: The School as a Social System.* Manchester:
          Manchester University Press.
    1977 *The Socialization of Teachers.* London: Methuen.
Lakoff, Robin Tomach, and Raquel L. Scherr
    1984 *Face Value: The Politics of Beauty.* Boston: Routledge and Kegan
          Paul.
Lakomski, G.
    1984 On Agency and Structure: Pierre Bourdieu and Jean-Claude
          Passeron's Theory of Symbolic Violence. *Curriculum Inquiry* 14
          (2):151–63.
Lambart, Audrey M.
    1979 The Sisterhood. In *The Process of Schooling: A Sociological Reader,*
          ed. Martyn Hammersley and Peter Woods, 152–77. London:
          Routledge and Kegan Paul.

Leacock, E.
    1969 *Teaching and Learning in City Schools: A Comparative Study.* New
          York: Basic Books.
Lees, Sue
    1986 *Losing Out: Sexuality and Adolescent Girls.* London: Hutchinson.
Levi-Strauss, C.
    1969 *The Elementary Structures of Kinship.* Trans. J. H. Bell, J. R. von
          Sturmer, and R. Needham. Rev. ed. Boston: Beacon Press.
Lewis, C. S.
    1936 *The Allegory of Love: A Study in Medieval Tradition.* Oxford: The
          Clarendon Press.
Lightfoot, Sara Lawrence
    1988 *Balm in Gilead: Journey of a Healer.* Reading, Mass.: Addison-
          Wesley.
Long, Elizabeth
    n.d. Feminism and Cultural Studies: Britain and America. Depart-
          ment of Sociology, Rice University.
Luttrell, Wendy
    1989 Working-Class Women's Ways of Knowing: Effects of Gender,
          Race and Class. *Sociology of Education* 62(1):33–46.
    n.d. Claiming Authority, Claiming Self-Worth: Black and White
          Working-Class Women's Ways of Knowing. Department of So-
          ciology, Duke University.
McCarthy, Cameron, and Michael W. Apple
    1988 Race, Class, and Gender in American Educational Research:
          Toward a Nonsynchronous Parallelist Position. In *Class, Race,
          and Gender in American Education,* ed. Lois Weis, 9–39. Albany:
          State University of New York Press.
MacDonald, Madeleine
 1979–80 Cultural Reproduction: The Pedagogy of Sexuality. *Screen Ed-
          ucation* 32/33:141–53.
    1980 Socio-Cultural Reproduction and Women's Education. In
          Schooling for Women's Work, ed. Rosemary Deem. London: Rout-
          ledge and Kegan Paul.
MacLeod, J.
    1987 *Ain't No Making It: Leveled Aspirations in a Low-Income Neighbor-
          hood.* Boulder, Colo.: Westview Press.
McRobbie, Angela
    1978a Jackie: An Ideology of Adolescent Femininity. Stenciled Occa-
          sional Paper, no. 53, Women Series. Birmingham, England:
          Centre for Contemporary Cultural Studies.
    1978b Working Class Girls and the Culture of Femininity. In *Women
          Take Issue: Aspects of Women's Subordination,* ed. Centre for Con-
          temporary Cultural Studies Working Papers in Cultural Studies
          96–108. London: Hutchinson.
    1980 Settling Accounts with Subcultures: A Feminist Critique. *Screen
          Education* 34(Spring):37–49.
    1981 Just like a Jackie Story. In *Feminism for Girls: An Adventure Story,*

ed. Angela McRobbie and Trisha McCabe. London: Routledge and Kegan Paul.

1982   The Politics of Feminist Research: Between Talk, Text, and Action. *Feminist Review* 12(October):46–57.

McRobbie, Angela, and J. Garber

1976   Girls and Subcultures. In *Resistance through Rituals: Youth Subcultures in Post-War Britain,* ed. Stuart Hall and Tony Jefferson, 209–22. London: Hutchinson.

Marcus, G., and M. Fischer

1986   *Anthropology as Cultural Critique: An Experimental Moment in the Human Sciences.* Chicago: University of Chicago Press.

Moffatt, Michael

1989   *Coming of Age in New Jersey: College and American Culture.* New Brunswick: Rutgers University Press.

Ogbu, John U.

1974   *The Next Generation: An Ethnography of Education in an Urban Neighborhood.* New York: Academic Press.

1978   *Minority Education and Caste: The American System in Cross-Cultural Perspective.* New York: Academic Press.

1985   Crossing Cultural Boundaries: A Perspective on Minority Education. Paper presented at symposium, Race, Class, Socialization, and the Life Cycle, 21–22 October, University of Chicago.

1987   Variability in Minority School Performance: A Problem in Search of an Explanation. *Anthropology and Education Quarterly* 18(4):312–34.

Painter, Sidney

1940   *French Chivalry: Chivalric Ideas and Practices in Medieval France.* Baltimore: Johns Hopkins Press.

Parry, John Jay

1941   Introduction to *The Art of Courtly Love (Tractatus de Amore),* by Andreas Capellanus. New York: Columbia University Press.

Patzer, Gordon L.

1985   *The Physical Attractiveness Phenomena.* New York and London: Plenum Press.

Peacock, James L.

1988   *The Anthropological Lens: Harsh Light, Soft Focus.* Cambridge: Cambridge University Press.

Philips, S.

1983   *The Invisible Culture: Communication in Classroom and Community on the Warm Springs Indian Reservation.* New York: Longman.

Quinn, N.

1982   "Commitment" in American Marriage: A Cultural Analysis. *American Ethnologist* 9(4):775–98.

Quinn, N., and D. C. Holland

1987   Culture and Cognition. In *Cultural Models in Language and Thought,* ed. D. C. Holland and N. Quinn, 3–40. Cambridge: Cambridge University Press.

Rapoport, R., and R. N. Rapoport
　　1976　*Dual-Career Families Reexamined: New Integrations of Work and Family.* London: Martin Robertson.
Reilly, Kevin
　　1980　Love and Devotion. In *The West and the World: A Topical History of Civilization,* 183–204. New York: Harper and Row.
Reiter, Rayna, ed.
　　1975　*Toward an Anthropology of Women.* New York and London: Monthly Review Press.
Rich, Adrienne
　　1980　Compulsory Heterosexuality and Lesbian Existence. *Signs* 5(4): 631–60.
Riley, Kathryn
　　1985　Black Girls Speak for Themselves. In *Just a Bunch of Girls: Feminist Approaches to Schooling,* ed. Gaby Weiner, 63–76. Milton Keynes: Open University Press.
Rist, R.
　　1973　*The Urban School: A Factory for Failure.* Cambridge: MIT Press.
Roberts, Joan I., and Sherrie K. Akinsanya
　　1976a　*Educational Patterns and Cultural Configurations.* New York: David McKay.
　　1976b　*Schooling in the Cultural Context.* New York: David McKay.
Rodgers-Rose, La Frances
　　1980　Some Demographic Characteristics of the Black Woman: 1940 to 1975. In *The Black Woman,* ed. La Frances Rodgers-Rose, 29–41. Beverly Hills: Sage.
Rothman, E. K.
　　1984　*Hands and Hearts: A History of Courtship in America.* New York: Basic Books.
Rougemont, Denis de
　　1940　*Love in the Western World.* New York: Harcourt-Brace.
Sanders, W. B.
　　1980　*Rape and Woman's Identity.* Sage Library of Social Research, no. 106. Beverly Hills: Sage.
Schofield, Janet Ward
　　1982　*Black and White in School: Trust, Tension, or Tolerance?* New York: Praeger.
Schur, Edwin M.
　　1983　*Labeling Women Deviant: Gender, Stigma, and Social Control.* Philadelphia: Temple University Press.
Schwartz, G.
　　1972　*Youth Culture: An Anthropological Approach.* Addison-Wesley Module in Anthropology, no. 17. Reading, Mass.: Addison-Wesley.
Schwartz, G., and D. Merten
　　1968　Social Identity and Expressive Symbols: The Meaning of an Initiation Ritual. *American Anthropologist* 70(6):1117–31.
Scott, James C.
　　1985　*Weapons of the Weak: Everyday Forms of Peasant Resistance.* New Haven: Yale University Press.

Sharpe, S.
    1976 *Just Like a Girl: How Girls Learn to Be Women.* Harmondsworth: Penguin.
Smith, L. Schacklady
    1978 Sexist Assumptions and Female Delinquency: An Empirical Investigation. In *Women, Sexuality and Social Control,* ed. C. Smart and B. Smart, 74–88. London: Routledge and Kegan Paul.
Smucker, Orden
    1947 The Campus Cliques as an Agency of Socialization. *Journal of Educational Sociology* 21(3):163–68.
Spradley, J.
    1979 *The Ethnographic Interview.* New York: Holt, Rinehart and Winston.
    1980 *Participant Observation.* New York: Holt, Rinehart and Winston.
Stoltenberg, J.
    1975 Towards Gender Justice. *Social Policy* 6(1):35–39.
Thomas, Claire
    1980 Girls and Counter-School Culture. *Melbourne Working Papers.* Melbourne.
Trueba, H.
    1988 Culturally Based Explanations of Minority Students' Academic Achievement. *Anthropology and Education Quarterly* 19(3):270–87.
Valli, L.
    1983 Becoming Clerical Workers: Business Education and the Culture of Femininity. In *Ideology and Practice in Schooling,* ed. Michael W. Apple and Lois Weis, 213–34. Philadelphia: Temple University Press.
    1986 *Becoming Clerical Workers.* Boston: Routledge and Kegan Paul.
Wallace, Michele
    1988 Review of *She's Gotta Have It* and *School Daze. The Nation* 246(22): 800–803.
Wallace, Walter L.
    1966 *Student Culture: Social Structure and Continuity in a Liberal Arts College.* Chicago: Aldine.
Waller, W.
    1937 The Rating and Dating Complex. *American Sociological Review* 2:727–34.
Weiler, K.
    1988 *Women Teaching for Change: Gender, Class and Power.* South Hadley, Mass.: Bergin and Garvey.
Weis, Lois
    1985 *Between Two Worlds: Black Students in an Urban Community College.* Boston: Routledge and Kegan Paul.
    1988 High School Girls in a De-Industrializing Economy. In *Class, Race, and Gender in American Education,* ed. Lois Weis, 183–208. Albany: State University of New York Press.
Wexler, Philip
    1987 *Social Analysis of Education: After the New Sociology.* London: Routledge and Kegan Paul.

Weyr, Garrett
    1988 *Pretty Girls.* New York: Crown Publishers.
Whitehead, Ann
    1976 Sexual Antagonism in Herefordshire. In *Dependence and Exploitation in Work and Marriage,* ed. Diana Leonard Barker and Sheila Allen, 169–203. London: Longman.
Willis, Paul
    1977 *Learning to Labor: How Working Class Kids Get Working Class Jobs.* New York: Columbia University Press.
    1981a Cultural Production Is Different from Cultural Reproduction Is Different from Social Reproduction Is Different from Reproduction. *Interchange* 12(2,3):48–67.
    1981b *Learning to Labor: How Working Class Kids Get Working Class Jobs.* Rev. ed. New York: Columbia University Press, Morningside.
Wilson, Deirdre
    1978 Sexual Codes and Conduct: A Study of Teenage Girls. In *Women, Sexuality and Social Control,* ed. C. Smart and B. Smart, 65–73. London: Routledge and Kegan Paul.
Wolpe, AnnMarie
    1978 Education and the Sexual Division of Labour. In *Feminism and Materialism: Women and Modes of Production,* ed. Annette Kuhn and AnnMarie Wolpe, 290–328. Boston: Routledge and Kegan Paul.
Wood, Phillip J.
    1986 *Southern Capitalism: The Political Economy of North Carolina, 1880 to 1980.* Durham: Duke University Press.
Yanagisako, Sylvia
    1988 Sex and Gender: You Can't Have One without the Other. Paper presented at meeting of Society for Cultural Anthropology, 20 May, Washington, D.C.
Zetterberg, Hans L.
    1968 The Secret Ranking. In *Sociology and Everyday Life,* ed. Marcello Truzzi, 42–55. Englewood Cliffs, N.J.: Prentice-Hall.

Glossary

Cheerleaders: A squad composed mostly of women, who accompany a school's (usually male) sports teams and lead cheering in support of the team. Chosen for their physical attractiveness and athleticism, they have high status on campus.

Dormitory, dorm: A building, as at a college, containing a number of private or semiprivate rooms for residents.

Fraternities. See Sororities/Fraternities

Grading scales: University grading policies use letter grades—A (outstanding), A−, B+, B, B−, . . . , F (failure)—to evaluate student performance in coursework. Letters correspond to a 4-point scale in which 4.0 equals an A, 3.0 a B, etc. Individual professors sometimes substitute another numerical scale for in-class work, using a 100-point scale: 100 percent equals a perfect score, 92 to 99 percent (roughly) an A, 88 to 91 percent an A−, . . . , below 60 percent an F.

Grammar school: A graded school intermediate between a primary school and a high school.

Greeks. See Sororities/Fraternities

High school counselor: A faculty member who advises students on personal and academic problems.

Homecoming: On campus, an annual event held to honor visiting alumni. In communities, an occasional event held to honor former residents.

Major: The subject or field of study chosen by a student to represent his or her principal interests.

Semester: A division constituting half of the academic year.

Sororities/Fraternities: Local or national organizations of women (sororities) or men (fraternities) serving primarily a social purpose on university campuses, with secret initiations, special insignia, and "houses" where members live together. Members of the system are generally referred to as "Greeks" because the organizations' names are composed of letters of the Greek alphabet.

Index

Acker, S., 34
Althusser, L., 6, 26, 29, 30, 32, 40, 239
  n.11
Anthropology: of education, vii, 17, 20,
  26–28; feminist, 35
Anyon, J., 26, 55
Apple, Michael W., 7, 26, 31, 51, 238
  n.2, 239 nn.6, 9, 240 n.14, 251 n.9
Arnot, M., 33, 41, 43, 46, 47, 242 n.11
Ashenden, D. J., 8
Attractiveness: contested images, _
  217–18; differential standards, 94–95,
  211–12, 245–46 n.14; hegemonic
  forms, 224, 229, 245 nn.11, 12, 249
  n.9, 251 n.6; meanings of word, 244
  n.2; and prestige, 95–96, 104,
  152–53, 206, 211, 219, 250 n.2 to
  chap.15; ranking, 95–96, 98–104,
  149, 159, 216–17, 245 n.9; rival styles,
  157–59, 229–30, 248 n.4; and
  romance, 8, 18–20, 84, 90, 117; as
  route to marriage, 106, 197;
  social-psychological research on,
  245–46 n.14; strategies of, 153–54; as
  symbolic capital, 102–5, 212, 213, 214,
  221, 230

Barrett, Michele, 6, 29
Bartky, Sandra Lee, 105
Beauvoir, Simone de: *The Second Sex,* 19
Becker, Howard S., 84
Bernstein, B., 33
Berscheid, E., 245 n.14
Bloch, Maurice, 251 n.7
Boggs, J. W., 26
Bookman, Ann, 252 n.12
Bourdieu, P., 6, 26, 27–28, 29–30, 32,
  103, 153, 221, 238 n.3, 239 n.8, 251
  n.7
Bowles, S., 6, 30, 32; *Schooling in
  Capitalist America,* 26

Boyfriends: problems with, 113–17,
  129–33; search for, 85–86, 97, 105,
  109–11, 125–29, 190–91, 213; as
  source of prestige, 90, 98–107, 118,
  123–24, 129, 152, 211, 216; strategic
  enactments with, 138–43; as
  substitute for academic success,
  191–92. *See also* Dating; Sexual
  auction-block
"Bradford" University, 3, 14–15, 16,
  64–66, 71–74, 77, 84–90; women's
  relationships at, 111–18, 150–51
Brake, Mike, 44, 80, 227–28, 250 n.2 to
  chap.15, 252 nn.13–15
Brown, Julie, "'Cause I'm a Blonde,"
  210–11, 212, 215, 218, 250 n.1 to
  chap.15

Cain, C., 249 n.2 to chap.9
Campbell, A., 45, 46
Campus cultures, 79–85, 93, 244 n.3 to
  chap.6; and romance 93–94. *See also*
  Peer culture; Peer groups; Student
  cultures
Capellanus, Andreas, 93
Careers: "choices," vii, 4–6, 13–14, 20,
  59, 67, 181–82, 243 n.15;
  "derailment," 14, 179; and grades,
  173; identity, 173–74, 179–80,
  196–97, 200; marginalized, 4–5, 68,
  85, 178, 181–84, 187–88, 190, 200,
  224, 250 n.4 to chap.13; math/science,
  3, 13, 63, 243 n.4
Categorical theories of gender, 38–39,
  41, 46
Centre for Contemporary Culture
  Studies, 30, 34, 240 n.16, 241 n.1
Clark, Burton R., 31, 83
Class: cultural politics of, 34; and
  differential educational outcomes, 26;

267